MY
KIND OF
COUNTRY

ALSO BY CARL CARMER

Stars Fell on Alabama

Listen for a Lonesome Drum

The Hurricane's Children

Dark Trees to the Wind

The Hudson

America Sings

Genesee Fever

The Windfall Fiddle

The Susquehanna

The Tavern Lamps Are Burning, Compiler

MY
KIND OF
COUNTRY

Favorite Writings about
New York

by

CARL CARMER

DAVID McKAY COMPANY, INC. · NEW YORK

MY KIND OF COUNTRY

For permission to reprint the following material by Carl Carmer, grateful acknowledgment is made to:

American Heritage, for "O the Ee-rye-ee Was Risin'." Copyright © 1952 by American Heritage Publishing Company.

American Home, for "America's Victorian Homes." Copyright © 1964 by *American Home.*

The Atlantic Monthly Company, for "Hanging Day." Copyright © 1936 by The Atlantic Monthly Company, Boston, Massachusetts.

Columbia University Press for "Fiorello LaGuardia" from *The Greater City: New York, 1898-1948.* Copyright © 1948 by Columbia University Press.

Grace Church in New York, for excerpts from *The Years of Grace.* Copyright © 1958 by Grace Church in New York.

Hamilton Alumni Review, for "A Reminiscence of John V. A. Weaver—Notes for a Biographer." Copyright © 1938 by *Hamilton Alumni Review.* For "Melanchthon Woolsey Stryker," a commencement address delivered at Hamilton College, 1964. © 1964 by *Hamilton Alumni Review.*

Harper's Magazine, for "The Climber." Copyright © September, 1932. (Reprinted in *Best Poems of 1933,* Jonathan Cape Ltd., London.)

Holiday Magazine, for "Upstate Is a Country." Copyright © June, 1957 by Curtis Publishing Company. For "The Champlain Valley." © 1959 by Curtis Publishing Company.

Holt, Rinehart and Winston, Inc., for "To Make a River" and "Hudson River Aesthete" from *The Hudson.* Copyright © 1939 by Carl Carmer.

Alfred A. Knopf, Inc., for "Philetus Bumpus" from *America Sings,* copyright © 1942 by Carl Carmer; for "Bride of Apollo," "The Ghost of the River Octagon," and "The Wraith on Cedar Street" from *The Screaming Ghost,* © 1956 by Carl Carmer; for an excerpt from *Windfall Fiddle* by Carl Carmer, © 1950 by Alfred A. Knopf, Inc.

To Elizabeth

TABLE OF CONTENTS

❦ Introduction

Carl Carmer's kind of country is a hilly land traversed by shining rivers; sizable patches of tall trees still stand, and brooks are rimmed by wild flowers. In this country there are strange winds blowing and the dead are restless; the unbelievable is the most earnestly to be believed.

To be specific, Carl Carmer's country is—and only could be—upstate New York. There must be the land of the Finger Lakes where he was born, and Albion on the Erie Canal where he grew up, the Genesee country south of Rochester, and Rochester itself. There must be College Hill (where old Hamilton sits above Oriskany's stream) and the checkerboard of the dulcet streets of Cooperstown. And Irvington—just barely beyond the groping fingers of New York City—for him a refuge where the eight sides of his wonder palace and the spirit of his literary kinsman, Washington Irving, fend off the devils.

It was Carmer who first noted the broad band of wondrous happenings that have crossed New York State from east to west, from the Shakers at Lebanon to the Spiritualists in Lily Dale; and it was he who called this path the "psychic highway." The wayfarers on that highway were as disparate as they were amazing: Mother Ann Lee, Prophet Joseph Smith, the spiritualist Fox Sisters, The Publick Universal Friend. The rich history of this state has been Carl Carmer's delight— not merely the narratives of the religionists, but of all manner of men and women and the events they brought to pass. He sees history as a series of incidents to be told, and told well, that a new generation may savor them. Most particularly, he looks to the individuals at the core of each incident and comes to understand them and their motives and their groping acts.

Carl Carmer has paid especial attention to those who lived along or traveled on the waterways of his kind of country. His writing returns again and again to the Erie Canal, the Hudson (whose sage and defender he has become), the Susquehanna, the Niagara and, to a lesser degree, the lakes which dot our hinterland. It is no accident that he is the editor of the "Rivers of America" series (he sees rivers as the warp of history) and no mere happenstance that he also is editor of the "Regions of America" series.

Always he comes back to the individual. He is intrigued and delighted by octagon houses (of which he owns one of the noblest), but he is far more interested in Orson Fowler and the paths by which he came to fashion those eight-sided dwellings. More than anything else, Carl Carmer finds people the grist for his mill, not alone his literary mill, but the mill of life itself.

It is perhaps too soon to begin to evaluate Carmer's contributions to American letters, though it is not too early to take note of specific contributions. So far as I am aware, he created a new literary pattern, a way of looking at people and places as at a foreign country, which resulted in a new and true appraisal of events past and present. Beginning with *Stars Fell on Alabama,* he perfected the pattern in *Listen for a Lonesome Drum* and in *Dark Trees to the Wind.* In each of these he combines personal experience and documented research with the oral history of the people of a geographic area to emphasize events as the people remember them as having happened. What actually happened in the past is the great concern of most historians; but Carmer knows that what people *believe* to have happened can often have an equal influence on the course of events. He has sometimes been regarded as the most important recorder of the history of the American folk-fancy. "Folklore," he has said, "is the poetry of our common mind."

Not since Irving and Cooper has a writer treated New York State as a romantic land, full of mystery and unlimited variety. Others have written sympathetically of regions of New York, but in such pieces as *Upstate Is a Country,* Carmer has covered whole areas with a gossamer cloak of magic, delight and beauty. From my view, this was the discovery and statement of a truth by which Carmer lit a backfire to counteract the myth of New Englandism—that curious misreading of history that sees everything good, noble and significant as having happened in or derived from Yankee rocks and ice.

In retelling the folk history of Upstate, Carmer turned up scores of forgotten but significant incidents, movements, facts and people. His books have suggested subjects for studies-in-depth to young scholars, and this certainly had been one of his purposes. Such matters as the Anti-Rent Wars, the Cardiff Giant, the Hunters' Lodges, the origins of Mormonism, the influence of the Shakers, the crimes of the Loomis Gang, and Andrew Jackson Downing's cottages, to mention but a few, came into popular awareness only after his writings had made them known again, and then came under scholarly scrutiny.

Carmer brings to his prose the rhythms and qualities of a poet. I am delighted that this volume contains some of his poems, for they are hard to come by, but one will note that throughout his prose there are rhythmic tides. In general, these are the rhythms of our folk speech, often couched in the folk vocabulary. Once in a while he produces a piece—"Fiorello LaGuardia" is an example—that is in the clipped, efficient style of a good reporter; but the style we think of as characteristic of Carmer is the flowing, moody poetry of "To Make a River."

Some men are novelists, others essayists, others historians, but within the limits of his profession, Carmer is a master of many literary forms. If you start reading him with two facts in mind, this is more easily understood: he is a poet and a storyteller. His ability to give poetic values to good stories well told is at the core of almost everything here. This is why there have been loaded upon him many an admiring sentence such as *Time*'s statement that "Author Carmer maintains an aloof compassion, avoiding sentimentality as well as mockery....He [has] always tried to find, in the local customs, turns of speech, characteristics, meaningful survivals from the richly spiritual past."

Finally, one should speak of the dogged, cussed side of Carl Carmer. He is an old-fashioned liberal and has marched long and loyally in those ranks of his fellows. Each time our government has robbed the New York Indians, his voice has sounded strong protest. He has spoken out for a second chance for rehabilitated convicts, and has risen to defend Storm King Mountain, one of New York State's most beloved landmarks, from those greedy corporations which would ignore its history and disregard its beauty.

Why? Why does he spend weeks and months of his year in defense of people's rights or of the preservation of beauty? I think I know the answer—it is that his native state has nourished him and given him courage to battle against forces that would make the reality of his kind of country less noble than his dream of it.

LOUIS C. JONES
Director, New York State
Historical Association

October, 1966
Cooperstown, New York

Song for Orleans County

I have carried milk pails,
Silver in the dusk,
Over barn-to-house trails
Sweet with trampled husk.

The stars above the barnyard
Were white as the warm milk foam,
And the crickets sang hard
As I went home.

Let others sing of silk bales,
Gems, and ivory tusk,
I have carried milk pails,
Silver in the dusk.

Upstate Is a Country

The happiest entry into New York State, my grandfather
used to say, is to be born there. The only disadvantage, he would add,
is that you will not realize your enviable lot until you have grown old
enough to travel and see how much less fortunate the natives of other
regions are. Since he wore the long white beard of a patriarch and unfailingly served buckwheat pancakes and maple sirup for breakfast,
I received his every word as gospel. Indeed, my boyish pride in New
York was fortified on each of my frequent visits to his home in Dryden,
in the center of the state, especially when he reminded me, as he did

invariably, that my very birth might have occurred uncomfortably, high on a Tompkins County hill, had not his team of white-faced, York-State-bred Morgans made a record dash to the Cortland Hospital.

If a life is begun by a hopscotch jump into a state's middle, it is natural that the early years of it be spent in concentric circles. The Genesee Valley, my mother's former home, was the first perimeter. My earliest memory is of a cobblestone inn beside the waters of Conesus, a minor digit of the Finger Lakes about twenty-five miles south of the city of Rochester. I was wakened in a second-floor bedroom and carried to a balcony outside a window. Below me, horses switched nervously under blue-jacketed riders, and long-eared dogs, brown-spotted on white, padded about eagerly snuffling the ground. Such images lie far back in an adult's life; clouds surround them, then open for only a split second of sun. I would be a man before I knew that these riders of the Genesee Valley Hunt had eighteenth-century prototypes, that the Wadsworth family, who organized the Hunt in post-Revolutionary times, had chosen the blue-and-buff of Continental uniforms for their jackets rather than the conventional "hunting pink," which former riflemen of Washington's army might mistake for the garb of a British lobster-back. It was upon a latter-day unit of this same hunt that I looked down from the inn balcony.

My state is bright with glinting waters. That first glimpse of Conesus Lake was only a happy sample. Before too long I discovered that the winding Genesee River, pastoral in most of its reaches, raced so far below high bluffs at Mount Morris and at Letchworth Park that few dared stand at the edge of the Palisades to watch its white-water rapids and foaming cascades. At Rochester, the river was roofed over and went boiling under Main Street stores to make its long drop to the jagged rocks below. The waves of Ontario welcomed it a few miles farther north, making a wide blue ribbon border for the land.

I also discovered Niagara Falls, from the high wet spot where the Niagara thundered down past the Cave of the Winds and raced into the whirlpool beyond. My father and I once embarked on the little steamer *Maid-of-the-Mist*, whence we could see ahead of us the rushing mass of water leap from the high, sharp ledges and crash into the pool below, lifting clouds of spray which glittered into rainbows under the bright sun. "Why did you come here for your honeymoon?" my father asked of a couple standing beside us. "Because," said the bride, "it's the most wonderful place in all the world for a honeymoon," and I wondered why my dignified parent chuckled occasionally throughout the rest of the day. The mid-century elegance of the Cataract House impressed me, and I was awed when the desk clerk took an old register from the safe behind him and showed me the signature, "A. Lincoln."

And I discovered the bubbling springs that dot the countryside—springs that burn with a blue flame when ignited, like those in the Bristol Hills and in the little town of Cuba; waters that spurt hot from the depths of the earth and bring healing to men, like those at Sharon and Clifton and Lebanon; and others containing yellow sulphur of such repellent taste and smell that God-fearing folk agree it *must* be good for what ails them. Rambling, many-verandaed hotels grew up where people "took the waters"—not only at the famous spas in Saratoga and Ballston but even in little towns like Dryden where the taste of the springs was peculiarly abhorrent. My grandfather could recall when there was a cotillion almost every Saturday night in Dryden, and folks dressed fit-to-kill "promenaded" while the orchestra rested on the high balcony above the shining ballroom floor. Most of the guests were ladies, so there was always a need for extra gentlemen, and many a farm boy, if he had a clean shirt and a blue suit, received a little flowered card from the hotel management inviting him to foot it with the smart set.

In the red and gold of mid-October, 1825, came the opening of the great Erie Canal, with a boat parade that began at Buffalo and ended in New York Harbor. Governor Clinton's man-made river proved its worth by paying for itself promptly. It also scattered along its length the quick-grown settlements with the nautical names—Lockport, Middleport, Eagle Harbor, Brockport, Adams Basin, Spencerport, Weedsport, Port Byron—to compete with the older towns, those that had been given scholarly names years before by a lover of the classics—Syracuse, Ilion, Rome, Utica, Pompey, Homer, Marathon.

When I was seven we moved from the Genesee Valley to a canal town first named Newport but rechristened Albion, between Rochester and Niagara Falls. First I mourned the high hills we had left behind, then blessed the day we did. I learned to swim in a swift-running culvert that tapped the Erie to run a gristmill. I practiced jumping to the decks of the slow canalboats at one bridge and climbing back at the next. In the town's grimy newspaper office, whence a man of authority could spit through an open window into mid-channel, I heard tell of a day when a break in the canal bank left the water level so low that an Albion housewife, scooping out a washtubful, grounded all boats west of Rochester. And a certain carpenter, nearly seven foot tall and bearded like God—or Moses—sometimes came by to tell how he carried the Stars and Stripes through battle after battle in the Civil War and was never hit.

There was always work for a boy in Western New York State in the days that followed the turn of the century. Farmers had retired after a lucky run of five good harvests, industrialists had invested in the Suspension Bridge at Niagara Falls, speculators had risked a few hundred on Eastman Kodak stock at ten dollars a share, against the advice of their elders. ("It's only a passing fad.")

With their new wealth they had built big, rectangular, cupola-crowned houses far back from the wooden sidewalks, and hired boys to mow the level green lawns on Saturdays.

North toward the lake was more work, in the apple country—Baldwins, they keep well in the cellar; Greenings, nothing can beat 'em for pies; Pound Sweets, if you like 'em that way; Maiden Blush, pretty as they sound; Seek-no-furthers, they mean what they say; Northern Spies, best flavor in the world. Through the autumn days, pickers rode the swaying ladders, and when they emptied their pickbags into the barrels there was a hollow drumming sound. All night long the pickers tossed restlessly in their sleep as if their ladders were still bouncing on the resilient boughs.

Sometimes we bicycled nine miles to Oak Orchard, on Ontario's sandy shore. Our object was swimming and sunburn, but there were rewards en route. The road led through the "Land of the Cobblestone Houses," dwellings with local fieldstones, rounded and smoothed by the waves of Ontario, set into the mortar walls. Some are reddish because their walls hold only disks of a local rust-colored sandstone; others are striped in alternate red and white rows or have the stones slanted in herringbone patterns or set alternately deep and shallow to give a dappled shadow effect. Finding enough stones took as long as three years, even with neighborhood "gathering bees" which ended in feasting and dancing.

Oak Orchard today holds a more solemn mood than when I pedaled the country miles to its refreshing beach. The covered bridge that sang echoing welcome when a team trotted through and also offered deep shade to canoeing couples—("Paddle from under quick when a wagon comes, those floorboards don't sprinkle talcum powder")—has now been replaced by sullen steel and concrete. The Victorian dwellings no longer look upon green lawns. Wind-blown whitecaps have dug under the banks on which they were founded, and the gabled structures seem to waver in precarious balance as if they were about to dive into the rolling surf.

Other communities on the southern shore of Ontario have a gayer and more lasting look. Follow the coastline east to Sodus Bay and you will see stable, commodious summer residences sporting whimsical labels ("Our Social Security"), and boathouses sheltering fast sleep-in cruisers and faster speedboats. Westward, in the neighborhood of Buffalo, lakeside communities are numerous and crowded, and there are still others on the southern shores of smaller, more treacherous Lake Erie. Inland, along the slim streaks of blue water called the Finger Lakes, towns that until recently took their water-vacation advantages as personal blessings, have realized that people will travel long distances to enjoy cool breezes, fishing, sailing, water skiing, swimming, yacht-club life.

The most irresistible of all lures to vacationing Yorkers is culture. In summer months the whole area teems with it. New Englanders were the chief settlers, and an inherited Yankee conscience makes their descendants so uneasy over idling during their vacations that they demand intellectual "improvement." How strongly this attitude persists can be seen on the shores of one of the state's westernmost small lakes, Chautauqua, where the famous Chautauqua Institution has been functioning since Victorian times.

Life changes somewhat once you have entered the gates of the Chautauqua Institution. Its taboos are simple—no automobiles, no cats, no alcoholic beverages. You may live in one of the old cottages that shoulder each other along the brick-paved, leaf-shadowed streets—which were built long before the first horseless buggy and are too narrow for two-way motor traffic—or in a hotel, possibly in the dignified Athenaeum, the last American tavern, so far as I know, to abandon the custom of serving cornmeal mush and milk for supper every Sunday night.

You soon discover that the taboos at Chautauqua are balanced by intellectual and spiritual blessings. The loud-speaker in the sunken Amphitheatre, center of the most important activities, carries morning hymns and the sermon of a distinguished prelate. In the intervals between events the bells of the carillon down by the lake tumble appropriate tunes into the quiet air, and the morning program continues with an economist, a sociologist or an explorer at the Amphitheatre microphone. Comes then the cacophony of an orchestra (made up mostly of artists from the New York Philharmonic) tuning up to run through the evening's concert.

In the meantime, the distinguished artist who is head of the Art Center has sought a dell where light streams from the north upon the canvases of his elderly pupils; the Chautauqua Repertory Theatre rehearses a comedy (there are few demands for heavier fare); the writers giving courses in the Writers' Workshop strive mightily to tell the ambitious amateurs ("I've always thought I could write") how to compose and sell their works.

To facilitate adult improvement, the clubs of Chautauqua are remarkably active. The Bird and Tree (it exiled the cats) now works continuously at beautifying the grounds. The Woman's Club is active in good works. The W.C.T.U. (it has tried, not always with success, to keep the liquor out) still wields a powerful influence. One Amphitheatre speaker, according to local folklore, tried to recommend an occasional cocktail to his white-haired audience and was ushered from the platform to the gate, where his suitcase awaited him, packed by an efficient member of the W.C.T.U. The Literary and Scientific Circle, oldest book club in the United States, has been prescribing reading to its thousands of members for more than three quarters of a century. Those who complete its four-year course are graduated at Chautauqua each year on Recognition Day with ceremonies that are impressive if somewhat sentimental and dated by now.

Far to the east of Chautauqua, a little over an hour's ride southwest of Albany and inaccessible except by automobile, lovely old Cooperstown curves about the southern end of Otsego Lake, known as Glimmerglass in the *Leatherstocking* novels of James Fenimore Cooper, whose father founded the town. No gate or fence guards the treasures of this cluster of historic houses, quiet and luxurious hotels and a half-dozen museums, but the small population is used to seeing automobiles from all over the Union pour into Main Street, park for an hour or two, and move on.

The Baseball Museum, a modest red-brick building, is not easily identifiable, but a Cooperstonian can spot a pilgrim unfailingly and issue directions almost before he is asked. The cars are crowded, and they have baggage tied on top, and there's pretty sure to be a boy inside. Once past the ticket office, the family scatters. Mother and the girls look at the paintings and the old programs, and soon tire. Grandpa finds a photograph of Christy Mathewson, who pitched a game he saw in the old days. Father sentimentalizes over Lou Gehrig's uniform, and sonny dashes from the cleated shoes of Babe Ruth to the ball Mickey Mantle socked over the center-field fence in Washington.

Not all the baseball enthusiasts visit the other educational showplaces of Cooperstown. One of these is the Farmers' Museum, which houses fascinating relics of rural New York before the Civil War and also serves as the last resting place of the Cardiff Giant. Yorkers love the story of this stone man who was carved in Iowa and buried in 1869 behind Stub Newell's barn in Cardiff, a midstate village not far from Syracuse. The figure's "discovery" led to controversy and controversy to fortune for Stub and for David Hannum and the rest of the conspirators who plotted the magnificent hoax. Many a noted scientist lost his reputation by claiming the "grand old sleeper" to be the petrified body of a man who lived when giants walked the earth. Even today the curious wait in long queues to look upon his passive form, and since an admission is charged, he is still making money for his custodians.

Most rewarding of Cooperstown treasures is Fenimore House, once an elaborate private residence, now a treasure house of Americana. Here you will see early paintings, both skilled and primitive, that show the nation as it looked long ago; the remarkable life masks, made by J. H. I. Browere, of the great men of America's beginnings (some of them the only true likenesses we have); furniture made by Shakers, whose prohibitions of ornament led to clean lines and exquisite curves. For two weeks each summer, in the auditorium of this building and in make-do assembly rooms nearby, large groups attend the New York State Historical Association's Seminars on American Culture.

Yorkers approve all this so strongly that the state is fairly peppered with exhibitions of their pioneering past, yet they squirm a little when reminded of all their ancestors who were stricken with moon madness. Consider the Shakers, who whirled, danced, marched in the "square order" or the "quick manner," and spoke strange gibberish when endowed with "the gift of tongues." Their sturdy dwellings had two doors—one leading to the men's dormitory and the other to the women's—because they believed that only when all sexual practices ceased would the Kingdom of the Lord arrive. They increased their numbers only by conversion and by adoption of orphans. They believed all adornments wicked, wore plain costumes, and made furniture and utensils so beautiful in functional simplicity that they are cherished by a grateful posterity. "Hands to work and hearts to God" was their creed—and through the streets of their villages, neat and quiet, drifted the odors of their herb gardens.

Eventually the Shakers moved into Ohio, where a section of Cleveland still remembers them with its name, Shaker Heights. The last of those who remained in New York died only a few years ago, held in warm affection by other Yorkers, who hope that in Shaker heaven the Sisters are wearing the promised gowns "of twelve different colours," with colored handkerchiefs about their necks, blue silk gloves, silver shoes, and bonnets "of silver colour trimmed with white ribbon," and that they are marching in the square order and the quick manner with Shaker gentlemen dressed in sky-blue jackets with gold buttons, "beautiful fine trousers, as white as snow" and adorned with shining stars and sky-blue glass buttons, neck scarves of white silk bordered with gold, flawlessly white shoes and fine fur hats of a silver color.

While the Shakers were moving toward Ohio, a ten-year-old boy named Joseph Smith left Vermont with his mother and came to the bustling York State town of Palmyra. Twelve years later, on a September midnight, he climbed to the summit of a nearby drumlin and found, or claimed he found, a book of golden pages. This was the Book of Mormon, which he translated with the aid of diamond-lensed spectacles that were lying beside it. Then he organized the Church of Jesus Christ of Latter Day Saints, which considers the words of Mormon an authentic complement of the Christian Bible. While Shakerism died because it denounced propagation of the race, the Mormon faith succeeded, aided partly by an early tenet (discontinued in the 1890s) which encouraged polygamy. Today the disciples of Joseph Smith and his successor, Brigham Young, number more than two million.

In 1847 another prophet came out of Vermont, this time to Oneida and with another idea regarding human continuance. Exiled by his Yankee neighbors, John Humphrey Noyes, Dartmouth graduate, arrived with his disciples to put into practice his theories on Perfect Living. Noyes believed that spiritual and physical love were parts of a unified quality, and that all Perfectionists must love one another equally well. Monogamous love he denounced as wickedness and sin.

If any man or any woman in the colony desired to mate, it was necessary only to ask the Central Committee's permission—usually granted if the prospective partner agreed; and thanks to a contraceptive technique called "male continence," only four out of fifty-eight births at Oneida were unintended. When the object of mating was parenthood, the Central Committee held a solemn meeting to discuss the health, background and temperaments of both parties. The children were raised in a separate house as wards of the entire community, and parents were advised to show no preference for their own offspring. Pierrepont Noyes, one of the founder's nine children, each by a different mother, has delightfully described the life of the youngsters in his book *My Father's House, an Oneida Boyhood*.

The Oneida Community's eugenic theories died out in 1880. One reason was that the younger people objected to the sexual proposals they received from their elders. Another was the disapproval of many neighbors, who proclaimed the colony a hotbed of sin. But not to this day has there been so meticulous an experiment in breeding humans. Researches indicate that the Oneida Community's children had physical and mental endowments far above the average in their vicinity, though fifty-four examples of planned births would seem to be too few to justify grand generalizations.

Now that the boy remembered in earlier paragraphs has long been a man, I am glad to live no farther from the surroundings of my youth than the width of the state. Here in eastern New York, the towns that are nearest me are older than the towns of my boyhood, and the land more thickly settled. Crowds flow daily back and forth in this area, as inevitably as the tidal waters of the Hudson River. Morning takes them southward to New York City, the many-towered metropolis that most of them regard as alien territory. Evening brings them back to the river-town stations, where queues of automobiles await them, each piloted by a pitying wife bent on reacclimating her husband to restful greenery and the contentments of family life.

There is, however, a wavering boundary beyond which the crowds move north to their work. The line falls across the Hudson at a point where the Catskill Mountains lift blue summits into the sky of its western banks. North and west of this line lies a cherished land called upstate.

The Catskills are the most gregarious and hospitable of American mountains. Neither high nor steep, they suggest no climbing ropes, no spiked shoes. Each spring they welcome thousands of happy companions to the almost countless hostelries hidden within their comfortable folds. A cheerful uproar prevails, provided partly by the hotel guests, who are mostly from New York City, and partly by the hotel managements, which offer lavish entertainments. Professional entertainers, theatrical troupes, dance orchestras, famous basketball teams, tennis players, golfers travel the profitable trail known as the Borscht Circuit. Once happily described by Arthur Kober's comedy, *Having Wonderful Time,* this vacationland is crowded with people who are openly enthusiastic about people. An air of carnival rises from these hills that were named for squalling wildcats. Rip Van Winkle would find a long sleep difficult here today!

Ride north along the Hudson, beside the Catskills, then leave its shores at Rip Van Winkle Bridge and make west for Cairo, a country town proclaimed cosmopolitan by its pizzerias, cafés, beer halls, delicatessens. Roads join in a star here. One goes north to more Catskill caravansaries. Another, branching south, leads to the hill-circled hamlet of Purling, where the Old Heidelberg and the Bavarian Manor invite to dark elegance and darker beer. Take the northwest route numbered 145, the Sharon Road, to the old village of Leeds, and at midtown you will see a building labeled Jerry Shea's Irish Center. Roll on a few miles and suddenly Ireland has confiscated the hillsides. Here, in fittingly named Greene County, stand the Emerald Isle, the Shannon View, the Shamrock House. Here the O'Neills, the Weldons, the Hagans, the Kearneys, the Mooneys, the Donellys are hosts to families whose old-country names are their best references. Turn in for an Irish stew at Erin's Melody, caper a bit at Blarney's Star Casino and go to early Mass next morning at the tiny chapel of St. Mary's.

"New York State has everything" is a familiar boast among New Yorkers, and sometimes they add, "even two kinds of mountains." North of the Catskills lie rolling hills and the river plain of the east-flowing Mohawk, and beyond that lies rising land again—the foothills of the Adirondacks. Steeper and higher than the Catskills, the tree-lined slopes of the Adirondacks offer silence, the companionship of nature, the shade of balsam, spruce and hemlock, and hidden lakes where the only sounds are those of fish jumping and the whisper of wind riffling the water.

While the Adirondacks are not high compared with Western mountains, more than two score of their countless peaks rise above the four-thousand-foot level. The highest, to which the Adirondack Indians gave the name of Tahawus (the cloud splitter), is over five thousand feet and provides on its steep sides not only a level nook for Lake Tear-of-the-Clouds, where the Hudson rises, but also an iron mine.

The "uphisted lands," as lumberjacks call this country, fill most of the northeast corner of the state. The towns of Lake Placid and Saranac Lake are in the busiest vacation areas, with palacelike clubs and inns and sophisticated shops where people can spend money when they are bored with other diversions. But such places are far from characteristic. Simple log dwellings, even log inns, are not infrequent in the Adirondacks. In many towns, by mid-August, stores are displaying checkered mackinaws, wool shirts, red-flannel underwear, lumberjack peaveys and snowshoes. "Summer up here," said one native mountaineer, "lasts about twenty minutes and *that* seems to come around noon dinner."

Three roads leave Albany, the York State capital, in an east-west course across the rolling hills and river flats that separate the Catskills from the Adirondacks. The northernmost is the Schenectady-Utica-Syracuse turnpike, which runs along the north bank of the historic Mohawk. The southernmost is the Cherry Valley Pike, one of the world's most beautiful highways, which sweeps up and down the mile-long hills as if it were the track of a magnificent outsized roller coaster. Between the two, at least part of the way, runs the new Thruway, the comfortable speedway that unhappily bypasses the fine old towns and buildings and the restaurants that serve the distinctive foods and wines of the region.

This is the upstate area. Only the inhabitants, legend claims, can define its boundaries, and they are not given to exactitude in matters of geography. The late Samuel Hopkins Adams, the distinguished author who lived all his years in the area, once said, "Upstate is west of Albany," and considered the subject closed. Upstaters sniff scornfully at New York City's society-page headlines that say, "Upstate Wedding at Peekskill-on-Hudson." They look upon the island of Manhattan as a subject city-state which very properly pays heavy tribute to Albany. As for that other island, called Long, they regard its people as a salt-water breed more closely akin to New England Yankees than to people dwelling beside pure, fresh lake waters.

Some writers claim that the upstater can be distinguished by his physical, mental and social attributes. Not so lean as the New England Yankee (he is too well fed), his manner indicates that he will never stoop to dieting for the sake of vanity. He is hearty and friendly, and his conversation is intelligent and sometimes penetrating except on the subject of fine arts, which he regards as unmanly or at best a lot of foolishness, even if he is a college graduate. ("My wife does the reading for the family.")

Refusal to conform is a cardinal sin to the upstater. He will not let himself be called pretentious by his neighbors. He avoids fancy clothing, nor does he want his wife to be conspicuously dressed. He may go all out in business or in sports without fear of ridicule, but in other areas his shelf-expression is hampered because he may fail and be laughed at or else succeed and be regarded as one who has tried to set himself above his fellows. Once I heard an upstater admit to a group of friends that he felt that he had done "a pretty good job" on a project. The remark caused a shocked silence.

While the upstater is greatly moved by the subject of food, his tastes run generally to meat, mashed potatoes with gravy, green vegetables and pie. Generous helpings are as likely to win his praise as skilled preparation. Visitors sometimes wail that they cannot find rare beef in the restaurants. ("I'll have rare roast beef," said one. "There isn't any," said the waiter, "and it isn't rare.") Few places serve French or Spanish dishes, and a *spécialité de la maison* is not usually offered. The chief influences on upstate restaurants are Italian, German and tearoom.

Despite their regard for "the usual," upstaters follow many side trails. Ask Lansing Christman, who lives on a farm in the Helderberg Hills southwest of Albany, and I suppose he would reply that he is a broadcaster working at Schenectady's WGY. Yet he keeps the farm turning out crops, and in addition he turns spare evenings to good account by writing poetry, just as his farmer father, the late W. W. Christman, did before him, and actually selling it.

As for his broadcasts, his essays on the joys of rural life have been published in books because farmers like to have them around.

Ask Jeff (Charles Lucius) Kilborne what his business is and he will tell you, "Depends on what bank of the lake I'm on." Stocky, gray-haired and in his middle fifties, Jeff lives alone in Boscobel, a sprawling, cottagelike home on the east side of Owasco, smallest of the Finger Lakes. From his front porch he can see Ensenore, his 200-

acre dairy farm spread on the long slant of the western shore. Visit Ensenore at dusk and you will observe six dogs urging his hundred registered Holsteins toward the barns, where the milking machines will soon be at their rhythmic pumping while a dozen cats sit imperturbable but expectant.

At the north end of the lake Jeff and his brother own a farm-machinery business. ("We stand behind everything we sell except our manure spreaders.") One of Jeff's business tales is of a farmer who said to him one morning: "I can get one of those mowers in Auburn for two dollars less than your price."

"Why don't you buy in Auburn then?" said Jeff.

"They're out of 'em."

"Hell," said Jeff, "when we're out of 'em, we *give* 'em away."

The number of upstaters who can turn a hand to more than one job is legion. Bill Gratwick, of Buffalo, retired to the little town of Pavilion to devote himself to sculpture. His works failed to win prizes because, the judges said, they lacked style. Then Bill raised imported Merino sheep and entered them at county-fair exhibits. They won no ribbons because, the judges said, they lacked style. Now he grows outsized peonies, and in addition he and his wife have organized a neighborhood chorus which performs Gilbert and Sullivan. Both products have style.

Upstate cities follow a pattern, too. Through the old part of town runs the chief residential thoroughfare. Here, in lawn-girt rows, stand the sprawling dark Victorian piles built by the old families who made their money early—the tribes referred to, with some awe, as Old Amsterdam, Old Herkimer, Old Rome. Inevitably, some of the elegant mansions have been converted to funeral homes. Others have been sold to enterprising immigrant families—and their colorful alterations of conservative façades sometimes startle their neighbors. On the side streets, near this major aisle of aristocracy, stand the expensive new residences of the well-to-do come-latelies whose ranking is less sacrosanct. And on the "other side" of town, in thousands of homes varying little in design, live the employees of the big industries.

Of the smaller upstate cities, many are identified with a single industry. Troy, upriver about ten miles from Albany, is widely recognized as the source of shirts and collars. Schenectady is associated with electric appliances, Gloversville and Johnstown with gloves, Rome with copper, Endicott with business machines, Johnson City with shoes, Little Falls and Herkimer with dairy products, Jamestown with furniture—and so on. All of these vary little from the usual upstate pattern. Three, however, differ very markedly.

The first is Albany. No one who has ever seen wide State Street rise from the Hudson River docks to the Capitol building is likely to forget the sight. It is a sweeping and majestic approach to ornate nothingness —to the three-acre, $25,000,000 gingerbread castle in whose façade the period influences come and go as raggedly as do political influences within. But politics aside—and architecture, too, for most of Albany's other streets are lined with dull look-alike houses of dark red brick or brownstone—Albany has one surpassing distinction. This is Keeler's, the best year-round city restaurant in all upstate, an eating house that feeds sophisticated Manhattanites, rural politicians, foreign diplomats whose palates can be weaned from exotic dishes—and all come away singing the praises of the food. Upstate contains only two other like establishments, and both are in small towns—the Krebs in Skaneateles and Halloway House in East Bloomfield.

The second atypical city is Syracuse, now a center for electronics products and a boom town so overextended that it has hired city-planning experts to ease its growing pains. Syracuse University, city-sized itself and surrounded by the seething town, has retreated sky-ward—with its 21,000 students—from the slopes where it began to the summit of Mount Olympus, where its newest dormitories look out over the vast reaches, tumbling hills and water-streaked valleys of upstate.

Third is Geneva, the most distinctive of upstate cities. Nowhere else in the Northeast are such gracious city houses standing like Godey's *Lady's Book* matrons in a close row, presenting faces of unquestion-able fashion toward the street. Behind them, on sunny days, long nar-row Seneca Lake accentuates the white of sails with the blue of water. A genteel provincialism flavors both the houses and their occupants, so that Geneva is something like South Carolina's Charleston, complete with Church of England touches and an "old Geneva" Shintoism of its own.

The two largest upstate cities are Rochester and Buffalo, and the smaller of these, Rochester, is the better organized and the more homogeneous. Although a few miles separate it from Lake Ontario, it has profited from Great Lakes commerce for more than a hundred and fifty years and now seems stabilized on a high level of genial and genteel conformity. Samuel Hopkins Adams, who was brought up there, pronounced Rochester (from his eyrie on Owasco Lake about sixty-five miles away) as nearly perfect as a city may become. Others are not so sure—like the young executive who told me this: "The city hasn't changed. Yesterday I was summoned to an immediate staff meeting. I showed up wearing a yellow shirt under my jacket. I didn't mind that I was the only one in a colored shirt, but I *did* mind that every mother's son there mentioned it."

Until recently downtown Rochester looked much like an enlarged village with an ill-inspired yellow-brick department store standing like a medieval cathedral at the top of the mall. Now it is in the process of such drastic change that native citizens lose themselves in the labyrinth of new streets. It is a town of beautiful shade trees and comfortable homes however, and in spring its many parks are green and white and purple pleasure-grounds when more than five hundred species of lilacs perfume the whole area and canoes drift in a sun-tinted haze on the river.

Rochester remains the Kodak City, of course, and George Eastman lavished more than $30,000,000 on making it a city of culture. His dream was to provide an art center where his fellow citizens could enjoy fine paintings and great symphonies. In this area Rochesterians sometimes find themselves quite as bewildered as in their new downtown streets, but they are delighted with their progress. Rochester continues on its way, satisfied and comfortable.

At Buffalo, the port may not be denied. Long ships, the ore-bearing "whale-backs," dock in the shadow of towering grain elevators. The lake winds roar into the wide streets. Nights are peppered with the yellow glares of steel furnaces. Delaware Avenue—"Old Buffalo"—is losing face as trade crowds in where society elegants once lived. Impromptu quartettes send *Zwei Herzen im Drei-Viertel Takt* out through the swinging doors of malt-scented German restaurants. And thousands of weathered houses shelter one of the largest Polish populations in the world—a group not to be inhibited by a drab environment. The proof is to see them on a Sunday, walking to their churches with the bulbous spires, or to be a guest at one of their wedding festivals, which run to three full days of gaiety.

Buffalo has a freer "feel" about it than any other York State city. Possibly the wild gusts from the lake, the port atmosphere, the heartiness and *Gemütlichkeit* of the music-loving Germans, the humor and excitability of the Poles are responsible for this. Possibly, too, the English spoken here may be a clue. It abounds in the flat *a* sounds and protracted *r's* used by the town's Midwestern neighbors, and this would make Buffalo the place where the Midwest begins.

The affection and admiration in which Yorkers hold their state is of a distinctive nature. The breezy enthusiasms of Texans, the lush poesy of Californians and Floridians, the dry assumptions of Down East Yankees are not emulated by natives of my state. Their feeling is articulated by a small voice deep within themselves. The language that a region speaks to its inhabitants is not easily translatable. To a child who discovers all new things in an ecstasy of wonder it is not at first understandable. But to an adult Yorker, who knows that the time of becoming one with the soil inexorably advances, the voice of his own landscape is clear.

Yorkers hear this voice and sometimes, on appropriate occasions illumined by wood fires or by stars, they talk about it. They are, they say modestly, a common-sense people, realistic, thrifty, healthy minded, humorous and easygoing, the very antithesis of mystics. Nevertheless, in those unguarded moments, the honest Yorker will confess that he sometimes feels a "something unnatural" that comes from his natural surroundings. Whether most of his days are spent in the sharp Adirondack clarity of Keene Valley, or among the misty vineyards that line one of the Finger Lakes, or beside the level orchards on blue Ontario's plain, or in the forest shadows where stand the cabins of the Cattaraugus Reservation Indians, this is true.

Your Yorker will point out that, from the time the tribes of the Iroquois Confederacy realized that the Onondagas were more psychic than other Indians, and chose them as the keepers of the eternal fires through whose informing flames the messages of the Creator are translated, men have known that the land which is now upstate holds a peculiar enchantment. He will add that Shakers, Perfectionists, Mormons were only three of more than a dozen religious sects that have burgeoned on the forty-mile-wide east-west strip where beings from another world have spoken to his fellow Yorkers. And to clinch his argument he will assert that drumbeats punctuate the windless air above the Finger Lakes on certain magic days, though no living person has ever beheld the instrument or its player. He will say, truthfully, that he has himself heard the lonesome drum and he will laugh at the science departments of the many colleges roundabout which have considered the phenomenon and propounded several learned explanations, no two alike.

Scoff at him and he will tell you *sotto voce* that, while most of his neighbors have their feet on the ground, like himself, he knows some who appear as sane now as their grandfathers did before they joined the Oneida Community, but who might at any time surprise him— and themselves—by surrendering to mystic influences which never cease to hover in the otherwise salubrious upstate air.

In no other region, I believe, is there a more comprehensive rapport between inhabitant and environment. To its people, rivers and lakes mean boundaries, water traffic, irrigation, pure drinking water, and an intangible something more. Mountains, and valleys between, mean vacation lands and tourism, bottom lands mean fertile soil and rich harvests, cities mean vast industries and wide employment, but all these blessings have an added indefinable and mysterious quality that banishes monotony from York State life.

❦ Author's Note

I had intended the project entitled *Windfall Fiddle* to be a truthful account of an upstate New York boyhood—my own. A survey of my early years made me realize, however, that long periods were spent in thinking, in non-thinking, in dreaming and in effortless grow-ing. A narrative which included these intervals, I decided, would be dull indeed, and so I set about squeezing the more active events of my youth closer together. This led perforce to a kind of patchwork quilt of clear authenticity and mist-hung fiction.

❦ Windfall Fiddle

One day a dark man with long curly hair that hung down to his shoulders got off the train at the depot. He was carrying two big suitcases which were very heavy, but he did not check them with the station master. He carried them over to Main Street and opened them up not far from Bob's home. They were full of bottles that contained a reddish liquid. When Bob came by, the man stopped him and told him that his name was Red Eagle and that he had until very recently been a medicine man of the Onondaga Indian Tribe on the reservation near Syracuse. He said that the bottles in the suitcases contained a secret Indian cure for rheumatism, baldness, indigestion and heart trouble, and that he needed a boy to distribute his handbills. These would tell people all about the wonderful things the cure did. Because this was his first visit to White Springs and because he thought it was a lovely little town, he was going to sell the liquid for just what it had cost him to make it up. He said he hated to see the lives of any of the nice people of White Springs made unhappy by any disease whatsoever, and Bob would be doing all of them a real service by taking the handbills around from door to door. Naturally, he added, Bob would be willing to do this just to help his friends, but because he was such a nice honest-looking boy he would be paid twenty cents as soon as all the bills had been handed out.

When Bob had done the job and everybody had had time to read the handbills, Red Eagle said that he would personally call at every door and offer each family a bottle or maybe two bottles if they really needed them, although he ought to be careful about letting any one buy more than he needed because that might use up the supply, and somebody who needed the cure badly would not be able to buy any.

Then the man pulled out of the top of one of the cases the handbills which showed pictures of himself in an Indian suit, wearing a feathered headdress. Below it were printed parts of letters from people who said they had suffered a great deal from many kinds of diseases before they had taken this secret Indian cure and that they now felt better than ever before in their lives. Red Eagle's eyes were very bright and there was a very strange and frightening look in them when he counted out a hundred of the handbills and gave them to Bob.

"Remember," he said and his long curls shook as he said it, "one only to a house and I will know it if any of them get lost or thrown away. Don't ask me how I will know. I have powers that few men have; do not force me to use them."

Bob was so scared by the man's strange look and his queer words that he wanted to give up the job right then and there. The only difficulty with doing that was that he was too scared to say what he wanted, and so he took the handbills and began slipping them under front doors or into mail boxes. He worked all the rest of the morning at this and by time for his lunch he had only a few of the bills left. On his way home he went by the spot where he had left the man but the suitcases and their owner had disappeared.

When he reached home, he found his father had already begun eating his lunch. Bob sat down beside him and told him all that had happened. Mr. Carson laughed:

"I'd not count on being paid, Bob," he said. "A policeman saw him and asked him if he had a license to peddle on the streets. He said no, but that he thought Indians could peddle in this state without a license. So the policeman, whose name is Jerry Two-Kettles and who was born on the Tonowanda Reservation, asked him what tribe he belonged to and he said Onondaga. Jerry asked him a question in the Onondaga language and the man couldn't answer it. So Jerry took him down to the courthouse and he asked Dr. Norton to look at one of the cure bottles and tell him what was in it. Dr. Norton took a bottle over to his office to test it and came back in an hour and said there was nothing in it but water and Easter-egg dye. Jerry thought that was very funny, but the Justice of the Peace, Judge Seymour, didn't. He sent your friend to jail for three days."

Bob felt very badly over doing so much work and losing the twenty cents payment, and he was a little surprised that he did not feel very angry with the long-haired man. He wished he could see Red Eagle and talk to him because he talked so strangely and told things that were very interesting. He would probably never have seen him again if he had not walked by the jail that afternoon, not planning to go inside, but just wondering how he would feel if he had been arrested for helping Red Eagle and put in a lonesome cell. As he walked by one of the barred windows he heard a sudden hissing noise from inside. He looked through the bars and could just make out in the darkness of the cell the bony face and long curls of the cure-seller.

"Listen, my boy," said Red Eagle earnestly. "I was given my choice between paying a five dollar fine or spending three days in jail. As it happened, I did not have the five dollars with me at the time." He laughed a very deep and solemn kind of a laugh.

"Think of it," he said. "Here I am—a very rich man—and I am put in jail because I am so careless about money that I did not think to change the hundred dollar bill I usually carry in my other pair of pants."

Bob said, "Are you really rich?"

"I am very rich," said the man eagerly. "I have hidden in the false bottom of my trunk which is now in Rochester a great fortune in twenty dollar gold pieces. It was once paid to the Onondaga Nation by General Washington for helping him to win the American Revolution. My great-great-grandfather, who was a great warrior, received it and it has been kept in my family ever since. Oh, I knew what that Onondaga policeman said to me all right. I just wanted to throw him off the track. All the bad Indians are trying to get that money away from me. There are many thousands of dollars in the bottom of that trunk."

The man stopped and laughed again in the same hollow, serious way as before. Then he said very suddenly, looking straight into Bob's eyes with a very piercing glance:

"Have you five dollars?"

"Y-y-yes," said Bob weakly, remembering the money he had earned for his violin and not wishing to lie.

"Good!" said the man. "Go get it and bring it to me so that I can pay my fine!"

"B-but," said Bob.

"And do you know what I'm going to do for you?" said Red Eagle impressively. "I'm going to give you not twice or five times or even a hundred times your five dollars. I'm going to give you one thousand dollars from the bottom of my trunk, which is checked in the parcel room of the New York Central Station in Rochester.

"But I don't need all that money," said Bob. "All I need is twenty dollars."

"You are an honest lad," said the cure-seller, gazing at him strangely, "and I shall insist that you keep the thousand that I give you as soon as I get at that trunk. In the meantime may I ask you a simple question and expect an honest answer?"

"Y-y-yes—I guess so," said Bob.

The man lowered his voice to a sharp whisper.

"How much money have you got?" he said.

"Seven dollars and sixty-seven cents," said Bob.

" 'Tis enough," said the man strangely. " 'Twill serve."

"What?" said Bob.

"I suppose you don't have it with you?"

"No, sir, it's home in my bank."

"Well, boy, run home and get it and I will repay you a thousand silver dollars before tomorrow's sun shall set."

"Are you very sure?" said Bob doubtfully. If it's really true, he thought, I could pay for my violin tomorrow night and I would have nine hundred and eighty dollars to do with as I please. I could buy my mother a new dress and my father that expensive fishing rod he wants, and I could buy myself a pinto mustang with four white feet and I could have cowboy boots and a silver-studded saddle.

"Put your ear close to these bars, and I will tell you something," said the man very seriously and in a very low voice. "Is there anyone near you on the street who could overhear what I am about to say?"

"No," said Bob.

"Good," said the man, "for I have never told this secret to a living soul. Though I may seem to you to be every inch an Indian brave, though all the six nations of the Iroquois believe me to be a direct descendant of the great Hiawatha, the founder of their great federation, there is in my veins the blood of the first gypsy ever to come to the shores of America. He was a stowaway on the flagship of Columbus—the *Santa Maria*. When discovered, he was put in irons and later set ashore on a barren island, left to starve. Friendly Indians rescued him and took him to the mainland. Ever a wanderer, he joined a hunting party bound north and while trapping beaver in the Hudson valley he was captured by a raiding party of Senecas who brought him to this very neighborhood. A Seneca Princess saved him from being burned at the stake and he was adopted into the tribe and became her husband. No doubt you are wondering, my dear Bob, why I am telling you this greatest secret of my life."

"No," said Bob, "or I guess I mean yes."

"Of course you mean yes and I will tell you. I have already mentioned my extraordinary occult powers. Because of my gypsy blood I can sometimes see into the future. I am also clairvoyant. Your seven sixty-seven for example—it is in a small metal bank hidden under a pile of old clothes in a dark closet. Is that right?"

"Why, yes!" said Bob, astounded.

"You see," said the man triumphantly. "And now I will tell you what else I see. I see myself, freed from this foul and loathesome dump, returning from Rochester on the afternoon train tomorrow. You are waiting at the depot as it pulls in. I descend: I take out my wallet and count out into your hands fifty twenty-dollar gold pieces. You are almost overcome with gratitude. You can now buy for your father and your mother and yourself things that have always been needed. You laugh, then almost cry; we embrace. And all for seven sixty-seven."

"Do you mean it?" cried Bob, gazing deep into the man's blazing eyes.

"I, Red Eagle, have said it," said the man in his deepest and most sincere voice.

"Then I will get the money for you," said Bob, and he raced for home. With trembling fingers he emptied his bank and counted out the money. When he was through counting he thought of all the hours of hard work he had put in to earn it, and that made him think of how much more time he would have to work hard to earn twenty dollars, and he was glad that he would have so very much money right away and without having to work for it at all. He ran back down to the jail and pushed the money through the bars, and Red Eagle counted it eagerly and then said:

"My boy, you will never regret this," in his deep voice.

"If you pay your fine right away you can catch the after-supper train for Rochester," said Bob.

"What's that?" said Red Eagle. "Oh, yes. The after-supper train. That will hardly be necessary. There is a morning train, is there not?"

"Yes," said Bob slowly.

"That will do very well," said Red Eagle. "After all, the money is in my trunk right at the New York Central Station. I will go to Rochester in the morning, get the money, and return on the afternoon train just as I saw it when I looked into the future. As for this evening I have certain plans. Would you care to join me?"

"I could come downtown after my violin lesson for a little while," said Bob eagerly. By now he was completely fascinated by the Indian-Gypsy—or was he a Gypsy-Indian? He thought he had never met anyone quite so romantic, so full of strange adventures....

"I think I will dine here," said Red Eagle calmly. "After a leisurely meal I will summon the jailer and arrange to pay my fine. Let us meet at the Clinton Street bridge over the canal at—shall we say, eight o'clock?"

Bob did not tell his father and mother of his plans to meet Red Eagle. Nor did he tell Miss Adelaide. He realized afterwards that he should not have kept it a secret and that he must have had a guilty feeling about it, or he would have told all that had happened that afternoon. At the time, though, he assured himself that the reason he said nothing was that he wanted to surprise everybody the next evening when he came home gaily tossing gold pieces high in the air and able to buy his violin and anything else he wanted.

He was so excited that he could hardly eat and his mother said anxiously: "Are you sure you feel all right? Have you been eating between meals? Is your forehead hot? I believe you have a fever."

As for his violin lesson, he made so many mistakes that even sweet Miss Adelaide got a little out of patience and dismissed him early saying: "Bob, you really must learn to pay attention to what you're doing if you are ever going to learn to play the violin."

Red Eagle was already waiting on the Clinton Street bridge, leaning over the railing with head bent and long curls dangling.

"Good!" he said. "I see you are a man of your word. Now, if you will join me in a stroll along the towpath, we shall see what we shall see."

The two set off at an easy pace along the north bank of the canal on a trail made grassless and hard by the hooves of many horses and mules. Bob found himself enjoying the walk hugely. Red Eagle talked easily and he told of the days when he rode in Buffalo Bill's Wild West Show and made a tour of the great cities of Europe. Kings and princes sat in the front boxes and applauded his daring horsemanship and queens and princesses smiled down at him. "That was when I first began wearing my hair long," said Red Eagle. "They liked it that way."

The canal curved in a slow bend just outside of town and beyond the County Fair Grounds. As Bob and Red Eagle reached the far side of the bend they could see a long rectangular canalboat moored there in the deepening spring dusk. Beside it a pair of patient mules were tethered to a strong post, heads bent and stretched forward toward the weeds and grass that lined the towpath. A light winked on in the little square windows of the cabin. Yellow and clear it poured out into the darkness, revealing the dark red blooms and green leaves of the geraniums in the tidy window boxes. Bob could hear a mouth organ playing a sprightly tune as he and Red Eagle approached and then a man's tenor voice sounded out loud and clear:

> "When I came to this wonderful country
> It filled me with greatest surprise
> To see such a great undertaking
> On the like I ne'er opened my eyes
> To see full a thousand brave fellows
> At work from the Spring to the Fall
> A'drivin' along the old towpath
> Their mules on the Erie canal.
>
> "I joined up with them for a season
> My Saturday pay for to draw
> And soon I had learned how to holler
> More words than plain Gee and Haw
> Our food it was all very plenty
> To complain we'd no reason at all
> I had money in every pocket
> While workin' upon the canal.
>
> "While at night we all rest from our labor
> Begorra, our rent is all paid
> We stop and we haul in the bowline
> In the cabin our beds are all made
> We all set a-jokin' together
> There is nothing our minds to enthrall
> If happiness be in this wide world
> I am sure it is on the canal."

By the time the voice had finished the song, Bob and Red Eagle could see the music makers. They were seated on stout wooden chairs that were tilted back against the wall of the cabin, their feet dangling in the air. The player of the mouth organ was a woman—the biggest, Bob thought, that he had ever seen. By the light that streamed from the windows he could see that she was dressed in a flowing dress of red background on which were printed a torrent of white and yellow daisies. On her head she wore a yellow sunbonnet and the light from the window occasionally was reflected in a gleam from her glasses.

She was not really so fat, Bob thought, as just plain big all over. Her legs were long and her head was an unbelievable distance from the seat of the chair. She was wide, too, and anyone could see that she would weigh more than most men, even fat men. The man was scrawny and his face was small except for a big nose which slanted from left to right, beginning at the middle of a narrow forehead and ending above and somewhat right of the center of his wide mouth. He wore no hat and his hair was scant and wispy. His clothes apparently consisted of a faded and frayed red-checkered shirt and a pair of worn and faded blue overalls. His feet were bare. As he suddenly saw two dark figures at the foot of the narrow gangplank that led to his boat the man tilted his weight forward and the front legs of his chair hit the deck sharply.

"Who'll that be?" he said softly.

"It is I, Red Eagle," said Bob's companion, "with a young friend."

"Begorra and it's the King of the Injuns," said the man and there seemed to be relief in his voice, "or the King of the Gypsies—and which is it being this fine spring evening?"

"The King of the Gypsies, of course, when the twilight is deepening into dark and the swallows have just stopped their flitting," said the woman, and Bob was surprised that the voice which came from her enormous body was as clear and fresh as that of a girl.

"Whichever it be, ye are welcome," said the man. "For a moment I was thinking that instead of you it might be that other red man, that limb of Satan, the Injun officer of the law. Deliver us all from a policeman that's not an Irishman. It's unnatural."

"This is my friend and partner, Bob Carson," said Red Eagle. "He has aided me this day in a way which I can never repay."

"Nor will ye," said the man cheerily. He rose from his chair and shook Bob's hand solemnly and the woman behind him did not move but said simply in her sweet girl's voice: "Hello, Bob Carson."

"I'm Dion O'Brien," said the man, "and the woman is my wife, Molly. And have ye both had your supper? There's what's left of a chicken in the galley."

"Yes, thank you," said Bob.

"I dined as a guest of the town," said Red Eagle.

"I heard ye was in jail," said Dion O'Brien, "and may I say it was no surprise. After I took three full bottles of that cure ye left us in payment of that bad debt, my rheumatiz was much worse than before."

"And my hair began falling out," said Molly O'Brien.

"Speaking of that debt now paid in full," said Red Eagle, "it came to me that I would be able this evening to place you under a similar obligation."

"Ye're sure of that now?" said Dion O'Brien. "Ye wouldn't be deceivin' us?"

"I looked into the future," said Red Eagle simply.

"And how much will we be owin' ye?" asked Mr. O'Brien heatedly, "so I can tell Molly to get it out of the sock."

"I did not see the exact sum," said Red Eagle, "but it was enough that I felt justified in buying a new pack of cards at Clarke's Drug Store in town." He reached into the breast pocket of his black coat and brought out a small new cardboard box sealed shut with a big blue stamp.

"New cards!" said Molly O'Brien, as if she were a small girl receiving a doll. "How nice! Do let me see them." She took the box from Red Eagle and ran her long fingers over it, then held it up into the light streaming from the window.

"These cards were bought," she said with a giggle, "at the Hearty Enjoyment Shop on Front Street in Rochester. 'Magic and Card Tricks a Specialty.'"

"O—ho!" said Dion O'Brien, "and ye would be treatin' us to a brand-new pack of slippery cards, would ye, ye spalpeen? It's mighty kind of ye and I'm much obliged but we'll be playin' with the same old pack."

"When I looked into the future," said Red Eagle, "we were playing with this pack."

"Well, ye'd better take another look," said Mr. O'Brien, "and ye'll see we're playin' with our old cards and that we won't be takin' Red Eagle's Cure for rheumatiz, baldness, and indigestion in payment of just debts."

"Very well," said Red Eagle. "It will make no difference in the result." He turned then to Bob.

"What time, my boy, are you accustomed to retire?"

"He means," said Molly O'Brien helpfully, "when do ye go to bed?"

"Half-past nine," said Bob, "sometimes I stay up until ten."

"I have been wondering," said Red Eagle, "whether you would not enjoy sitting here on the deck in the moonlight while my friends and I enjoy a somewhat competitive game in the cabin. You could then inform us if anyone were happening to be strolling down the towpath so that we might prepare a welcome for them. If no one comes I believe I shall be ready to walk back to town with you before ten o'clock."

"And he'll be walkin' light," said Dion O'Brien.

"Mr. Red Eagle," said Bob desperately. "Are you going to play a betting game with my money?"

"Bob," said Red Eagle, "you have wisely entrusted seven dollars and sixty-seven cents of your funds to my care to be expended as my judgment sees fit in order to bring you large returns. Five dollars of that money unfortunately had to be spent to give me freedom of action. I am about to make a judicious use of the remainder. You need have no fear. I have looked into the future."

"But the money in Rochester," said Bob, and he felt a lump rising in his throat at the same time the bottom of his stomach seemed to be dropping like a stone. "What about the thousand dollars I am to have tomorrow when you come back on the afternoon train?"

"It shall be as I have said," spoke Red Eagle in his deepest tones. "And now if you will be good enough to keep a watch for evening strollers I would like to enjoy a quiet game with two old friends."

"I will get you some cookies," said Molly O'Brien, "and you can sit here and eat them."

"I can't eat anything now," said Bob miserably.

"They are very good," said Molly, "and I think you will like them." She stood upright and Bob saw that she was obliged to stoop to enter the door of the cabin. The two men followed her inside. In a moment, she returned with a plate full of big round sugar cookies.

"I baked them this afternoon," she said. "Eat hearty" and she stooped again to enter the cabin door.

Bob thought he had never been in such utter despair; he knew now how greedy and how stupid he had been. As he sat munching on Molly's cookies, which were very good, indeed, he realized that he had never trusted Red Eagle completely and that he had gambled with his own money much more foolishly than the cure-seller was gambling in the cabin at that very moment. He was sure now that the story about the gold pieces in the false bottom of the trunk in Rochester was wholly false. Red Eagle had deceived him with fancy talk and his deep sincere voice. Yet Bob could not bring himself to blame the strange man: if only he were really bad all through, he thought, if he were only a burglar or a tough and wicked man who took other people's property by force, then he could hate him and he would not feel so guilty himself. He thought of all the hours of really hard work that had now gone for nothing because he had listened to Red Eagle, and he knew suddenly that the reason he had been so silly as to believe him. He wanted to get out of earning the money, of deserving it by giving honest hard work in return. He wanted his violin and at the thought of it his despair seemed unbearable.

He would have to begin all over again and he would never be able, at the rate he had been going, to earn enough money to pay for it in the months remaining, before the time set by Miss Adelaide. He thought of asking her for more time and knew that since his loss of what he had earned had been his own fault that he could never do so. Tomorrow, he thought, I will take the violin back to Miss Adelaide and tell her it is unfair for me to keep it and practice on it when I can never own it. Then he thought of his father and mother and of how little money his father had because school superintendents of small towns are not well paid. And he thought of how hard his mother had to work because she could not hire a girl to help her, as the richer ladies of the town did, and how kind they were to him and how much they wanted him to have the violin and learn to play it.

A little breeze rippled the dark waters of the canal and stirred the geraniums in the window boxes, and his cheeks that had been burning with embarrassment and humiliation felt cool; he knew that they were wet with tears from his brimming eyes. For the first time he was aware of the spring peepers, the tiny frogs singing all about him from the waters and the banks of the canal so loud that they sounded like sleigh-bells on a cold, clear winter night. Then he felt the overpowering desire to go home and tell his father and mother all about what had happened. He knew that they would be disappointed in him and he squirmed in his chair in the misery of knowing it, but he felt he must go to them at once and by telling them, lighten the pain of knowing what a fool he had been. He knew that they loved him and that they would say so and he would be comforted.

There was a step on the gangplank and Bob realized that he had not been watching the towpath as Red Eagle had told him to. The light from the window struck a bright brass button and Bob, watching a slim, tall, dark figure move swiftly up the plank, recognized Jerry Two-Kettles.

"Hello, Bob," said Jerry softly. "Thought you might be wanting to walk home now and stopped by for you."

"Hello, Jerry," said Bob. "How did you know where I was?"

"Figured it out," said Jerry. "Asked myself where I'd be if I was twelve years old."

"You mean you were looking for me," said Bob. "Why would you be looking for me?"

"Because your dad came downtown and told me you usually are home by nine-thirty and in bed by ten. It's almost eleven now."

"Was he worried?"

"Yes, I think he was—at least until I told him I'd find you."

The door of the cabin opened and Red Eagle peered out.

"Bob," he said, "are you keeping good watch? I thought I heard voices."

"You heard 'em all right, you imitation Indian," said Jerry. "If you're an Onondaga, I'm a Hottentot."

"Officer Two-Kettles," said Red Eagle in an injured tone. "I consider this persecution. No sooner have I arranged for my liberty after a most unjustifiable arrest and settled down for a sociable evening's game with two respected friends than you again appear, threatening tax-paying citizens who are trying to make an honest living. I consider it an outrage, sir, an unpardonable and, may I say, stinking outrage. Why—why—why—"

"A sociable game, is it?" said Jerry Two-Kettles stepping up to the door and looking beyond him where the O'Briens sat at a table. "I can see cards and money in there and if I did my full duty I'd run you all in for gambling."

At that Molly O'Brien rose from her chair in the cabin and stooping to avoid bumping her head as she came through the door she stood upright on the deck. Her hands on her hips she faced the policeman and spoke in her clear little girl's voice.

"Ye spalpeen," she said, "ye outlandish savage with a painted face and no clothes, ye tomahawker of babes and defenseless women, ye dancer around the pagan fires of the haythen. Ye've burnt good Christians at the stake and ye've worshipped strange gods and now ye stand there keepin' honest and hard-workin' folks from enjoyin' the rest they've earned by the sweat o' their brow. If there's one thing I can't abide it's a wild man o' the woods, a speaker of a crazy language no self-respectin' human ever heard before, a redskin with a black heart an' a yellow belly and—and—" she paused to get her breath, "and a furriner at that."

As she stood there Bob thought she was almost terrifying, for the light streaming out the door behind her made her shadow before her so large that it covered most of the long narrow boat. He held his breath wondering what Jerry Two-Kettles would do after she had heaped all her insults upon him. He was astounded at that very moment then to hear Jerry laughing.

"Molly O'Brien," said Jerry, when his laughter was under control. "I know you and your mouth organ and that sweet-voiced, song-singin' husband o' yours. Your boat ain't the cleanest on the canal but it ain't the worst either. I'd be willin' to pass by your breakin' of the law if it wasn't for the company you keep. You may not think much o' my folks a while back but you're consortin' with a lyin', thievin' long-hair that pretends to be an Indian when everybody knows he's nothin' but a hand-readin', fortune-tellin', card-crookin', jail-breakin', cure-sellin' gypsy."

"I am Red Eagle," said the cure-seller loftily, "and I did not break jail. Though I was unjustly accused, I chose to pay my fine."

"With whose money?" said Jerry.

"With mine," said Bob.

"I thought so," said Jerry, "and how much more of it has he got?"

"Two dollars and sixty-seven cents."

"Hand it over," said Jerry to Red Eagle. The long curls of the cure-seller twitched in an annoyed gesture.

"I am for the moment financially embarrassed," he said. "Perhaps at a later time."

"Where's the money?" said Jerry firmly.

"He lost all of it fair and square in an honest poker game," said Dion O'Brien defiantly, "except twenty-three cents and that's on the table inside."

"Tell you what I'll do," said Jerry. "If you three will give back to this boy that two sixty-seven the gypsy stole and be out of the county by tomorrow noon, I'll take Bob here back home and forget this happened. Otherwise you'll all be sleeping in the jail-house."

"I did not steal the money," said Red Eagle. "It was entrusted to me as an investment."

"Did he tell you about hundreds of twenty-dollar gold pieces hid in a trunk?" said Jerry to Bob.

"Yes, he did."

"I thought so," said Jerry. "He's a dirty swindler. I can't get the five dollar fine back but by the Lord Harry that two sixty-seven had better show up or—"

"I'll pay it," said Dion O'Brien hastily. "That is, all but twenty-three cents."

"Okay," said Red Eagle, looking injured and noble, "though it leaves me penniless, I will pay my just debts."

"We'll take you on to Medina tomorrow morning," said Molly, "and give you your breakfast."

"I'll go get my suitcases, then," said Red Eagle promptly. "I hid them under the grandstand at the fairgrounds after I got out of jail."

Dion O'Brien stepped inside and came back out with the money which he counted carefully into Bob's hand.

"Come on, Bob," said Jerry. He turned to Molly O'Brien. "I can forgive you all those things you said about me, Molly, except that crack about me bein' a furriner."

"Guess I'll have to take that back," said Molly smiling. "Goodnight, folks."

Bob and the policeman walked back along the towpath toward the glow in the sky made by the lights of downtown. They were about halfway there when they heard singing behind them and the sound of a mouth organ. Bob recognized the song and he listened happily until Dion O'Brien's high tenor dwelt on the final words:

> "If happiness be in this wide world
> I'm sure it is on the canal."

✿ The Civil War and Me

On a cloud-hung Decoration Day when I was ten I wakened to the treble of fifes and the beat of drums. I dived into my clothes, gulped my cereal, and set out down Main Street. I was near the high-domed courthouse when sudden rain silenced the band and drenched my shirt. I dashed between white pillars and through a door into the courtroom. There Tom Kirby in Prince Albert coat, gray and white striped pants, white vest, a high collar, and a black necktie was speaking:

"There is little need to say more. Here in the front row sit our aging heroes of the desperate Civil War. We honor these living few and through them the thousands who fell. To them we say we have not forgotten. Shiloh, The Wilderness, Antietam, Gettysburg are more than names to us. I dare say there is not a family in this town which does not remember one of them with an especial sadness."

I do not remember what else Tom Kirby said. I had been moved by that one idea and I thought about it until the drums and fifes began raising echoes. Then old Sam Francis, town carpenter, rose to his full height of six-foot-seven, lifted the colors which he had carried, miraculously without injury, up the slopes of Missionary Ridge, and marched to the door. Sunlight suddenly poured through the windows. The

From *New York State and the Civil War*, published November, 1962, by the New York State Civil War Commission.

white-haired fifer began to play "Marching Through Georgia" and the
two old drummers took up the beat. Now we were marching—veterans,
audience and all—down toward the Erie Canal. In ten minutes we had
crossed the bridge to the baseball lot where the town team and the
traveling Cherokee Indian team were warming up.

At supper that evening I said to my parents, "Was anybody in our
family a soldier in the Civil War?"

"Why, of course," said my mother. "Your Grandfather Lamson enlisted when he was only twenty. He was wounded in the leg at the
first battle of Bull Run."

My father smiled wickedly. "Next time you see him ask him whether
it was the shin or the buttocks," he said to me.

Mother's blue eyes turned a bleak look on Father. "I'm his daughter,"
she said, "and I guess I ought to know. It was the shin and not that
other place."

My father's teasing led me later to a history and a chapter describing the headlong flight of Federal units at Bull Run.

I was not to see Grandfather Lamson until after a social event, the
Griswold Family picnic, at Dryden, the Tompkins County town where
my Grandfather Carmer and my grandmother (born Sarah Griswold)
were hosts.

The Carmer house was not big as farmhouses went in the township,
but it stood high on the bank of Fall Creek and that made it possible
for a photographer to stand down near the water, slant his camera
upward and get a picture of the whole kit and caboodle of Griswolds
and their relatives. The Carmers were outnumbered about ten to one
but my father's generation, loyal to their mother, all appeared, and
I was proud to see that Grandfather Carmer had the biggest and
whitest beard of the lot. I still have a print that proves it.

Taking the photograph was always the last event of the picnic. All
at once the road was choked with democrat wagons and surreys and
even lumber wagons all stuffed with Griswolds. I soon found Grandmother Carmer in the cool woodshed surrounded by great yellow
circles of cream risen from the round shallow milk pans.

"Did Grandfather fight in the Civil War?" I said.

"They wouldn't take him," said my grandmother, skimming the

wrinkling surfaces and emptying her spoon into a pitcher. "A horse stepped on his foot when he was a boy and the recruiting officer said he'd give out on long marches."

"Didn't any Carmers go?"

"Well, now let's see. There's your Uncle Charlie. He enlisted three times in all and got wounded at Petersburg. He gets so much pension he hasn't done a lick from the time he came home. Every good day, and a good many that aren't, he goes fishing."

"Does he catch many?" I said.

"No, I wouldn't say so. I guess fishing's more a kind of religion with him. He'd have gone over to Dryden Lake today except he likes picnics, too."

Disappointed at not finding a family hero, I said, "Didn't any more of the family go?"

"There was your Cousin Oliver Carmer," said Grandma. "When he enlisted he was twenty-one and the strongest man in the county. Folks used to come from miles around to see him wrestle and lift weights at the fair. He was captured and sent to Andersonville Prison about the same time cousin Bezaleel Griswold came there. Bezaleel was fifteen years older and Oliver did the best he knew how to take care of him but it didn't do any good. Bezaleel died and Oliver came home so peaked he looked like a living skeleton. His brother Dan came safe through seven battles but lost a leg in the first charge at Gettysburg. Then he learned to be a tailor. That gave our village two one-legged tailors. The other one left his leg behind at Gettysburg, too. They were both lucky, I guess, for five Dryden boys were killed on that same day."

By this time, attracted by my grandmother's talk and my small-boy interest, Uncle Charlie and my father had come up to listen.

"I was a youngster then, but I remember most of those who went," said my father, "and the best of them all was my Uncle Nathan Griswold. He was so young they set him to drilling recruits at Elmira. Then he was ordered to New York City to help stop the draft riots. After a three-year stretch he vowed he wouldn't go back unless they sent him to the front. I can remember him when he came home on furlough. He was tall and blue-eyed and wore a moustache and when he stood up in his uniform to sing 'Just As I Am Without One Plea' in the Presbyterian choir or to play a cornet solo in the Dryden band,

'Take Up Your Gun and Go, John,' the whole town was proud. He made a lot over me when I was little and I loved him."

"Everybody did," said my grandmother.

Then Uncle Charlie spoke up and I could tell by the startled looks of my father and my grandmother that he was breaking a long, long silence.

"I was shot at Petersburg the same day as Nathan," he said. "When the mine under the Rebs exploded, it left a big crater. Two white regiments poured in and tried to climb out the other side to take Cemetery Hill. They couldn't come it. Then two regiments of Negroes charged in behind them. I used to drop in on Nathan—being he was brother to my brother's wife—and he had told me he'd been drilling the colored boys and would be leading a company of them. When they were given the word they went right through or maybe over the whites and began climbing out of the crater. But by then the Rebs had lined the top and were shooting them down by the hundreds—like shooting fish in a barrel."

Suddenly Uncle Charlie stopped, and I saw he was looking at my grandmother. She had snatched her handkerchief from her apron and put it to her eyes.

"He was my dear, dear brother," she said.

My father said, "You musn't take on about it now, Mother. That was a long, long time ago."

"It will always be yesterday," she said. "He died with them because he loved them and because he hated slavery so."

"There were other reasons for the war," said my father.

"Not here," his mother said fiercely. "That was the *only* reason in Dryden." Then she dropped her skimming spoon and walked unsteadily toward the front parlor.

Autumn came to our home in the Western New York fruit belt a few months later, and with it came news from Wisconsin. My great-uncle Albert, my grandfather Lamson's brother, was on his way east and would visit us for a few days. Even my father seemed somewhat impressed by this.

"He's the one that escaped from Libby Prison," he said. "And your mother has a picture of him he had taken as soon as he hit the Union lines. He *would*."

When Uncle Albert arrived from Wisconsin I was amazed to discover how much he looked like the wartime photograph. Though he now wore a beard, I realized that I would have recognized him once I had seen the picture. I remember being troubled for fear he would be as unlikely to talk as Uncle Charlie, but I need not have worried. He loved to tell about his escape, and I only wish I could remember all he said about it.

From his enthusiastic account I gathered that Uncle Al had been mustered into the Wadsworth Guard (104th Regiment of Infantry) as a sergeant in the autumn of 1861. He was a second lieutenant by July 1, 1863. On that first day of Gettysburg his company was in line to the right of Seminary Ridge.

"The Rebs were behind a dilapidated stone fence along the woods. Our line charged them and took some prisoners. The Rebs were reinforced and came at us. This time we gave way and it was reported we retired in good order. That meant we all kept up with the fastest runner in the regiment."

When Uncle Al returned so swiftly to town he was astounded to discover it had been occupied by the enemy. He and his companions hastily assumed the roles of attendants in their Division Hospital and busily "played nursy" to the wounded, but the Johnny Rebs were not fooled. Uncle Albert was soon under guard and held a prisoner at the headquarters of General Pickett. He saw that officer stride out with a full staff and bodyguard on the way to his desperate charge, and later saw his forlorn return with a lone aide.

Never having suffered from hunger, filth, and human cruelty and their attendant effects, I could not fully realize them in my child's imagination, though my parents were horrified by Uncle Albert's narrative of life at notorious Libby. I was, however, greatly pleased with his anecdote of how two Union men escaped from the march to its gates by secreting themselves in an outhouse behind a southern mansion, and a little puzzled by his description of it as an "old-fashioned place." (Apparently modern plumbing had blessed his Wisconsin farmhouse before it had reached my own home.) I was also delighted with his story of a Genesee Valley private nicknamed "General Guinea Pig," who secreted a tiny stars-and-stripes banner so successfully throughout three years of frequent searches that he was able to present it to General Wadsworth's wife with appropriate ceremony at the end of the war.

Best of all of Uncle Al's tales, I thought, was his report of the Libby Prison Minstrel Show put on by the inmates on Christmas Eve of 1863. Uncle Albert had brought the program with him all the way from Wisconsin and he read excerpts from it proudly.

"Performance to commence at 6 o'clock. Admission free. Children in arms not admitted." The show began with "The Overture to the Opera 'Norma'" rendered by the whole troupe. Then followed a melange of classics, comic songs, and dialogues. "Drafted into the Army" preceded a violin and flute duet "Serenade from Lucia," and "Root, Hog, or Die." The sadness of "The Dying Girl's Last Request" was alleviated by a clog dance and a list of the Dramatis Personae which intimated the content of some of the sketches: "Black Swan to be played by Lieutenant Morgan, Broadway Swill [sic] by Lieutenant Burnett, Richard III by Captain McWilliams."

My mother had told me that her "Uncle Al" was known in Geneseo as "The Man who Escaped from Libby" and I was greatly surprised to hear him deny that he had done so. As the tide of war turned against them the Confederate authorities had shipped many prisoners from Richmond first to Macon, Georgia, and thence to "Camp Sorghum" in Charleston, where they found themselves under the fire of fellow-Yankee besiegers. There they became so hungry that when a razorback sow wandered aimlessly into camp she was literally torn apart and devoured by those fortunate enough to have a "good holt" on her.

Possibly given encouragement by their pork-chop dinner, three Yankee officers on the next morning forged for themselves three paroles to leave the camp to obtain firewood. They had taken the precaution of covering their shoes with red pepper, and the bloodhounds summoned to track them, when the escape was discovered, lost interest in their mission. Captain Edward Sill and Lieutenants William Shelton and Albert Lamson had set out for "God's Country."

Uncle Al said that Shelton was such a good writer that he would leave it to me to read his account of the trio's return to safety which was published in the *Century Magazine,* Volume XL, 1890, under the title "A Hard Road to Travel Out of Dixie." My father and I immediately set out for our town library where we obtained the issue containing it. I spent most of the next Saturday and Sunday reading the melodramatic adventures described therein.

Hidden and protected by courageous Negroes, the three fugitives made their way northward—sleeping in the day, walking at night. Eventually in North Carolina they became separated. Then sympathetic hill folk guided Sill and Lamson over Great Smoky Mountain trails to the Federal troops in Chattanooga. Thin, weary, ragged, the two friends had enough spirit left to go at once to a photographer and have him make a record of how they looked when they rejoined their comrades. The picture was reproduced in the *Century* article by Shelton, who reached Chattanooga a month later.

Late on the night of the Sabbath, while Uncle Al snored comfortably in our guest room, I told my parents I had completed my researches on my family in the Civil War.

"Well," said my father, "they didn't do so badly for a lot of average farm boys. All enlisted at the bottom. None was promoted farther than first lieutenant except Uncle Nathan just before he was killed."

"They did their duty," said my mother. Her husband looked at me.

"You're lucky your mother's mother and her fighting Hebridean clansmen didn't come to America in time," he said, "or you'd have to turn full-time genealogist."

🐝　Boy Reading

Down in the meadow where the dim path meandering
Finds at last the watercress greening on the brook,
Waterlilies lift their gold for reckless squandering
Of bumble-bees encamped in an alder nook.

There in the twilight where the gay rout crowds,
Flecked by filtered spotlights from the dodging sun,
A boy is sitting quietly, eyes on sailing clouds,
Ears alert to gossip of the ripples as they run,
Hands on the covers of a new-found book.

Here the sky is water-blue, tossing silver galleons,
And the hollow rumble beyond horizon's rim
Is not the somber echo of the summer thunder
But the brassy volleys of their sullen guns.

All about his body shine materials of wonder,
Each colored pebble is a talisman to him,
Each flash of light comes from leveled lances,
Every leafy tree is a whispering spy,
The butterflies are priestesses performing mystic dances,
Each robin's note is a Druid prophecy.

> A book can be a time-machine, turning back the years
> To a violet-girl in bombazine,
> A surly knavish Byzantine,
> A buccaneering brigantine,
> A monarch in arrears.
> A book can be a cry through a sky that's moonsick,
> A bead-eyed bat in a shadowy place,
> The whistling sigh of a sound-quick broomstick
> In space;

A wind-swung lantern at a pitch-black crossroads
A snowball rolling toward obesity,
> The secret blossom of a rock-hid moss-rose,
> Twin old maids at the manse for tea.

> A book can be a diamond (facets without end),
> A baking-powder biscuit, a bow to bend,
> A white town dreaming in a hill's high pocket,
> An eagle screaming over legions to the wars,
> The jet-sped arch of a wild skyrocket—
> Burst into stars!

Down in alder-shadow by a chattering brook
A boy has just opened a new-found book.

🐝 Bride of Apollo

My European ancestors were Holland Dutch, and after moving to heterogeneous America they stubbornly kept on marrying spouses of the same breed. The earliest of these immigrants found the trip across the Atlantic to New Amsterdam so disturbing that they never trusted themselves to water transportation again, and they seem to have transmitted their distaste for it to their descendants. My great-grandfather broke a tradition of long standing, however, by marrying a girl of English antecedents, and her son, my grandfather, apparently liked her so much that he wed one Sarah Griswold, whose ancestors left the scene of Sir Walter Scott's *Kenilworth* to establish themselves in a Connecticut town which they called Killingworth. This genealogical introduction should explain my presence as a little boy at annual Griswold picnics in Tompkins County, New York, around the turn of the century.

Some of the first Griswolds in this country were seagoing men, and it was from a grizzled, full-bearded descendant of these that I heard in my tenth year an after-picnic narrative he thought some of his younger kin should be acquainted with.

There was once, he said, a handsome and powerfully built young Captain Griswold who had been so successful in his early voyages to certain of the West Indies, then known as the Sugar Islands, that he ordered built at his own expense and according to his own specifications a slim, fast schooner which he named for his bride of a few months, *Asenath*. Before the ship was completed he placed an order with the cleverest wood-carver on the Connecticut coast for a magnificent figurehead to adorn the pointed prow. The wooden figure was to be a representation of Apollo, and it would show that god with hands outstretched before him as if the waves of the sea were horses and he were holding a tight rein on them as they raced ahead of his water-chariot.

The wood-carver had no sooner looked upon the handsome captain than he realized he need seek no further for his model, and he carved a likeness so perfect that it was immediately recognized by all the Yankees of the shore towns. Though some of these who were scholarly —the schoolteachers, the ministers, the lawyers—objected that they had never seen an Apollo with a black beard, the carving was approved with delight by Asenath and hundreds of friends who soon came to identify it with the master of the vessel rather than the classic god.

The first voyage of the *Asenath* to the Sugar Islands and return was made in amazingly good time, and the profits of the venture were so great that the captain and his lady left New England and removed to that section above New York Harbor now known as Brooklyn Heights. Here, on a tall bluff that looked down on brownstone Hudson-River-Gothic city houses, the young couple ordered to be erected a glittering white New England mansion.

The second voyage, too, was highly successful, and the captain built his own dock below his home and began to think of acquiring other vessels. On his third, however, a hurricane struck the *Asenath* when she was a few days out from the Sugar Islands, and she was lost with all hands.

When Asenath realized that the captain would come back no more, her grief was so intense and so prolonged that for three years her Brooklyn neighbors worried for fear she would lose both reason and health.

Then, on a bright and blowy day a Gloucester captain put in to New York Harbor for a minor repair. He met the young widow and courted her so ardently that after six months of decorous protest she set the day for their wedding.

On the evening before that day came the greatest storm that could be remembered in the history of the harbor. When it had finally blown itself out and the morning was clear and bright, Brooklyn folk were horrified at seeing far up on the shore, where apparently it had been driven by great waves, what seemed to be the lifeless remains of a human. The face was toward the sand, but head and shoulders were

held from it by stiff arms as if, at the moment of death, there had
been one last despairing effort to rise.

When the first onlookers ran up the slope they saw that the seem-
ing corpse was a wooden image of a black-bearded man, though at a
little distance it looked exactly like a body cast up by the sea—a body
which still had possessed life enough to crawl toward a longed-for
goal, for it was directly lined up between the Griswold dock and the
house of the Widow Griswold on the hill.

When Asenath rushed down the slope and saw the figurehead, she
threw herself upon it as if it were the fleshly remains of her lost husband. Her betrothed found her there, and the two of them held a short
colloquy. Then the man lifted the image and, staggering under its
weight, followed the frantic widow into her house. He came out later,
looking grim, and ordered the wedding plans canceled. Then he
boarded his vessel, cast off, and put to sea.

In the succeeding months the widow became silent and frighteningly morose. There was considerable speculation along the waterfront
as to what had become of the figurehead until a ship's painter, hired
to "freshen up" the outer walls of the white residence, reported seeing
it through a window. "She's got it tied up on the dining-room chair
the captain used," he said, "and it's his spittin' image! There's a
blanket below the table so you can't see there's no legs, and the arms
stretch out along the upper surface. Sets out her meals with her, but
don't say much."

The widow lived there with the likeness of her late husband for
forty-odd years before she died. The heirs of her property were distant
cousins, and they sold the figurehead to a museum that prided itself
on its collection of scrimshaw, harpoons, and other seagoing Americana.
I have not found out where the figure is, and so, whenever I enter an
exhibit of this sort, I wonder if I shall soon be face to face with the
carved wooden likeness of an ancestor whom genealogists would describe, I believe, as collateral.

❧ Melanchthon Woolsey Stryker

Our class of 1914 came to Hamilton at the height of the career of its president. Melanchthon Woolsey Stryker had already made himself a legend and we both feared and honored him. He was a stocky man of florid face and thick graying hair. His black moustache bristled. So did the man behind it. He drove his shiny black buggy and brown mare with a flourish. He walked with a flourish. When he sang we knew what Shakespeare meant by the stage direction— a flourish of trumpets. In his teaching he frequently moved so far ahead of us that we had no idea of his meaning. He was the only man I ever knew who used seriously the expression "the whatness of the which" and made it seem rational.

He was the poet who wrote and set to beautiful hymn music the verses we sing to Alma Mater—"Dear is thy homestead glade and glen" —and their spell still brings to even our most cynical alumni lumps in the throat, tears in the eyes.

He was the most complete individualist we were ever to know and we, who had herded through the usual routine preparations for college, were disturbed, even stunned by his emphatic and eccentric (I use the word in its exact sense) opinions.

He was—or could be—a speaker who created silences in our unruly Chapel—suspenseful silences of deep feeling. I suppose each of us remembers different snatches from his sermons: after the disaster of the *Titanic*—"those two noble Jews, refusing to be parted, lying clasped in each other's arms on the ocean's floor"; after the torpedoing of the *Lusitania*—"I have ordered the flag lowered from its staff on this campus. It will not fly again until our nation makes answer."

Most impressive, and shocking to us, of all the sermons he preached us, arms flailing, feet stamping:

"Whatever the path you choose," he shouted, *"be* somebody. If you decide to be a villain, then be the wickedest villain you can possibly be. *Be* somebody!"

Melanchthon Woolsey Stryker hated sham and hypocrisy. Most of all he hated mobs. Some thought him an intellectual snob because he despised mob-thinking—the most ominous of all dangers to a democracy.

We heard the legend when we came to College of his preaching a sermon on the choice which vacillating, guilt-ridden Pontius Pilate offered a mob—to set free either Jesus or Barabbas, a common criminal. As I remember the story, when Dr. Stryker came to his last paragraph he had worked his way to the rear of the podium. "The mobs have always made sinful choices," he roared, and then, impersonating the mob before Pilate, he moved forward in three great strides. With each step he yelled at the top of his voice: "Barabbas! Barabbas! Barabbas!"

A week or so later an undergraduate with the incredibly Latin name of Rex Titus ended an oration on the Republican high tariff, or something equally irrelevant, on a dull note from the back of the platform. Then to the electrification of his sleeping classmates he stormed toward them.

"Barabbas!" he shouted "Barabbas! Barabbas!"

Prexie (as we called the great man) immediately demanded the expulsion of the offender, but the Hamilton faculty has always been a democratic governing body and the majority of them regarded Titus's offense as more impudent than insolent.

"It has always seemed to me," said the guttural voice of Schnitz (Dr. Herman Karl Brandt, professor of German to you), "that a man who subjects himself to ridicule is bound to receive it." Titus remained.

There were other moments during our years at Hamilton when Dr. Stryker failed to recognize the climate of the student body. Once he kept us all after morning Chapel to learn a new baseball song he had composed to the tune of a then popular song "Yip-i-addy-i-ay." The first two lines ran:

> *They're* the laddies for me, they are,
> They're the laddies for me.

We forgave him—do you forgive a god?—and the matter was never mentioned again.

Prexie was a master of Latin but he learned to pronounce it in the days before the scholars decided how it had been spoken in the days of Horace. This led to a number of misunderstandings. He conducted our commencement exercises in Latin. Whenever he announced a choral number he said, "Musica sit," and the sitting choir stood up.

He was an incurable punster and on one occasion when, for a reason I have forgotten, I was invited to dinner, two roasted ducks on a platter were brought to the table.

"Carmer," said my host briskly, "what's the Latin for 'I am a leader'?"

I blushed and stammered and he answered his own question. "Some ducks," said the president of Hamilton College.

Though Hamilton needed more students during his whole administration Prexie would never compromise in any way to obtain another matriculant.

"Dr. Stryker, do you smoke?" said a pious father desiring to protect his son from sinful influences.

"Sometimes," said Prex, "when I go fishing."

"Dr. Stryker," said the parent, "I would not allow my son to go fishing with you."

Prexie slammed his fist down on his desk.

"He has not been invited, Sir," he shouted.

One other virtue I would emphasize before I end my essay on this great man. Through his choices (and perhaps the choices of his predecessors), he had a highly distinguished faculty with which to work. Among them was a professor of French who so aroused an undergraduate to the beauties of Provençal that the young man became a mighty influence on the whole course of American Poetry.

Our professor of economics held a "moonlighting" job as a member of the New York State Legislature.

Our professor of philosophy wore a frock coat and striped pants to class—the very model of a learned old-time professor.

Our professor of chemistry was also president of the American Peony Society, an instrumentalist who imported the best chamber music quartettes to Hamilton and played along with them, president of the Society for the Breeding of Sealyham Terriers, and the originator of a series of Saturday night readings in the works of George Bernard Shaw, then regarded as a dangerous radical.

Our first instructor who aimed at creating physical competence in us was a bouncy little man with a curly white moustache, whom we knew as "Uncle John." His sole qualification for the job, as far as we ever knew, consisted of his having belonged to a circus in which at every performance he raced a galloping and intelligent horse—intelligent because he knew how to slow up in time for Uncle John to break the tape just ahead of him.

A former professor at Hamilton has recently informed me that as he was climbing to the college campus early one morning he was hailed by Dr. Stryker and ordered into the presidential mansion for breakfast. His host had discovered in the morning newspaper a paragraph which disturbed him and the silence around the domestic board indicated that he had expressed a positive opinion. As the guest sat down to await the reaction of the family, he heard Mrs. Stryker venture a hesitant remark.

"Melanchthon," she said, "I find it very puzzling that you so utterly disapprove of Theodore Roosevelt. He reminds me so often of you."

The guest has ever since believed that only his presence prevented a memorable outburst.

It is my thesis today that it was this group of unique and incorrigible characters, led by a master eccentric, who produced the Hamilton class of 1914.

❦ A Reminiscence of John V. A. Weaver—Notes for a Biographer

John Weaver had impact. Meeting him meant feeling the smack of a personality. Impression was inevitable and usually, though not invariably, pleasant. An important professor plodding down College Hill on enrollment day in the fall of 1910 never quite forgave freshman Weaver's hearty slap on the back and his high-voiced demand for a match. Neither did his classmates—for no Hamilton class ever bowed to college conventions more obsequiously. Standardized minds, we came in a uniform set, accepted the world as it was, and were sure that we were preparing ourselves for it—the world that turned upside down as soon as we graduated.

A philistine is not often happy in a college. Weaver had an inquiring mind, practically no tact, and an embarrassing directness. Neither the faculty nor his fellows made his life at Hamilton easy. He became the symbol of brashness, and "Now, Weave!" was a college byword with which to rebuke anyone who overstepped the lines of accepted conduct. Professor Brandt, kindly and lovable beneath the mannerisms that made him "cross and crabbed Schnitz" of freshman year, became a really menacing bear of the Dark Forest whenever Weaver approached. John went on being brash and electing German. In the days when the disciplining of freshmen by sophomores and upperclassmen was frequently corporal he got more correction than was his share. His wide grin, shining like a crescent moon from a Milky Way of freckles, often concealed an unhappiness both physical and mental, but discipline never reformed him. Not even his enemies (and he had a few) ever questioned his courage.

He had a lot of fun in college, too, particularly after his freshman year, but he had to be reminded of it sometimes. Not so very long ago he said to me, "Why do I like Hamilton? I was never happy there." We decided that he loved the Hill because it is one of the most beautiful spots in the world. We remembered sitting on the Alpha Delt back porch on June days when the valley below was a bowl of misty light that purpled the low hills beyond, speeding down the long hill to the Psi U House through an aisle of deep snow—our sled tilted on its inside runner as we caught the curved rail and swung through the stone arbor—walking dirt roads on spring Sundays with a stop now and then surreptitiously to tilt a farmer's big pail (left beside the road for a collector) and drink from its big bowl-like cover long drafts of foamy milk. College Hill was a beautiful exciting place, we decided, and Weaver had fallen in love with it as a place. We had to revise our judgment a little later, however, when we recalled that the 1914 *Hamil-*

tonian had been influenced by a current comic strip (depicting the struggles of a pair of impoverished young men to get along in high society) to call us two "The Hall-room Boys," basing the insult on our practice of attending Utica dances clad in finery that many brothers of Alpha Delta Phi and Psi Upsilon had willy-nilly sacrificed to our sartorial splendor. That led to other amusing anecdotes and Weaver was obliged to admit that there were things about Hamilton other than locale that were to be remembered with affection.

The honesty that characterized John Weaver's writing showed itself in college immediately. He talked a great deal about writing and he was hungry for experiences which might serve as basic material. So far as I know he never wrote anything which he did not believe to be true to living as he knew it. He made a good deal of fun of me because I avoided experience and tried to write stories and verses out of sentimental conceptions I had gained through reading. He enjoyed being merciless in his criticism. When I did something he liked, however, it put him in a black mood. He never tried to convince himself that it was not good, as a less honest person might do. He had set a very high standard for himself and it disturbed him even to suspect that it could be approached by any other undergraduate.

In September of 1914 Harvard felt the impact I mentioned at the beginning of this article. While I was trying to avoid the piercing eye of George Lyman Kittredge, Weaver was bearding George Pierce Baker, telling him that he had written a melodrama better than most on Broadway. Baker read portions of the play to his class in his detached, ironic way. It turned out to be based on a degenerate's sex crime (committed not far from Clinton a few months before) and the class, with the exception of Eugene O'Neill, who had not yet had the opportunity of training American audiences to accept such subject matter casually, found it wholly distasteful. Baker sent Weaver packing at the end of the first semester and had the professorial bad judgment to prophesy that he had exiled a tyro who would never write a play. Weaver kept on trying and took the delight of a small boy in recalling Baker's remark when his *Love 'Em and Leave 'Em* became a comedy success years later.

I did not see Weaver for many years after he left Cambridge. I heard that he had gone into business of some sort, that it had been interrupted by the war, that he was working on a Chicago newspaper, that he had gone to New York. In 1921 I left the faculty of Rochester to teach at the University of Alabama. At about the same time came the publication of *In American,* and the book pages of newspapers related the story of its author's correspondence with Henry L. Mencken on the subject of a distinctive American language and of his attempts to write poetry in it. I read *In American* to my class in verse writing and felt as important as only a young English instructor who knows an important writer can feel. The class was enchanted by the poems. We accepted with hearty approval the sincere little monodramas that somehow made poignant the inarticulate shopgirls, druggists, stenographers, teamsters, of Weaver's city world with its cheap sentimentalities and pathetic poses. We agreed with Henry Mencken, who had written in *The Smart Set:* "Weaver opens the way for a ballad literature in America, representative of true Americans and the American dialect." Several of my students wrote verses in imitation of Weaver. I sent them to him and began to make arrangements for him to come to Tuscaloosa to lecture.

When he came I was amazed to see that ten years had made no noticeable difference in his appearance and manner. He was still slight, nervous, given to sudden enthusiasms, as vital as a sophomore. My students, inured to the peculiar personal eccentricities of other contemporary American poets, found Weaver's simple, eager, human qualities delightful, and they spent as much time with him as he would allow—a generous portion. He talked a great deal about his beautiful wife, Peggy Wood, and her fine influence on him. He never seemed to get over his wonder that so lovely and charming a person had become his wife.

During his University of Alabama visit the two of us went over to Columbus, Mississippi, to make a joint appearance before the students of Mississippi State College for Women. Weaver talked about the American language and I talked about American folklore, and the two subjects went together so well that we spent the hours of the return journey planning a joint tour in which we would attempt to make America aware of its own native expression, quality, and background.

When we got off the train at Tuscaloosa the ambitious dream had faded from our minds and we never spoke of it again.

The honesty that made Weaver's work always worth considering made itself known outside his writings in many ways. He was as loyal to his friends as to his artistic standards. He insisted on taking a sonnet of mine—not a very good sonnet—back to New York with him from Tuscaloosa and somehow he persuaded John Farrar, then editor of *The Bookman,* to publish it. That got him, and John Farrar, too, into more trouble, for, encouraged in a measure entirely out of proportion to the importance of this first triumph, I began to think of trying to become a writer. Four years later I presented myself at Weaver's Connecticut doorstep. I had given up teaching, had been fired from a New Orleans newspaper, spent my last dime, and decided to try to find a job in New York. Two days later I was assistant editor of *Vanity Fair.* Just what sort of black magic Weaver had used on editor Frank Crownin-shield and managing editor Donald Freeman to get an upstate small-town product with a few years of experience in rural Alabama a job on a journal that prided itself on being the nation's most sophisticated voice I never knew. Somehow he had communicated to them more enthusiasm than I deserved. He had great faith in his friends.

While I visited Weaver in Stamford, Peggy Wood was playing *Candida* on the road and we were taken care of by Peggy's Aunt May Wood with almost as much earnestness and affection as she lavished on David, son of John and Peggy, who was then just beginning to walk. This gave us much time to talk and John used most of it in a discussion of his career. I was more than ever convinced of his sincerity, his desire to interpret the millions of underpaid and underprivileged Americans. By that time *Love 'Em and Leave 'Em* had run its happy course on many American stages, *More in American* and *Finders* had been added to his first verse studies of the kind of folks he loved and wanted to understand. *Her Knight Comes Riding* had been a not too successful attempt to carry some of his poignant character studies over into the form of the novel, and he had helped to make *The Crowd* into one of the most moving and significant dramas the silent motion pictures had produced. His brain was boiling over with plans for the future—all based on his desire to write, out of the lives of ordinary

Americans, the joys and tragedies of ordinary living. He would make more great motion pictures, write more novels, composed more poems that would make America conscious of itself. When I left Stamford his energy and purpose had cheered me mightily at a time when I needed cheering.

After that Weaver was in Hollywood much of the time. We got together in New York for lunch on his visits to the East. Peggy Wood, who was writing a book for my publishers, brought me happy messages from him. The Carmers and the Weavers ran into each other at a theatre one evening and we decided we must see something of each other. But Stamford and New York are almost as far from each other as both are from Hollywood in the conceptions of Stamfordites and New Yorkers. We did not see each other as often as we planned. I was shocked when I learned that Weaver had gone to Colorado for his health but I was sure that his love of life and his courage would pull him through. Now I wish I had seen him oftener.

I would like to feel that in this article I have kept a proper balance and not fallen on the side of a too hard objectivity or a too soft sentiment. In writing of a college friend, one whose life never ran tangent to my own without my being benefited, the tendency is naturally toward the latter fault. The opinions of less prejudiced writers than I bear out, however, what I would say about John Weaver. In a simple and beautifully written editorial published in *The Saturday Review of Literature* last summer, William Rose Benét summed up Weaver's artistic life by saying that he was an able, honest, consistent laborer in those fields he had chosen to till. Some of his work, in my opinion, went beyond this appraisal, invading high places, and it surely had wide influence. It is now too early to make a satisfactory judgment of his place in the history of American letters, yet I feel sure that he will be set down as one of the poets of the late American renaissance which brought our national poetry back from Victorian artificiality to the natural and beautiful vernacular, and as a forerunner of the important group of contemporary American writers who find injustices in our national life and want to influence their readers to correct them. He tried very hard to say something that would help the people he wrote about, and I believe his poems deserve a place on a very special shelf devoted to the works of Hamilton College writers who have done like-wise—a shelf on which appear, among others, the books of Arthur Bullard and Joseph Vogel.

In the poem "L'Envoi" which ends his first book John Weaver wrote a line that reads:

"Fight for the ways of seein' fresh and true."

He always practiced that bit of uncharacteristic preaching. No college could ask more of one of its graduates.

❦ Fiorello La Guardia

Fiorello La Guardia became a legend in his own life-time. Now, after his death, he seems alive because of the legend's vitality.

They called him "Butch." They called him "Little Flower." They called him "The Hat." Waves of laughter swept the movie theaters when the stout short figure under the broad brim of a black Stetson appeared in the newsreels, the button-bright eyes flashing with eager sincerity, the round face working with deep emotion, the high voice squeaking in righteous indignation. But the laughter held such affec-tion as has been accorded to few public figures.

The people of New York knew he was one of them, and that he fought their battles with everything he had. If John Purroy Mitchel had been their plumed knight, La Guardia was their Don Quixote, and when he tilted at windmills he sometimes won. He was at once an epitome of the frustrations of each poor and insignificant citizen.

The blood of fighters flowed in him. A grandfather battled through Italy with Garibaldi's Red Shirts and married a descendant of a Jewish refugee from the Spanish Inquisition. La Guardia's father, who joined the United States Army after coming to this country as accompanist for the great soprano Adelina Patti, was bandmaster of the 11th United

States Infantry and became one of the many casualties of the deadly "embalmed beef" served at Tampa in the days of the Spanish War of '98.

Though Fiorello La Guardia was born in New York City, his "home town," if the term may be defined as "the place where a man grows up," was Prescott, Arizona. It was typical of the frontier army-post villages. Cowboys and Indians and soldiers were accepted common-places of its simple life. Its schools were excellent. The family subscribed to the New York *World* in order to be informed on events of national and international importance, and it was from the editorials of that journal in the '90s that young Fiorello obtained a lasting distaste for Tammany.

Fiorello La Guardia tried to enlist in the war against Spain but was rejected as too young. It was hard to convince the editor of the St. Louis *Post-Dispatch* that he should make a sixteen-year-old boy an accredited correspondent, but Fiorello did it and set out to accompany his father. Thanks to Tampa's bad beef, neither reached Cuba. The elder La Guardia was honorably discharged with a small pension and brought his whole family together under a New York roof. In 1901 he died.

In 1912, young Fiorello, who had garnered experience as American Consul at Fiume (then part of Hungary), as interpreter at Ellis Island, as a student in the night sessions of New York University Law School, hung out the shingle of F. H. La Guardia, Attorney-at-Law.

After two years of enthusiastic if unpaid work in behalf of the garment workers, then on strike, the new lawyer was given the nomination for Congress in the 14th District against Congressman Michael Farley, President of the National Liquor Dealers Association. Farley won in a sure district but lost 14,000 of his usual 16,000 majority.

Two years later, in 1916, before the unbelieving eyes of his own party, La Guardia defeated the unbeatable Farley. Then, because war threatened, he learned how to fly a plane before setting out for Washington.

In Congress he fought, during the early days of World War I, for civil liberties, for woman suffrage, for food control, for conscription. Then he set off for Italy where, in command of a squadron of United States flyers, he gave his superiors fits of exasperation with his indifference to official brass-hat procedures. After two years of combat service the Captain returned a Major and kept his seat in Congress by defeating the Socialist-Pacifist candidate Scott Nearing.

In the House of Representatives he fought many of Woodrow Wilson's policies but stoutly defended the League of Nations. He became the implacable foe of Volstead and his Prohibition Amendment. He introduced a resolution informing the new republics of Russia and Poland that the United States considered their persecution of the Jews within their borders a disgrace and that they could expect nothing from this country until it ceased.

He was re-elected again and again. He became so popular with the polyglot population of New York that the Republican leaders yanked him, protesting excitedly, out of the House and ran him for President of the Board of Aldermen. He was elected and immediately became so busy in liberal causes that a clash with the Republican Old Guard was inevitable. When it came, La Guardia attacked the party that had put him in office as violently as ever he attacked Tammany.

Nevertheless, he expected the Republican nomination for Mayor in 1921. His wife and his little girl were dying as he campaigned for it, bitterly charging that he was being betrayed, that solemn promises were being broken. The Republican leaders refused him the nomination and named able, honest, whimsical Henry H. Curran, who was defeated by John F. Hylan.

Both major parties and a considerable proportion of the press rejoiced that the firebrand radical was now politically dead. He came alive immediately and so vigorously as an independent Republican that the party could not refuse him nomination to Congress from the 20th District. When the Tammany nominee (of Jewish blood) accused him of being anti-Semitic he sent out postcards printed in Yiddish, demanding that his opponent (who was unacquainted with the language of his ancestors) meet him in a debate to be conducted entirely in Yiddish.

He was elected and continued his independent career in Congress, laying about him vigorously, regardless of party lines. He fought Prohibition, the Ku Klux Klan, the Mellon tax bill. When horrified Republicans objected to his attacks on the national administration, he went back to Harlem to make his annual report to his constituency. "I would rather be right than regular," he said.

Then he helped found and organize the Progressive Party. When the organization lost its power, he took over the Republican control in his district without a fight and finally in 1929 wrung the nomination for Mayor from a reluctant Republican leadership. He was soundly trounced in the election by Mayor Walker, then pathetically confident in his indifference to La Guardia's charges of corruption in city government.

La Guardia's temperament permitted no biding of time. He went back to Congress for his seventh term, with the disappointment of his failure of election to the mayoralty burning within him. Bitterly he attacked the hypocrisies of prohibition. The opponents of copyright reform received a tongue-lashing that endeared him to all creative artists. With honesty that would cost him many votes he opposed the veterans' bonus. A national sales tax bill that seemed sure of passage was defeated through his efforts. He denounced Wall Street bankers for offering bribes to writers on finance, flayed the writers for accepting the bribes. He aided the late Senator George W. Norris of Nebraska in the passage of a measure that outlawed "yellow dog contracts" (these prohibited employees from joining unions outside the company that employed them), and remedied the abuses of antilabor injunctions.

The Democratic landslide that swept Roosevelt into the Presidency and Herbert Lehman into the governorship in 1932 swept the Republican Congressman of the 20th District into the discard. For the first time in eighteen years Tammany Hall triumphed in La Guardia's own bailiwick. Utterly discouraged, he announced his retirement from politics. "I am going to get a little place in the country and settle down and raise chickens," he said.

A week later he called an anti-Tammany mass meeting at Town Hall.

Returning to Washington for the remaining three months of his term, the "lame duck" Congressman who had just proclaimed, "They got me at last. I am too old to start over and they have wrecked my political career," found himself the choice of Franklin D. Roosevelt to sponsor New Deal legislation which the President-elect felt should be adopted even before he took office. La Guardia worked at his new duties with diligence. Then he left Congress for his retirement and rented a cottage in Westport, Connecticut. From this vantage point he viewed the growing split between the Tammany forces for O'Brien and Edward J. Flynn's Bronx machine backing McKee. Here was an opportunity for a minority candidate to win, and no one has ever been more alive to opportunity. First he suggested a Fusion anti-Tammany ticket in a statement in which he named for the mayoralty ex-Governor Alfred E. Smith. The candidates he suggested for other offices included Robert Moses, Republican, Norman Thomas, Socialist, ex-Mayor Hylan, and Mayor O'Brien (for his old post as Surrogate). If Smith would not run, La Guardia said, he would himself. Neither Smith nor O'Brien (Tammany candidate to succeed himself) could possibly accept Fusion nomination and La Guardia knew it.

As the Republicans tried to head him off, first with Robert Moses, then with Major General John F. O'Ryan, La Guardia played his trump card—the support of Judge Samuel Seabury whose masterful investigation of corruption in the city government had made him the hero of all friends of honesty and integrity in public affairs. Again the Republicans found themselves in the familiar position of nominating La Guardia against their inclinations. They did it, and as ever he fought every inch of the way. And this time, though Joseph McKee gave him tough opposition, he won. He was Mayor of the City of Greater New York.

In his three successive four-year terms, while the Tammany Tiger starved, Fiorello La Guardia was the nation's busiest citizen. He was criticized for ridiculous inconsistency, for vulgar overstatement, for political opportunism. He might have hotly denied these charges, but there were moments of reflection when he knew them to be true. "When I make a mistake," he said during his third term, "it's a beaut."

His friends were more aware of his faults than his enemies were. The members of his official family at City Hall reported him confidentially as a testy tyrant, sure that he was right and that those who disagreed were for no good reason handicapping a righteous cause. His enemies admitted that he had integrity and that he was trying to give the city honest, efficient, and economical government. They had to content themselves with violent attacks on his errors and though, as he admitted, these were egregious, they were infrequent.

From the beginning to the end of his service to the city, Fiorello La Guardia fought its crooks and gamblers. He made Lewis J. Valentine, a career policeman and unpopular with Tammany, his Police Commissioner and told him to go after gangsters, racketeers, dishonest politicians, and grafting officers on his own force. Never able patiently to await the results of delegated authority, he could not help spurring Valentine with suggestions and with public denunciations of lawbreakers who should be "mussed up" or harried out of town by arrests on sight. He hated thugs and habitual criminals so much that, usually an ardent advocate of civil liberties, he intimated to a committee protesting police use of "third-degree" methods that the time to adopt regulations affecting such practices would be after he was no longer Mayor and unable to see to it that the methods were used with wisdom and discretion. Nevertheless, he brought honor and dignity back to the Police Department, which gradually became one of the finest municipal police services in the world.

The city, as a result of previous malpractices, was in an almost hopeless financial plight. By nonpartisan appointments of able executives and by vigorous personal effort, La Guardia brought it to a sound financial level and kept it there. He demanded a businesslike streamlining of the governmental structure and through charter revision and county government reforms, including the abolishing of many useless jobs and the revision (to avoid political pressures) of city buying, he got it. If the town could furnish no one sufficiently experienced and able to perform important duties, he appointed men of national reputations and persuaded them to come to New York. With amazing rapidity, after his appointees went to work, the city became a safer, healthier, and happier place to live.

But efficient administration of all existing departments was not enough for the fussy, excited, nervously active little man. He had creative vision and he had dreamed of a city of such beauty and happy living as few had ever imagined. He made the best appointment of his career in selecting Robert Moses as Park Commissioner. In the years that followed, while the Commissioner and the Mayor shouted at each other in ardent disagreement and then made up, the ugly approaches to the great town that lay between the rivers and the sea became tree-lined drives affording vistas of flowing waters, high palisades, picturesque islands, sky-piercing office buildings. New parks, green in summer, filled with elderly checker-players, young mothers pushing baby carriages, racing children. New playgrounds were crowded with eager young athletes. A tremendous airport was established on the meadows of Flushing. New sand beaches near the city welcomed millions to convenient parking, good food, sanitary conveniences, clean grounds, safe swimming.

To make New York a city in which neighbors get along well together the Mayor devoted his tremendous energies to slum clearance and low-rent housing, to the settling of labor disputes, to personal investigation of even minor complaints by individual residents.

When the subway fare had been set at five cents in the administration of Mayor Gaynor, no one could have predicted the decline in buying value of the American nickel. As it lessened, succeeding mayors were plagued by the fact that the subways were losing money. Raising the fare would work hardship on the masses of people of low income, and a corollary of that fact was that such action would result in loss of support from a tremendous number of voters. From political motives and because they were genuinely friendly to working men and women, Mayors Walker and La Guardia had opposed increasing the price of a ride. The latter realized, however, that the first step toward any common-sense solution of the subway problem was for the city to obtain ownership. Though he met with bitter opposition, he succeeded in achieving city purchase of more transit lines, thus unwittingly aiding his successor's bold winning fight to raise the fare.

From the first omens of coming war, La Guardia was belligerently on the side of the democracies, denouncing fascism and nazism and their leaders with sneering contempt. Many thought him overactive in his campaign to prepare the city for possible bombing, but he kept at it, insisting on careful organization and demanding perfection in black-out techniques. He tried his best to obtain an appointment to the armed forces or to war service as an administrator in an occupied nation, but high national authorities claimed that the job he was doing for the country's largest and most important city made him too valuable to be spared.

In the twelve years he served the city as mayor he was having more fun than most men can pack into the whole of their allotted span, and the people of the city were getting almost equal enjoyment out of watching a man with a real talent for living have the time of his life. He raced to fires, and a high helmet took the place of the Stetson. He stood before great orchestras and waved a baton expertly. During a strike when newspapers were not delivered he read the Sunday morning comic supplements to the children of the city over the radio, and his high voice and amused chuckles made "the funnies" funnier than they had been on the printed page.

When in the summer of 1945 Fiorello La Guardia said over the radio that he would not run for re-election, few of his hearers would take him at his word. Some suspected that his announcement was a political ruse. Others believed he was resigning because of his failure to obtain an important national appointment. Still others thought he was expecting such an appointment. All were agreed that after twelve years of his uniquely active administration it would be hard to imagine the great city without him at its head.

He could not leave office without a characteristic last gesture that proved him far from politically dead. Tammany and the American Labor Party had nominated to succeed him the experienced and capable Brooklyn attorney, William O'Dwyer, whom La Guardia had defeated in the last mayoralty campaign. The Republicans, advised by Governor Dewey, had named Jonah J. Goldstein, an honest and honored judge, hoping that his fine record and the fact that he was a Jew who could depend on receiving a large proportion of the Jewish vote (30 per cent of the city total) would bring about his election. La Guardia had proposed the names of a number of distinguished men, some of them Republicans, whom he would gladly support, and he resented the selection of Goldstein, who had been a Democrat until informed that he would be nominated as the Republican candidate.

With La Guardia to resent was to act. Suddenly a new party, the No-Deal Party, appeared on the New York scene, with Newbold Morris, President of the City Council, as its candidate for mayor.

Morris, whose character and capabilities were unquestionable and whose connection with one of the city's oldest and most prominent families made him a sentimental choice of the town's aristocrats, was enthusiastically supported by La Guardia, whose political acumen undoubtedly told him that his candidate could not be elected and that, by splitting the Republican vote, he was immeasurably aiding the campaign of O'Dwyer. At the end of forty years of bitter warfare against Tammany, its most implacable foe was making sure that the Tiger's candidate would be elected!

O'Dwyer won the greatest plurality in the history of the city, and the man who had defeated him four years before did not seem unhappy. No one could know William O'Dwyer without believing him honest and difficult to deceive. La Guardia had never believed that a man's political party mattered much when compared with those attributes. His beloved city was in safe hands and he had much to look back upon with pride. He had been a record-breaker—the only reform mayor of the City of Greater New York ever to be re-elected, the only mayor of any party to serve three consecutive terms.

Immediately on an office door in Rockefeller City, midtown Manhattan, appeared a sign: "F. H. La Guardia—Thinking, Writing, and Talking," and, as immediately, the door was locked as the lessee took over the job of head of the United Nations Relief and Rehabilitation Administration from former Governor Lehman, who was retiring for considerations of health. Again the little man was everywhere—in Washington, in every grain-producing state, in Europe. He talked United National Relief with Stalin, Tito, and the Pope. He demanded a food fund of $400 million to be administered by the United Nations.

When he did not get the money, he resigned and went back to the office where the sign told what was going on inside. He wrote a column for an afternoon newspaper with all of his accustomed vigor. For a smart furniture store which paid him for the use of them in its advertisements, he wrote stinging editorials against the things he hated. *Liberty Magazine* hired him to broadcast his opinions on national affairs and then, embarrassed by his characteristic forthrightness and his passionate utterances, fired him because of what the magazine chose to call "reckless and irresponsible statements." He sold milk over the radio by stating his point of view on city affairs. Then the strong body he had developed in his boyhood under Arizona suns began to fail him. For a few months he fought as bravely as ever, knowing that he was dying. On September 20, 1947, he died in his sleep. The world mourned.

The Exile

Farewell to the Adirondacks

Y'all have been sure 'nough polite to me
An' I'm right smart obliged, I want yuh t' know.
Somehow I wish that I could make yuh see
Why I can't stay. My words won't seem to go
T'gether right for that. I can't explain,
But Alabama's the only place I fit
An' I won't be a-feelin' right again
Until I'm back and livin' close to it.
Y'see I ain't been smart since Henry died,
An' the country round about here is so still
An' clear an' different, I can't abide
Bein' alone in it! I reckon it'd kill
Me if I stayed here long. Now back at home
There's *something* all the time; sometimes black boys
Fish in the yellow lake an' then songs come
A-floatin' up t' our shack; always *some* noise—
A gar breaks water with a lazy splash,
An' the locusts buzz right loud in the hot noon,
Or a mocker quits his foolin' quick to flash
A real song on the heavy air that soon
Will gather into grayish mists that smell
Too sweet of the shady marshes. All the night
There's rustlin's, *livin' things around*. C'n yuh tell

The difference? Why, take your sunsets even,
They come too still and with too much of gold.
There's near a hundred different voices weavin'
With a hundred colors 'fore our sun's lost hold
An' darkness comes. Lake water here is black
An' yuh c'n see, too real, white birches in it
Like silver streaks in an old black stone. The crack
Of one dry stick is scarier in a minute
Than a night of noises. There's magic here;
Your pines crouch close an' dark, they whisper things
In a strange air, not real, an' much too clear,
While mine cut through a perfumed air that clings
About their high-up tufted tops and caresses
Them to swayin'. Take your laughin' crick—
A crazy woman laughin' while she dresses
A doll, screamin' in the quiet. (The trick
Of fancyin' things, so Henry said, ain't good
For me, but this place somehow stirs up my mind.)
Now our crick's just the slow old branch. It would
Dry up in summer; jes' a hummin' blind
Old stream. An' then yuh've heard the little trout
A-jumpin' in moonlight? Well, they frighten me;
They skip, like the little men I've heard about,
I'd rather hear the gar a-splashin' heavy,
That's all. Oh, can't yuh see I've got to go?
D'yuh really feel why now? D'yuh reckon so?

🐚 To Make a River

From rocks as old as any in the world fresh waters rise
into a little lake beside the highest Adirondack peak, Mount Marcy.
Before the mountains, folding, raised island heads above the Grenville
Sea these rocks were there. Once they were higher, when molten masses

burst their crust to force tongues upward, lifting steeper summits to the sky. But the old rocks sank again and, in the years that followed, tilting and warping the surfaces of the earth, tropic oceans washed them smooth and streams of ice, miles deep, made scars upon their sides.

The little lake is younger than the rocks and younger than the glaciers, but older than man. In the whole state of New York it is the highest body of water to feed an ever-flowing outlet. When the naturalist Verplanck Colvin, in 1872, climbed through woods of spruce and balsam and white cedar to its bank it had a lovely name. He was so overcome with the emotion proper to his period and the occasion, however, that he wrote, in a sentimental report to the New York State legislature: "Far above the chilly waters of Lake Avalanche, at an elevation of 4,293 feet, is *Summit Water,* a minute, unpretending tear of the clouds, as it were—a lovely pool shivering in the breeze of the mountains...." The lawmakers were so overcome by this coincidental flowering in their midst of literary effort and the "pathetic fallacy" that lovely Summit Water soon officially became *Lake Tear of the Clouds.*

The rocky peak of Marcy, once called Tahawus—the cloud splitter—by the Indians, looks down into the mirror of Lake Tear. East of the peak, beyond Panther Gorge, stands the dome called Haystack, to the north stands Table Top, to the south Skylight, and westward rises Mount MacIntyre.

The clear water of the ancient rocks spills from the lake to shallow Feldspar Brook. Through its ripples shine the stones of its bed. Green, gold, blue, they glitter with iridescent labradorite. Down the crystalline slope the water plunges to join with other brooks, the Up Hill and the Upper Twin. Another fork descending in the shadow of Calamity Mountain from Flowed Lands and the Falls of Hanging Spear meets it to form the swift Opalescent River. And the Opalescent, running south and then west, at the hill town of Newcomb becomes the Hudson.

Flowing south then to Indian River Junction and between Bad Luck and Kettle mountains, keeping east of the steep sides of Ruby and Balm of Gilead, the thin stream meets the splashing Schroon. There the Hudson widens into a strong river running south between gentler shores broken by the mouths of streams: Stony Creek, Wolf Creek, the Sacandaga River. Below the last of these it flows east in level meanders, dropping after a few miles into an old and broad north-south channel. To this, for more than the first hundred miles of its course the Hudson has been in actuality a tributary.

The channel runs almost straight south, deepening as it goes. The last towering ice sheet that slid down from the north over most of New York State, blocking the St. Lawrence outlet and making the Mohawk River and the Great Lakes drain through the Hudson, was split by the Adirondack heights; its southern portion was forced into seaward progress between the high folded hills. It deepened the course of the great river as it moved.

From the point of its southward turn into the old glacial channel the Hudson flows through a gorge within an older valley. The floor of the gorge from almost as far north as Albany to its mouth lies below the level of the sea, creating a fiord or estuary where the fresh waters are ever subject to the invasion of salty ocean tides. Through a land of ice-built terraces the Hudson runs south to the northern gate of its highland canyon. On the west behind the terraces the Catskills lift the folded floors of ancient tropic seas, sediments bearing corals, starfishes, sea lilies which once had life beneath warm waters. East of the river and its eastern terraces lie the Taconics, which moved up into the sky before the Catskills were born.

There was a time, some of the scientists say, when the Hudson, before it reached the highland barrier, wandered off to the southwest through Pennsylvania where it joined the Susquehanna and emptied its waters into Chesapeake Bay. Another stream, whose source was far to the south, gradually by headward erosion moved its beginnings northward until it captured and incorporated the runaway and straightened its course oceanward. That course led through a barrier of ancient mica-laden rocks upreared into the high ridges of the Appalachians. The Hudson worked its way through those ridges, aided by the glaciers that forced their masses southward through its valley, smoothing the northern slopes, carrying boulders away from the southern, leaving behind high-frowning cliffs, digging a channel so deep that its floor is in places nearly a thousand feet below sea level.

Through the gateway peaks, Storm King and Breakneck, the river flows southward past Mount Taurus on the east, Bear Mountain on the west, and emerges from the gap between the mountains known as Dunderberg and Anthony's Nose. A few miles farther along, after passing between High Tor Mountain and Prickly Pear Hill, the gorge widens and the river spreads to its greatest width, more than three and a half miles at Haverstraw Bay. For the next dozen miles the stream narrows gradually and the west side becomes a sheer columned wall of hard basalt rising 350 feet in its lower segments, 550 feet at its full height. This rock poured from the earth's interior as molten liquid and inserted itself in a thick hard sill between layers of sandstone, forming a giant sandwich. The sandstone cover has been worn off near the river, leaving the hard brown wall towering above the water in an awesome vertical precipice, the Palisades.

The river runs past the narrow island called Manhattan into New York Bay, thence between Staten Island on the west and Long Island on the east to the Atlantic. But the end of its channel is not yet. Cut into a floor of the ocean, it extends far out to the southeast. A generally accepted theory is that at some date before the existence of man the water level of the Atlantic dropped ten to fifteen thousand feet. When the last of the four great ice sheets was on the land, a mighty river gushed down from the end of the glacier that had covered the Hudson valley and roared downward, cutting deep into the soft sediment of the former ocean floor, to a new shore line nearly 150 miles farther out than the old one. For thousands of years the great stream ran, constantly lowering its level and digging one of the deepest canyons the world has ever known. From a shallow beginning, as scientists have discovered by soundings, the floor of the gorge dropped steeply until in some places it reached a depth of 3,600 feet, several hundred feet deeper than the Grand Canyon of the Colorado. Had there been human life then, a traveler in a boat on the Hudson might have looked up to the blue sky between walls more than two miles high. But no man has yet seen, or probably ever will see, this stupendous natural phenomenon. After the river had created it, the salt sea returned and buried the canyon thousands of feet below the tossing waves.

The most recent surveys of the United States Coast and Geodetic

Survey do not completely confirm or contradict this theory. They point out that the Hudson Submarine Channel begins about three miles southeast of Ambrose Lightship where it is a flat-bottomed valley a mile and a half wide and twenty to thirty feet below the ocean floor. It runs in a sweeping curve, continually broadening and deepening until, ninety miles from its beginning, it is obscured by a delta formation.

Three miles southeast of this delta lies the beginning of the great canyon. The government survey soundings have shown that it slopes downward at the average rate of 150 feet a mile and that when it has reached its amazing 3,600-foot depth below the ocean floor its width from rim to rim is about five and a half miles.

In that canyon where once apparently the Hudson ran in sunlight and shadow between walls almost inconceivably high there is now only the twilight of the great sea depths. The naturalist-explorer William Beebe has sent his nets far down into that water-dusk and has written that in the Hudson gorge there swims a blind fish, whose eye-sockets are glowing headlights to attract smaller fish close enough to be caught and swallowed, and "a tiny white thread of a fish," with eyes "far out on the ends of impossibly slender stalks." Another dweller of these submarine depths is a round fish of glowing silver that keeps "all its batteries of green and violet lights turned downward while it stares unmovably and piously upward." Here are pale-violet humpbacked shrimp, and shrimp exuding clouds of scarlet flame, "active opals, gleaming and scintillating as they twist and turn," and a long bronze and black "scimitar-fanged sea-dragon."

Near the edge of the continental shelf—the elevation a hundred miles wide above the ocean floor, which geologists believe was once dry land —the Hudson channel makes one last plunge downward. The grade is so steep that the 1,200-foot drop has been called the "undersea falls." Actually, in the days when the river dashed through the gorge there must have been furious rapids here. At the seaward limit of the most recent surveys 135 miles southeast of Ambrose Lightship, the bottom of the canyon is 7,500 feet below the water's surface and 1,500 feet below the ocean's floor. Somewhere beyond that point the Hudson channel finally ends in the immensity of the Atlantic.

Apple Pickers

They are walking lonesome up the south road,
Their leathery faces turned to the low, wide trees,
And the farmer calls them into the reddening orchard,
Every last one he sees.

They lift the ladders to their certain pointing—
Two fingers each to the mist-circled sun;
They beat the barrelheads to syncopation
Till the day's whole stint is done.

Only at noon comes stillness for an hour
To spread across the fields in shimmering waves,
Then apples roll again from swollen pick bags,
Dull thundering on the staves.

On Saturday they load the truck with barrels,
Ride gay astride them all the way to town,
But girls wave from the porches by the depot
And they shyly shinny down.

When the late button clicks, puts out the street lights,
And front doors close on shadows down the walk,
Folks snug in bed hear pickers hollering homeward,
And it's no sort of talk.

The night freight, screaming, couples their piled
    loadings,
Grinds past the crossing, car by groaning car,
While sudden plumps from full, high-hanging branches
A windfall star.

🦋   Proud Lady-Ghosts

I have had a feeling about this region around us for
many years. As some of you may know, I believe in the psychic effect
of landscape—that landscape has a definite spiritual influence on the
lives of those who inhabit it. And nowhere is that land-spirit more
strongly felt than in this smiling York State. If these premises were
true, we could, by studying the spiritual trend of those who have lived
here before, discover what influence this region wields, what land-feel-
ing our predecessors followed in their lives among these rivers and
these hills.

Philosophers have at times suggested to us that the past and the
present coexist—that we are possibly contemporaries of those whom we
have learned to call dead. I wish you would accept that thesis for this
afternoon and receive as visitors a group of females who, though
invisible, are most assuredly living influences here. The first of these
is a short, slight woman who bears her head bent forward because she
has for many years carried heavy burdens with a strap placed across
her forehead. Her face is lined by ninety years of living but her eye is
bright and her talk is quick and a little Irish. When she was sixteen
years old she was living some miles south of us in Pennsylvania. One
morning when she was at breakfast with the members of her family
and friends she heard shots outside the door. Then Indians rushed into
the house and made her parents and all the other white people their
prisoners. The Indians set off in mad haste with their prisoners and
the slight girl felt the lash on her back as she and a boy companion
were driven like captured cattle in a wild dash to get out of white
man's territory. A few days later the horrified children saw the Indians

Commencement Address, Elmira College, Elmira, New York, June 14, 1937.

cleaning and drying scalps which they recognized as torn from the heads of their murdered parents.

Adopted into the tribe of the Senecas, this girl became the wife of a Delaware, "a noble man, large of stature, elegant in his appearance, generous in his conduct, courageous in war, a friend to peace and a great lover of justice." They lived happily on the banks of the Ohio River until her husband died and then she walked, paddled, rode through an almost pathless wilderness six hundred miles to this York State country. "My clothing was thin," she said afterward, "and illy calculated to defend me from the continually drenching rains with which I was daily completely wet, and at night with nothing but my wet blanket to cover me, I had to sleep on naked ground and generally without shelter.... I had to carry my child, then about nine months old, every step of the journey...I sometimes felt that I thought it impossible for me to go through..." In this country she married again—a six-foot-four Seneca—and with him she lived for nearly fifty years, bearing him two sons and four daughters before he died of tuberculosis at the age of 103.

She did not marry again but lived alone on the flats beside the Genesee River. Even after she was eighty she planted, tended, and gathered her corn, she chopped wood, she fed her cattle and poultry. Clad in Indian garments she won fame as an oracle among the Senecas, as a wise and great woman among the whites. The site of her home is submerged by deep waters now, but high on the bank of the river stands a statue to Mary Jemison, "The White Woman of the Genesee," whose fame will not be drowned by the years.

> Degenerate sons and daughters
> Life is too strong for you
> It takes life to love Life.*

Beside Mary Jemison on the invisible bench which holds our invisible visitors today sits a blonde, fair-skinned blue-eyed woman. Slight of body and sensitive of mind she worked in an English cotton factory

* From *Spoon River Anthology* by Edgar Lee Masters. Copyright 1915, 1916, 1942 by Edgar Lee Masters. Reprinted by permission of Mrs. Edgar Lee Masters.

once. Then she married a blacksmith and bore him four children all of whom died in infancy. After they had died she saw visions of such a nature that she believed herself inspired by a divine message. In England she was mobbed and her life was saved only by the intervention of a nobleman. Then she was thrown into a madhouse. When she was released she came to America and worked as a domestic servant for a time. Then in upstate New York she found a country which promised much to her and her followers. Thither they journeyed and began to worship as her visions bade them—by dancing and song. In the country about Albany and in the Genesee country north of us here where a group of her followers settled, wayfarers might often see grown men dancing down the dusty turnpike or grave young whirlers gyrating underneath the moon, lost in the rhythmic physical expression of the religious ecstasies that possessed them. Other Christian believers were very unchristian in their attitude toward these dancers. They beat them until their backs were raw. They tore down the walls of a house to get at the slight woman who led them and drag her by the heels outside to be tormented and mortified. Though her thin body wasted, her great blue eyes blazed out of their hollows with unquenched spirit. Earnestly she urged on her people the teaching she had given them. "Hands to work and hearts to God." "You will see peaceable times," she said. "Then you may worship God under your own vines and fig trees, and none of the wicked will make you afraid." And after Mother Ann Lee died her prophecy came true, for an observer wrote of one of the settlements of her followers words which could equally well be said of all of them—including that just north of us at the place where only the name Shakers Crossing remains to remind us:

No Dutch town has a neater aspect, no Moravian hamlet a softer hush. The streets are quiet; for here you have no grog-shop, no beer-house, no lock-up, no pound; of the dozen edifices rising about you —workrooms, barns, tabernacle, stables, kitchens, schools, and dormitories—not one is either foul or noisy; and every building, whatever may be its use, has something of the air of a chapel. The paint is all fresh; the planks are all bright; the windows are all clean. A white sheen is on everything; a happy quiet reigns around. Even in what is seen of the eye and heard of the ear, Mount Lebanon strikes you as a place where it is always Sunday. The walls appear as though they had been built only yesterday; a perfume, as from many unguents, floats down the lane; and the curtains and window blinds are of spotless white. Everything in the hamlet looks and smells like household things which have been long laid up in lavender and rose-leaves.

The third of our unseen guests today rode here in an open coach, its body shaped like an upturned half-moon, its seats covered with golden tapestry. Richly colored curtains hung from its top and on its front panels were engraved the letters U. F. It is the same vehicle in which she rode from Philadelphia to the west side of Seneca Lake to join her followers and direct their homemaking there.

When Jemima Wilkinson was eighteen years old in 1776 she caught a plague spread by the discharged British prisoners of the American Naval Ship *Columbus* and died. Her young body soon lost the fever's heat and stiffened in cold rigor, then grew warm again and arose from the bed in which it lay. A mouth that had once been Jemima's spoke saying that Jemima Wilkinson of Cumberland, Rhode Island, had left the world of time's reckoning, that her earthly form had been chosen to serve as the vehicle of that Spirit of Life from God who should be known henceforth as The Publick Universal Friend.

It is The Publick Universal Friend whom we welcome today—a tall, straight, graceful woman with sparkling dark eyes. Her hair, parted in the middle above her broad forehead, is thick and dark and falls in curls about her shoulders. She wears a broad-brimmed low-crowned white beaver hat and from her strong neck, encircled by a white knotted silk scarf, hangs an unconfined robe of white linen. A few miles to the north of us she built her big house whence she rode forth on a beautiful horse, her saddle and stirrups studded with silver. Jemima Wilkinson knew what it was to lend her strength to the ax or the swift alternations of the crosscut saw. She also knew and taught to the women who followed her that they belonged to themselves and not to their husbands—in an age when a wife was too often looked upon as personal property. Persecutors arrested her once and she was tried for blasphemy in a Canandaigua court but she was so wise, so sure, so good, that even the judge recommended her teachings. When, swollen with dropsy,

Jemima Wilkinson died for a second time, she left behind her an influence and a strength that is felt in the York State lake country to this day.

The fourth of our uninvited guests wears a costume that seems to us overmodest and ungainly. When I tell you that her name is Amelia Bloomer and that she wears the bifurcated garment which was named for her I need add little to my description of her. The first woman publisher of an American magazine for women—*The Lily*—the first stanch agitator for dress reform at a time when the dress of American women was not only complicated but definitely painful and unhealthful—Amelia Bloomer of Seneca Falls received more ridicule at the hands of her fellow citizens than any American woman of any time. She is still ridiculed but American women must not forget that they owe her more than they owe to many another more prominent woman. It was Amelia Bloomer who struck the first blow at false modesty when America was full of it. The age of sunlight—the age of shorts and halters and sunburn lotions and bathing suits in which it is possible actually to swim—began with Amelia Bloomer. Health and wholesomeness followed in her wake.

Beside her and dressed in similar costume sits the last of the friendly upstate ghosts who have come here. Her name is Susan Brownell Anthony and she fought for the things Amelia Bloomer fought for and for many more. She knows what it is to stand before a mob of angry men and be howled down because she speaks for women's rights. She has felt the impact of rotten eggs and overripe tomatoes. She knows what it is to be arrested and tried by a judge who has written his opinion before he has heard the evidence. She knows what it is to be fined unjustly and to defy injustice even when it is administered by the authority of her own country's government. She knows what it is to be scorned and insulted by the very people for whom she fights, even her women friends and neighbors in Western New York. But she knows, too, the joy of seeing a cause win its way across the years to a final victory.

These are five living invisible women who have come here too, ladies and gentlemen. The hills of York State gave them strength and nurtured them. Whatever other influences this landscape about them may have had, it gave them communion with some spiritual force that hovered above them, a force that returned them to their respective battles refreshed and renewed. Mary Jemison's struggle was to live. Mother Ann Lee's and Jemima Wilkinson's to live reverently. Amelia Bloomer's and Susan Anthony's to live justly.

One thing beside the everlasting integrity of their own personal genius these women had in common. None of them was educated in a college. Each had to meet her adversary unequipped with the weapons that civilization can and should provide. That they met and conquered their enemies was due to their own unfailing courage and persistence.

Like the college world you are leaving the world outside has its standardizing processes. Our cities arrange life for us so successfully that it is a matter of wonder that we are not more like each other than we are. City folks eat the same breakfast—dash for the same hole in the ground—are poured into the same tightly packed tube—moved rapidly to the same stations—hurried out of the same exits. The buildings which they rush to are so much alike that they must be differentiated by numbers. Like elevators boost them to like floors where they find like offices. Noon finds them eating the same lunches—chocolate malted and ham on rye—in the same drugstores and five o'clock returns them to the tight packed tubes. Then they eat the same dinner, listen to the same radio—hundreds of thousands of listeners hearing the same jokes at the same time—attend the same movie—it may have a different name but it is the same movie.

The small town and the country have routines equally as deadly to the seeker of the rut of least resistance. Modern America provides a wealth of nothingness for those who desire it. The courage of an unflinching personal integrity is essential to combat it.

These five invisible spectators of whom I have told you may be laughing a little grimly at some of you. They had not the knowledge which is yours and which should give you power. Somewhere in these hills and valleys they got the strength to be themselves and to believe in themselves. Some of them were wrong—by the standards we accept today—but none of them was wrong according to the standards she set for herself.

In a short while, shorter than you are expecting, I shall be through with what I have to say and you will be young women of a college no longer but young women of the world. Two kinds of life are waiting. Some of you, already pained by the emptiness of your own living, will seek anaesthetics to keep yourselves unconscious until you die. This world provides them—the chloroform of the bridge table, the ether of Society, the novocain of the beauty parlor. I would not try to frighten you into another course by our ghostly visitants. I realize that some of you are thinking it is a crazy idea anyhow. But to those of you who would argue with me saying—these early women had a chance to do something, they were pioneers when there was a frontier—I can give you the assurance that there is still and always will be a frontier. There is a frontier for those of you who prefer ridicule to a quiet evening at the movies, rotten eggs and ripe tomatoes to the applause of the Wednesday Morning Literary Club, unfair arrest and imprisonment to the very unrevolutionary practices of citizens who give lip worship at American revolutionary shrines.

The hills in which our five proud lady-ghosts still walk have done their part. The same influences that inspired them to lives of courage are still at work. They are not to be put aside by those who would be honest with their country and with themselves.

❦   Nathan Meets the Prophet Elijah

(*Nathan Hart, having escaped after his capture as a Whiskey Rebel, made his way northwest along the Susquehanna and westward into the Finger Lake country. There he came upon certain members of the sect commonly known as Jemimakins, disciples of the Publick Universal Friend.*)

Nathan rode east and north along Codonus Creek until the brown waters of the wide Susquehanna gleamed through the trees ahead. Then he turned upstream. During the day he chose to ride close to the river, sometimes in it when the bottom was gravelly and the water not too deep. For two days' ride he could depend upon recognizable landmarks to guide him. He forded the little Conewago in the late morning and in midafternoon the rippling waters of Yellow Breeches. That night he tethered Lottie on the banks of the Conodoguinet not more than a quarter mile from the west end of Harris's Ferry and, when the lights in the cabins below had gone out, he hobbled her and let her graze a few hours in the high brown grass while he slept. His rest was fitful. His mind was still striving to realize the new condition of his life. Sometimes when he dozed he would waken with a start, reaching for his gun—certain that pursuers had come upon him.

In the morning, after he had bathed his face and hands in the stream and eaten sparingly of the boiled ham and wheat bread which his mother had placed in his saddlebags, he faced northward again. And as he rode he felt despair settle upon him, despair and shame and a heavy, spiritless lassitude. His stomach sank within him and his mind was one dull ache. He tried to imagine a life ahead for himself, wondering where he would first dare to join other men again. What would he say when they asked him of his past? Would they believe he was a painter? Perhaps he would have done better to give himself up. In jail there would be a bed and three meals a day. After he was let out he could go back to painting wagons.

Then he thought of his arrest and the long march into Philadelphia and his quarrel with the mother-ridden, mewling girl on the steps of her home, and he urged his horse forward.

He heard voices ahead of him when the sun was high and spurred Lottie away from the river, making for Paul Reider's ferry across the Juniata. The raft ferry lay on the south side of the river as he rode up and he saw Reider seated on a chair at the far end holding a fishing pole. He stood up as Nathan led Lottie aboard.

"Don't need no ferry with that horse," he said lazily. "Jest drive her into the river and walk across on her backbone." He was so silent and so impassive of countenance as he poled his craft across the swirling water that Nathan suspected him of knowing his passenger to be a fugitive. He was the more certain of this when Reider, having run the ferry on the shelving north bank, said suddenly:

"Mahantango's mighty riled. Better keep straight north from here if ye want to cross her. Ye kin meet up with the west branch o' the Susquehanna later if ye folly Penn's Crick down towards Northumberland."

Nathan did not reach the banks of Penn's Creek until the next morning. He bore eastward farther than he had intended and unexpectedly came upon the Susquehanna below the creek's entrance at a spot where bladelike rocks, just below the surface, drew a thin white line across the dark water. There, lulled by the chatter of the riffle, he slept.

He spent the third day on a slanting ride up the sides of the Laurel Mountains. Often he had to leave the river and try to find an inland passage that would bring him back to it at some less impassable point. More than once he was forced to retrace his steps and try again. There was snow on the crests of the Laurels and Lottie picked her way delicately and slowly. In the afternoon came a slow, drizzling rain. A steep cliff towering over roiling deep water once more turned him away from the river. When he came upon it again he could see by the vague glimmer in the west that the stream now flowed from that direction and he knew then that he must go on to the north without its friendly guidance. He found a shallow riffle, crossed to the north bank, and plunged into the forest.

He rode steadily through the continuous rain-whisper of the woods and at last the night was black around him. Realizing then that he could no longer stay on his course he looked for shelter. Complete darkness had come so quickly that he could not find even an overhanging ledge to keep off the rain. He tied his mare to a pine. She looked at him inquiringly. "Good night, Lottie," he said. "I'll do better by you after this. There'll be butterflies to shy at soon." He slapped her steaming flank assuringly and lay down a few yards away. He stayed awake, shivering, for a long time, while his mind went back to the old circling of the wall of events that had hedged him in. Grayness had begun to sift among the trunks of the trees before he slept.

When he awakened the ground was mottled with shadows, and rays

of light had found small openings through the high foliage. He discovered a pool of rain water and drank deeply. Then, munching on
his wheat bread, he rode north.

The sun was directly above him before he saw river water again.
He was puzzled at first because the stream on his left was flowing
north, but, after calculating as best he could the number of miles he
had ridden since he left the Susquehanna, he reckoned that he was on
the banks of the Tioga and rode downstream.

The river was smaller and seemed more friendly. The sun was
bright and warm and there was a smell of coming buds in the air.
From each patch of snow along the banks tiny drippings trickled into
the smooth stream. The trees stood wider apart here. The tamaracks
and hickories had been dark and close upon the mountains, but beside
the chuckling water now the willows and the beeches made creamy
patterns against the sky. Just at sunset he came to a cabin clearing. He
would have circled it if a little girl had not appeared in the path just
in front of him and said, in a language he identified as French, something he did not understand.

At the sound of the girl's voice her mother rushed from the cabin
and ran to her baby. She was a thickset, dark woman with a mobile
face and large brown eyes. A coarse, loose dress, caught in at the waist
by a leather belt, hung down to her bare ankles. She wore no shoes.
She smiled at seeing Nathan and said "Bonjour, monsieur." She motioned to him to tie the mare and follow her to the cabin. As he did
so her husband, dressed in tow frock and trousers, strolled out, his gun
under his arm.

Then by alternate gestures and shouting in French they bade Nathan
welcome. The woman at once set to work cooking supper in the cabin
fireplace. Nathan saw her make a paste out of corn flour and water,
roll it into little balls, and place them on an iron skillet which she had
greased with a piece of salt pork. Into her coffee pot she dumped water
and a handful of burned corn kernels. The cakes were soggy and un-
salted, the coffee was a muddy, weak mixture, and Nathan was glad
when supper was over. He felt safe with these people, but he was embarrassed at his ignorance of their language and his dislike of their

food. The woman chattered steadily—as if by very rush of words she could make him understand a portion of her meaning. The little girl flirtatiously offered him portions of her cakes and giggled delightedly when he took them.

After dinner the man motioned his guest to the only bed in the cabin —a wide broad structure over which lay two dirty woolen blankets. When Nathan asked awkwardly by signs and grimaces where the family was to sleep the woman pointed to herself, her husband, and her child, and then out of the door to a covered shed which sheltered a small stack of hay. Nathan pointed to it and then to himself and nodded vigorously. The outside couch was far more inviting to him than the bed. The woman seemed relieved. The haycock would obviously accommodate one sleeper far more easily than three.

This settled, the Frenchman and his wife both shook hands cordially with their guest and the little girl put up her cheek for a kiss. Immediately the man took off his pants, and the wife loosened her belt and fingered the button at the top of her one-piece dress. Nathan left the cabin and walked out to the shed. The hay needed leveling off if he was to sleep upon it. He lifted his right foot and kicked the pinnacle of the stack.

A rumble that came from nowhere filled the night and the stack suddenly came alive. There was a cascade of hay and out of its stringy veil something white arose. For a moment it was impossible for Nathan to connect all the elements of the picture in front of him into a unified whole. Apparently a ghost had materialized from the dry grass, and gradually it was taking the shape of a tall man, clad in the pure garments of sainthood. Now, out of a bushy beard, jet black against his white robe, poured roar upon roar of outrage. Stunned with astonishment and fright Nathan looked on, motionless.

"I—I didn't know you were there," he said lamely.

"By the Eternal," shouted the bearded one, "the prophets have ever been persecuted, but they have sometimes retaliated. Remember the bears who ate the children! Remember—"

"Sorry I kicked you," said Nathan, "but who are you and what are you doing here?"

The bearded one rose on tiptoe and lifted a bare arm toward the sky.

"I am Elijah," he said, "habitant of the body of the late James Parker of Rhode Island. I cry aloud in the wilderness where there are none to hear."

The door of the cabin opened and the Frenchman stood naked in the starlight—his woods rifle aimed at the bearded head.

"Don't shoot," shouted Elijah, *"C'est moi, le Prophète."*

"C'est ça," said the Frenchman with a sigh and closed the door.

"You may share my couch," said the Prophet abruptly and he began spreading the hay about with vigor. Suddenly he stopped and glared at Nathan and shouted, "Unless you follow The Friend."

"What?" said Nathan.

"No," said Elijah. "A young man, strong and right-minded, a young man, long-legged and lusty, would not be deceived by that profane blasphemer, that female deceiver of the weak, that Pretendress to Divinity."

He switched his white robe about and scratched his thigh.

"Perhaps you are a raven," he said mildly.

"I don't understand you," said Nathan.

"A raven. A raven. 'And the ravens brought him bread and flesh in the morning and bread and flesh in the evening.'"

"I have boiled ham and wheat bread in my saddlebags."

"Then you are a raven," said Elijah and he shook hands solemnly.

After the food had been fetched, the Prophet munched contentedly and talked less formally. The Genesee Country, he said, was but a day's ride northward. There was plenty of work there. There were houses to be built and seeds to be sown. The soil was rich and it could be bought cheap. In some sections there were many trees, and clearing the land was hard. But the great flats along the river and beside some of the smaller streams were almost treeless and there the grasses grew to a height far above a man's head. Dangerous animals—bears, wolves, and wildcats—had begun to disappear, though a trader could still make a good living from the furs of minks and foxes and muskrats. Flocks of wild pigeons darkened the skies above the river every spring. There were fish in the waters to be had for the taking. Indians were growing a hundred bushels of corn to the acre in their flatlands. Settlers were beginning to plant hemp and flax and tobacco, and all were doing well.

"Why don't you live there yourself," said Nathan, "if it's the heaven you say?"

"I do," roared Elijah, "and it was heaven until the Vale of Kedron was rent in twain. Until the Universal Friend betrayed herself and me, we dwelt beside still waters in a land of milk and honey." He went on for a moment matter-of-factly. "I've been in New Town buying seeds and now I'm going home. As soon as my spring sowing is done," his voice rose again, "my cry shall be heard through all the land proclaiming that sin has seized upon The Friend."

"Who is The Friend?"

"The Spirit of Life from God before she assumed the power of the Almighty. I came with her to the Vale—I and Rachel Malin who is the prophet Daniel operating in these latter days in the female line—and together we counseled the faithful and our words were good."

"But what happened? Why are you angry with her?"

"She cast me out because of a little child. For years she preached at me—a seventh child—that all must love God more than earthly pleasure. Time and again she told me I must leave my wife and live as celibate as she. And when my seventh child was born she took my mantle from me before all the faithful and proclaimed I was no more Elijah." The prophet's voice rose sharply to a sudden sob. He turned and lay face downward in the hay. The shed was silent, then, all night.

🍂 Cooperstown

The water brims steadily over the southern edge of narrow hill-bordered Otsego Lake and seeks a lower level in a walled stream bed. It follows a man-made culvert under a road and emerges, widening, in a lawn that edges the brick walls—faded salmon pink peppered with burned black—of a big and rambling house. That the Susquehanna begins in the "back yard" of Riverbrink, as the house is called, is meaningful. The lake water here, for all its long and winding journey of five hundred and twenty miles to Chesapeake Bay, establishes a definite character.

The Hudson, rising high among Adirondack peaks and long miles from any dwelling of man, has two distinctive river personalities. For half its length it is a shallow, trout-haunted stream. Then it makes a sharp turn to the south and becomes the Hudson as most people think of it, lordly and majestic, a channel of ocean-going vessels, one of the greatest rivers of the world.

The Susquehanna, though more than two hundred miles longer than the Hudson, is born among men. A few yards from the lake it is not quite four feet deep, and there children swim, shadowed sometimes by the high bank across from Riverbrink. Canoes drift here and fishermen, hardly expecting a catch, idle with short lines dangling in water so clear that the fish can see them. In spring and summer, lawn and stream and high bank across meld varying shades of green, making a lush and subtly arranged background for the fading hues of the house, like a landscape by a French painter, Courbet. And, somehow, always consistent, through other back yards and through coal towns, through deep chasms and wide flat bottoms, the Susquehanna always keeps a relationship to the men on its banks. Sometimes dangerous, sometimes friendly, it ever maintains its unique unchanging quality, minding its own business, a "character" among streams.

Otsego Lake was once made famous through the world under a different name—"Glimmerglass"—and the man who so named it was James Fenimore Cooper, writer of *Leatherstocking Tales*, novels of the American frontier, whose father, William Cooper, had given his surname to the town in which the river begins.

When William Cooper first came to this spot, in 1785, as he later reported in his *A Guide in the Wilderness:*

> ...there existed not an inhabitant nor any trace of a road; I was alone three hundred miles from home without bread, meat, or food of any kind; fire and fishing tackle were my only means of subsistence, I caught trout in the brook and roasted them on the ashes. My horse fed on the grass that grew by the edge of the waters. I laid me down to sleep in my watch coat, nothing but the melancholy

Wilderness around me. In this way I explored the country, formed my plans of future settlement, and meditated upon the spot where a place of trade or a village should afterwards be established.

William Cooper was far from the first visitor to this spot in the "melancholy Wilderness," though this paragraph might not lead a reader to think so. George Croghan was one of a hundred associated partners who in 1769 obtained patents to a vast tract of land stretching from Cherry Valley on the north to the shores of Otsego. A Dublin-born trader, he came in that same year to the foot of the lake and with the aid of fellow Irishmen and some Indians raised ten buildings, cleared four fields, launched a bateau and erected a bridge across the Susquehanna. Through such beginnings Croghan might have eventually achieved a real estate empire. He had already created a "place of trade or a village" where later William Cooper dreamed one, but western lands offered even greater opportunity and he moved on to further and more ambitious land schemes on the Ohio.

Other visitors to this lonely forest spot had been soldiers. More than fifteen hundred men under General James Clinton had encamped there only six years before William Cooper, "alone, three hundred miles from home," napped where they had bivouacked. While the level of the waters against the dam they had built crept slowly upward, the army had waited there impatiently for weeks against the time when they would ride the suddenly released floodcrest downriver to join the other forces moving toward them. And General George Washington, remembering this exploit, after Yorktown and setting out to visit the scenes of war triumphs he had not witnessed, "traversed the country to the head of the eastern branch of the Susquehanna, and viewed the lake Otsego."

Croghan was a man of failures to the end of his life. William Cooper was a man of successes. A year after his visit to the "rough and hilly country of Otsego," he offered forty thousand acres of his purchase of Croghan's lands at sheriff's sale, and so great was the demand that in sixteen days all were bought and by "the poorest order of men." In making his contracts with them the landlord adopted a policy much wiser, as Louis Jones, Director of the New York State Historical Asso-

ciation, has pointed out, than that of his friends, the Manor Lords of
the Hudson Valley, who "were selling no land but devising inden-
tures which gave their tenants the shadow of independence but the
reality of perpetual servitude. The sturdy Judge sold his land outright,
as much or as little as a man wished to buy, giving them seven to ten
years in which to pay off the cost." By so doing he avoided the land-
rent wars which plagued the Hudson's vast estates in the 1840's.

Partly because the poverty of these settlers prohibited their clearing
large areas, the first years of the community's growth were difficult:
"their grain grew chiefly in the shade; their maize did not ripen, their
wheat was blasted," but William Cooper would not let them fail. An
aristocrat by nature, a rigid Federalist in politics, he had an overwhelm-
ing sense of *noblesse oblige*. "I erected a storehouse, and during each
winter filled it with large quantities of grain, purchased in different
places....I procured...a credit for a large quantity of sugar kettles
...I established potash works....I gave them credit for their maple
sugar and potash at a price that would bear transportation."

These and other efforts turned the adverse tide. The poor among
whom William Cooper had chosen to live began to prosper, and their
ever-helpful landlord was idolized. In three years came the establishment of Otsego County; Cooperstown became the county seat, and
William Cooper, naturally, first judge of the County Court. He had
moved his family from Burlington, New Jersey, the year before (1790),
and the story is that when his wife refused to budge from her chair
to go into the wilds, he ordered her loaded, chair and all, into the
nearest wagon.

Judge Cooper was a hearty, physically strong man of violent opinions.
He was a good wrestler and once offered a hundred acres to any man
who could throw him, which he promptly and good-naturedly paid
when after several opponents failed, one succeeded. He also fought
with his fists a hated political enemy and thereby established a lasting
controversy, for witnesses of the street battle differed as to who won.
Like his fellow Federalists he was an ardent supporter of the Alien
and Sedition Act and, in the period when Judge Thomas Cooper of
the downriver town of Northumberland was convicted of violating it,
Judge William Cooper of Cooperstown at the river's source had

Jedediah Peck, advocate of free speech and free schools, arrested for urging the law's repeal. One-eyed and aged, Peck was carted off to Albany in chains on a ride that did more than all his spoken words to arouse its witnesses to fiery denunciation of the doomed statute. It was doubtless the extreme bitterness of Judge Cooper's political convictions that led to his death. In Albany, after having left a hall where he had delivered a stormy political harangue, he was murdered by a never identified enemy who, sneaking up behind him, struck him a crushing blow on the head.

William Cooper's son, James Fenimore, was twenty-two when his father was slain. He had arrived in Cooperstown at the age of one, had been ten when the family moved from their frame house into the grandeur of Otsego Hall which his father had ordered constructed as more suitable to the community's first family. He saw little of it in his early youth, however, for at about the time of the removal he was sent to Albany where he prepared himself for matriculation at Yale. He entered that college at thirteen, but in his junior year was expelled for a violation of college rules. He spent two months in Otsego Hall before going to sea in the merchant service from which he soon transferred to the Navy. He resigned in 1811 and shortly afterward married Susan De Lancey of a widely known landholding Tory family in the Hudson Valley. For a while they lived in Westchester County, New York, but the banks of the headwaters of the Susquehanna which he had wandered during his first decade had made such a lasting impression that he could never deny their claim on him, and he returned to Cooperstown and built, not far from Otsego Hall, such a stone house as a young country squire might consider fitting.

In 1817, he moved his family back to Westchester. He did not return to the loved haunts of his boyhood for seventeen years. Then, having become one of the most widely known literary figures of the world, having done his native country high honor by his popular novels of America's early days, having lived abroad where he was the welcome associate of Europe's great, he came home to Cooperstown.

To the amazement of his fellow townsmen who felt flattered by his continued love of their beautiful lake-and-mountain landscape, one of the returned author's first acts was to forbid them their long-accustomed use of Three Mile Point as a picnic ground. They protested that they had so used it in the days of William Cooper who had never discouraged their happy gatherings on this little wooded peninsula, which jutting out into the water, provided magnificent views both up and down the lake. The crotchety son of William Cooper said that he owned the land and he would have no further picnic trespassers. The citizens of Cooperstown, feeling that long custom had established a sort of common-law right, denounced him in public print. Many of the newspapers of New York State concurred and said so. Cooper sued them all for libel and won suit after suit. These cases, while occasioned by the landowner's insistence on his property rights, ended in decisions which established in the law of the United States that a man may not publicly attack the character of another without producing evidence of the truth of the charges.

But the neighbors of James Fenimore Cooper were not grateful for these benefits. They regarded his attitude toward them as arrogantly aristocratic and subversive to a democratic society. His espousal of the cause of the tyrannical Hudson River manor lords in their quarrel with their tenants in 1845 still further embittered the common people. When he died in 1851, James Fenimore Cooper, the man who had brought to the village its greatest fame, was not mourned by the descendants of the settlers who had looked upon his father as their great friend and benefactor.

The town at the headwaters of the Susquehanna, like the river itself, has run a consistent course through the generations. In 1815, another "big house," Hyde Hall, was built by George Clarke, Anglophile descendant of a lieutenant governor of the Colony of New York, and it was soon evident that there would be more than one "first family" in Cooperstown. Since that time the village, blessed by great natural beauty, has become representative of a type not unusual in upstate New York in which homes like those of English "County families" give aristocratic flavor to communities not otherwise distinguishable from neighbors they regard as less fortunate.

James Fenimore Cooper as early as 1838 foresaw with keen intuition the town's future. He prophesied "no mushroom city" but a "provincial town of importance." Its natural advantages, he felt, made

it suitable for a summer resort habitable during the warm months by
"those who live less for active life than for its elegance and ease." For
the past hundred and fifty years Cooperstown has been this and, recently, a good deal more.

As the town grew more prosperous and more of the big houses
appeared—Lakelands, Brookwood, Apple Hill, Fenimore Farm—the
vivid hues contributed by a generation of amusing nonconformists
faded away, giving place to the solid, if dull, colors of Victorian con-
servatism. Cooperstown went through the years of America's cringing
cultural deference to Europe without such serious damages as are still
visible along the Hudson. When her novelist first citizen returned
from his European wanderings to Otsego Hall, he added to that simple
building crenelations and other Gothic defacements. These, as depicted
in a contemporary painting, create a feeling of resignation to the fact
that the house burned down in 1853. Edward Clark, an attorney who
had married a Cooperstown girl and had later become the partner of
I. M. Singer, inventor of the enormously profitable Singer Sewing
Machine, built a summer home near the shore of Otsego in 1854, and
in 1876 reared a castle on a little promontory. European visitors had
condescendingly pointed out to Americans that they had "no sense of
antiquity," and castles were one of the New World's major answers.

"Kingfisher Tower," wrote Edward Clark, "consists of a miniature
castle after the style of the eleventh and twelfth centuries...it adds
solemnity to the landscape...it gives a character of antiquity to the
Lake....The effect...is that of a picture from medieval times," and
he recommends it to those "whose minds can rise above simple notions
of utility to an appreciation of art joined to nature."

Cooperstown is today a unique, many-faceted jewel in the treasure
chest of New York State. Enter it in summer (and this is advisable
since its winters are strenuous) and you will realize that it is a quiet
tree-shaded, well-to-do village. Its business section is not unlike that of
most of the state's communities of about the same population, except
that there seems to be less ambition; there is no bustle here. It has in
its past been avoided by canal and railroad. It may be reached easily
only by private automobile. Yet it is one of the most sought-out towns
in all of America.

The reason for its popularity lies not in its exquisite landscape nor in its beautiful old homes, but in the civic enterprise of Stephen C. Clark, descendant of the Edward Clark who built Kingfisher Tower. When Edward Severin Clark, bachelor elder brother of Stephen died in 1933, he left a record of benevolent paternalism seldom equaled. The success of I. M. Singer and Company had made Edward a very rich man, and he lavished noble gifts on his loved community. He built a gymnasium and recreation center for his neighbors' children, a verandaed hotel, the O-Te-Sa-Ga, with a portico lined with tall white pillars, and he established and endowed the Mary Imogene Bassett Hospital (named after a distinguished physician and greatly admired friend) which (with further aid from the Clark family) provides for the community, and rural districts of which it is the center, a medical service equaled only by the most favorably known hospitals of the nation.

When Stephen Clark succeeded to the control of the late Edward's properties, he made an effort consistent with more modern ideas of philanthropy to turn such of his brother's former properties as were suitable into assets of value not merely to the town but to the people of state and nation. This purpose has borne fruit in three astonishing museums that have brought millions of traveling Americans to this unpretentious town.

The most generally known, the most visited and, in some respects, the least valuable to the national culture of these educational institutions is the Baseball Museum. The story that the game, approximately as played today, was "invented" by Abner Doubleday in Cooperstown about 1840 has been discredited. The game known as baseball was being played under that title almost a century before Doubleday (who never claimed to be its inventor) wrote out his "scheme for playing it." Nevertheless, the nation as a whole has accepted Cooperstown as "The Home of Baseball," and tens of thousands of family-laden cars with license plates representing every state in the Union roll into the town each summer. The museum itself is a neat, architecturally uninteresting building and, to the everlasting credit of the management, it is blessed with an absence of exploitation and receives dignified promotion. While most other national shrines are approached on highways lined with one-story white shacks announcing "Frozen Custard," "Hot Dogs," etc., the motor-borne pilgrim frequently passes the baseball mecca without noticing it and is obliged finally to ask a pedestrian where it is.

The most publicized exhibit in the museum is "Baseball's Hall of Fame," several scores of plaques bearing on each bronze surface a likeness of a selected player, one of the game's "immortals." The first six of these were displayed at the grand opening of the museum on June 12, 1939, when the Postmaster General of the United States appeared with seventy postal clerks and, with the politician's insouciant disregard of historical fact, sold to eager collectors 500,000 stamps recording the National Government's recognition of the date as the hundredth birthday of a game which was already about two hundred years old.

Baseball's relics impose greater demands on the viewers' imagination than do those of the historic scenes of our past. The latter through costumes, settings, properties, stimulate the fancy to re-creation of dramatic moments. But the diamonds, the uniforms, the gloves, the balls, the bats, have been so nearly alike through the years of baseball's history that only the most sensitive minds may consider them evocative. The last ball pitched in a famous "no-hitter" looks identical with the first one to be pitched tomorrow. The bat that was responsible for a record number of Runs Batted In in a season is not easily distinguishable from one that a new pitcher will soon strike out with. One worn catcher's mitt looks pretty much like another. The most colorful materials in baseball history are not among the annals and old properties of the big league teams. Millions have attended the league games and more millions, though never present at them, have kept eager watch over fielding and batting averages, but the most widespread interest of the vast nation has centered on Saturday and holiday ball played by countless local "home-town" teams.

Late in the nineteenth century and early in the twentieth, traveling teams of professionals willing to meet town teams along the Susquehanna and elsewhere for not unreasonable fees were very popular. There were the Cherokee Indians who donned paint and war bonnets to leave their highly decorated private car and parade through town, then danced and howled about second base before playing almost error-less ball. The Cuban Giants, whose accents were more Deep South than Spanish, were another such team, and the Susquehanna country-side for miles around used to be empty of humans on afternoons when the locals met the Bloomer Girls who played quite as well as men after the female pitcher had been replaced, at the end of the first inning, by a male substitute. The posters, private-car decorations, and prop-erties of these itinerant teams may someday add exciting color to the Baseball Museum's nationally popular exhibit. But today, it must be confessed, little color is evident. Nevertheless, hundreds of thousands of Americans visit Cooperstown each year, hoping that by looking long at the objects there displayed they may recapture in memory the white-lined greensward, the brown of the bare base-paths, the sharp crack of a bat, the white ball in long trajectory against the blue sky, the high-leaping catch and the diving "shoestring" catch, the pitch so fast the eye loses it, the swelling roar of the big crowd—all the poetry of the game.

The great figures of baseball's past, moreover, do not live in the minds of succeeding generations. Grandfathers stand reverently before the plaque of Honus Wagner, fathers before that of Lou Gehrig, young sons before a ball that Mickey Mantle hit over the fence for one of the longest of measured home runs. The older men are pathetic in their puzzlement over the boys' lack of interest in their own idols.

Unfortunately, only a small percentage of the vast number who enter the Baseball Museum to stare at the plaques leave the Hall of Fame to visit the Hall of Life Masks in Fenimore House where they may see exact plaster likenesses, sometimes the only likeness we have, of many heroes of early American history. Made from masks which the sculp-tor, Browere, fashioned by applying plaster to the face of the subject, letting it dry for a while, and then removing it, these likenesses form a portrait gallery of inestimable value to the nation.

In the tremendous "cow-palace" barns which Edward Severin Clark built to house his blooded cattle, Stephen Clark established The Farmers Museum—the most comprehensive of its kind in the world.

Here American families come to see the agricultural utensils that their ancestors used in other years. They may also see weavers at work making homespun, a blacksmith shoeing a horse, and other processes once matter-of-course in American life. In the level field beside the barns stands an early New York State town, constructed piecemeal of especially representative buildings that have been moved from other parts of the state to this site—a schoolhouse, a doctor's office, a general store, a lawyer's office, a tavern.

Across the road from the mammoth exhibit is Fenimore House, built by Edward Clark for his residence but occupied by him for only a year before his death. This is now also a museum, but more conventional than the other two. It contains paintings of significance to our early history, a very important American folk-art collection, an exhibit of Shaker furniture, and the Hall of Life Masks already described.

And so it is that the headwaters of the Susquehanna begin their flow in a town that is a kind of epitome of the life that has been lived along the river's banks. Not that Cooperstown is a part of the past which the visitor may by some psychic process step into. Its inhabitants do not worship the good old days. They look upon them with affection and respect and, being folk of common sense, with a gratitude for the fact that a general interest in them brings many a spending traveler into their shops and tourist homes. Being prosperous and more homogeneous than many towns on main transportation routes, Cooperstown has little difficulty in achieving a happy democratic way of life. It has its Sunday night sings when crowds of its residents sing old hymns and sentimental songs, its square dances in which young and aged violently participate. It awaits each year with particular pleasure the opening, on July fifth as a rule, of the Seminars in American Culture, sponsored by the New York State Historical Association, the headquarters of which are at Fenimore House. Then, for five days or so, all the town becomes a sort of university campus. Scholars, museum directors, librarians, teachers, historians pour into town, and some phases of American culture get a good going over from their beginnings to day after tomorrow. The discussions are held in tents, under trees, on verandas. There is a panel of experts in front of each audience, but that body frequently contains experts also and arguments wax hot. The "courses," selected usually by the Director of the Association, have had such titles as "The Frugal American Housewife," in which those enrolled engage in churning butter, baking bread in beehive ovens, and other hard old-fashioned ways of doing things which result in products of better quality than we get now from mass-production techniques.

In "Looking at the Landscape" all enrolled go by bus to such towns at downriver Bainbridge or Afton, and there disembark to discuss how the history of a community may be deduced from the architecture of its houses and business buildings, the crops that surround it, its cemeteries, its location in the landscape, its roads and streams. A new course, title self-explanatory, has recently been added—"The Life and History of the American Parlor."

As the seminars progress, town and so-called gown become firmly enmeshed in a happy treasure hunt of the past. Laughter drifts across sunlit lawns, the inevitable concomitant of good talk. Folk singers, their guitars hung on straps over their left shoulders, amble from tree to tent to veranda, ever ready with apt music and song. Cooperstown has a good time with its profitable avocation.

❦ Hanging Day

The beat of a hammer sounded out of the mist that covered the valley flats east of Cooperstown on the dawn of July 19, 1805. Early risers on the river side of town peered curiously from their bedroom windows across the soft dull gleam of the Susquehanna, for they knew that the gallows for the hanging of Stephen Arnold had been set up the day before. Only a few strangers who had chosen to camp all night beside that grim angle saw two boys at work and heard them tell they were building a platform for granny to sit on so that she could see the hanging "easy and comfortable."

By seven o'clock the sun had burned the mists out of the valley and off Otsego Lake, and the town was crowded. The taverns, the Red Lion and the Blue Anchor, had been filled long before the previous night's bedtime. That moment had hardly existed, for William Cook, host at the latter, in his usual holiday costume—drab coat of the style of 1776 with buttons the size of dollars, knee breeches, striped stockings, buckles so big they covered half his shoes, and a cocked hat "large enough to extinguish him"—had served up hour after hour such punches and flips as only a former steward on a British East Indiaman knew how to mix. There was talk of a knife fight around midnight over on Pig Alley, and some folks said that in a "wrastlin'" down in Frog Hollow a "half-horse, half-man" from the wild town of Canisteo beyond the Steuben County mountains had put a slick Onondaga Indian on his back.

By eight o'clock streams of carriages were rolling along Pink Street and Mosquito Road. From the Jams, round-topped hills above Milford, and the Twelve Thousand, steeper heights east of Schuyler Lake, from Hell Town and Dogtown and Butternuts, strings of wagons, men on horseback, and men on foot converged on Cooperstown. At the head of Otsego Lake rowboats and canoes slipped out of the shadow of Sleeping Lion Mountain and caught up with others from Hurry Harry and Muskrat Castle to make a scattered flotilla steadily advancing toward the shelving beach where Front Street rims the water. Groups of curious countrymen strolled past Otsego Hall, manor house of Judge William Cooper, whose hell-raising son Jim had been sent home from Yale College that spring; past Apple Hill, the home of Richard Fenimore Cooper; past Henry Bowers's just-completed Lakelands; past the new stone house (the only one in the region) that Judge Cooper had had built on the southwest corner of Water and Second streets for his daughter and her husband George Pomeroy.

Although the parade was not announced to start until noon, the yard across from the jail at Main and Second streets was spang full by nine o'clock. Folks tried out the stocks, looked respectfully at the whipping post, and stared across the street at the door that was soon to swing open for a murderer on his way to his fitting and proper doom. They said that Stephen Arnold ought to hang, all right. He had whipped his six-year-old ward Betsey Van Amburgh so hard that she died, "and him an educated man and a school-teacher." All because the poor child could not help pronouncing the word "gig" as "jig" he had taken off her clothes and seven times had driven her outdoors, where he had whipped her until the bitter cold of the night had made him go back to his fire.

The crowd got so excited talking that hardly any of them noticed when Jacob Ford of Burlington galloped up on a tired horse, dismounted, and ran into the jail. A few remembered afterward that he came out in a moment with the sheriff, who was frowning over what seemed to be a letter, and that the two went off in the direction of the center of town.

By eleven, when the sheriff came back to the jail, Cooperstown, with only five hundred inhabitants, was host to eight thousand, according to the best estimators. Suddenly there was a blare of brass and a tattoo of drums, and Lieutenant Commandant Mason's company of artillery and Lieutenant Commandant Tanner's company of light infantry marched up to take their places as guards to the wagon on which Stephen Arnold would ride to the gallows. Governor Morgan Lewis's love of military pomp was already losing him votes throughout the state, but nobody would kick at his detailing soldiers in full dress for so extraordinary an occasion as this.

Now the civilians who were to take part in the ceremonies were arriving at the jail door. In the little knot about the step stood the Reverend Mr. Williams of Worcester, imported to deliver the invocation at the exercises, and the Reverend Isaac Lewis, Presbyterian pastor whose flock was finishing up the first church in the township. Here was the loved dean of the town's physicians, Dr. Fuller, and, in old-fashioned knee breeches, the eccentric Dr. Nathaniel Gott, recently succeeded to some of the unpopularity of Dr. Charles Powers, who had been run out of town a few years before for putting an emetic into the punch at the Red Lion's New Year ball. Dr. Gott's offense had been an attempt to collect his bills by writing and sending to his debtors a poem:

> Says Dr. Gott
> I'll tell you what
> I'm called on hot
> All round the Ot-
> Segonian plot
> To pay my shot
> For pill and pot
> If you don't trot
> Up to the spot
> And ease my lot
> You'll smell it hot.

Elaborately indifferent to each other in the small group were Dr. Gott and Mr. Elihu Phinney, bookseller and editor of the Otsego *Herald or Western Advertiser,* whose pen was soon to describe the remarkable events of this day. Ever since a jovial evening when they had engaged in the dangerous game of suggesting epitaphs for each other's gravestones there had been a coldness between these two. Gott thought he had scored when he intimated that Phinney's soul was so small that ten thousand like it could dance on the point of a cambric needle. But Phinney had replied:

> Beneath this turf doth stink and rot
> The body of old Dr. Gott
> Now earth is eased and hell is pleased
> Since Satan hath his carcass seized.

They did not speak to each other after that. Gott was the more annoyed since Phinney, founder of *Phinney's Calendar or Western Almanack,* had won fame as a prophet when, through a typographical error in that popular journal, he had foretold snow for the fourth of July, only to find on that day, to his own secret amazement and the loud-mouthed astonishment of his neighbors, that nature was heartily co-operating by fulfilling his prediction. Perhaps it was the successes of his clever enemy that led the fiery physician to enlist in the War of 1812. Reported missing when it ended he was assumed to have died until some years later an American traveler in Spain, seeing on a doctor's shingle there a familiar name, took steps to identify the bearer.

Dr. Gott sighed and came back to his considerable family in Cooperstown. Phinney in the meantime had been loading book wagons which
he sent rolling over the state to tempt farmers and villagers to buy his
publications. After the Erie Canal opened he launched a fleet of book
boats which sold their wares at canal towns from Albany to Buffalo.

At almost the stroke of noon the big jail door swung open. The
sheriff strode out first, mounted his horse, and waited for his aides to
assist the pale, heavily chained prisoner into an open wagon. Then
he rode ahead. Behind him walked the ministers, the lawyers, the doctors, and a few important citizens. The band struck up a dirge as the
infantry and artillery companies formed in front of it and began to
march forward with the rolling wagon in their midst. As the slow
procession moved along Second Street and turned down Main, the
crowds that lined the way fell in behind. Along the aisle of witch trees,
"tall and lanky—pressing toward the east," past the Main Street stores
they went. Soon the boards of the Susquehanna bridge were complain-
ing beneath the wagon's wheels. The gallows were in sight on the river
flats a little below the red-brick house that stood near the east end of
the bridge. High above them in the distance rose the Vision, the peak
that marks the termination of the mountains that form the eastern
rim of the valley. At the foot of the gallows lay a wooden coffin, and
in front of both, on a tiny platform of her own, sat an old woman rock-
ing as she knitted and waited.
A few days later Elihu Phinney's Otsego *Herald* described the scene
as the wagon drew up to the place of execution and the condemned
man, his chains removed, dismounted to sit forlorn on his coffin:

Unconnected with the solemn occasion the appearance of such an
extraordinary collection of the sexes was beautiful in the extreme.
The ground at a small distance from the place of execution, which
was a small flat, arose towards the east in such a manner as to afford
every beholder an uninterrupted view of the interesting spectacle.
It seemed when viewed from the high western banks of the river,
a vast natural amphitheatre filled with all classes and gradations of
citizens from the opulent landlord to the humble laborer. The dis-

play of about 600 umbrellas, of various colors; the undulating appearance of silks and muslins of different hues; the vibrations of thousands of fans in playful fancy; the elevated background of the landscape interspersed with carriages of various construction and filled with people; the roofs of the buildings, which commanded a view, covered with spectators; the windows crowded with faces, every surrounding point of view occupied, and the gleam of swords, bayonets &c. in the centre afforded, whenever the mind was detached from the occasion, real satisfaction to the contemplative mind; but on reversing this picture, and reflecting that all those blooming nymphs, jolly swains, delicate ladies, and spruce gentlemen, fond mothers and affectionate sisters, prattling children and hoary sages, servile slaves and imperious masters would be, in all probability, incorporated with their native dust in 100 years, it strongly enforced the truth and pertinence of a maxim of one of the ancient sages, that *pride was not made for man*. A recurrence to the occasion increased our humility.

The Reverend Mr. Williams of Worcester opened the formal program. He climbed the steps of the platform, lifted a hand, and prayed for God's mercy on all present and particularly upon their unfortunate brother whose life must soon be forfeit to justice. Then the Reverend Isaac Lewis stepped forward. The crowd was still as he read his simple text:

"And he said unto Jesus, Lord, remember me when thou comest into the kingdom.

"And Jesus said unto him, Verily I say unto thee. Today shalt thou be with me in paradise."

Pastor Lewis preached his sermon, a "pathetic, concise, and excellent adapted discourse." When it was over, at a signal from the sheriff, Stephen Arnold rose from his seat on the coffin and spoke. He was a man of learning, he was penitent, and he spoke well, ending his remarks with the sentence:

"It appears to me that if you will not take warning at this affecting scene, you would not be warned though one should raise from the dead."

Granny, sitting on her little platform in front of the poor man, was obviously much moved by his words. While he was speaking, her needles flashed more and more swiftly in the sunlight and she rocked back and forth more and more violently. A strained silence encompassed the crowd now. The sheriff's boots sounded loud on the platform as he brought forward the rope and adjusted its noose about the neck of Stephen Arnold. There was a single warning cry. It came too late. A feeble scream, a crack of splintering wood, and Granny had rocked off the platform and broken her neck!

The old lady's death caused only a slight delay in the proceedings. The frail wizened body had been lifted and carried away before many of the crowd realized what had happened. The crescendo of questioning voices soon died out. Once more there was silence and the sheriff, standing beside the doomed man, spoke the last words the miserable fellow expected to hear, exhorting him to make his peace with God and bidding the spectators take warning from his fate.

Now, at the moment when nothing was left to be done save the suspension and strangling to death of Stephen Arnold, the sheriff took a few steps forward, drew from his pocket an official-looking paper, and read it aloud. It was a reprieve from Governor Morgan Lewis. While the crowd was still quiet, unable to grasp its meaning, the reader hastily explained that he had received the governor's message that morning around nine o'clock, but, after conference with several leading citizens, had decided that he could not disappoint the thousands of visitors who had come from far and near to witness the day's spectacle. Possibly he did not think it necessary to add that the sudden departure of all these people in the early morning would not have allowed Cooperstown's merchants to garner all the rewards that the day's brisk trading had given them. Simply out of respect for the town's guests, he said, he had allowed the scheduled exercises to continue thus far. Obviously they could not continue further. *115/39*

The purport of the sheriff's words reached the minds of the crowd and of Stephen Arnold at the same time, but their separate reactions varied widely. Arnold slumped to the floor at the foot of the gallows. The crowd roared its wrath. "Some swore, others laughed, but all were dissatisfied." Many had come a long way, lost at least two days' time, been put to considerable expense for which they felt they had had no corresponding return. "They acted and talked as if they must have a substitute." They seemed to think that either the sheriff or the absent governor would do nicely. Toward Stephen Arnold, however, they exhibited little animosity. He had done his part well and in good faith. For a few moments a riot was incipient, but the sheriff avoided it. He ordered the band to play a quickstep, the soldiers to fall in, and he headed a noisy parade back through the town. It drew the whole throng into its wake.

When it had reached the jail, the sheriff held up his hand for silence and granted Stephen Arnold's request that he be allowed to make the last speech of the day. From the wagon, before the jail received him, Arnold said he wished to thank Jacob Ford, who had brought the good news from Albany, and other friends, who had worked for his reprieve. Again he warned the multitude that had followed him on his joyful return from the gallows that they must control their passions. Anger, he said, had brought him to his shameful condition. Then he entered upon an incarceration which was to last the rest of his days, for his sentence was commuted the following year to life imprisonment.

Still enraged, shouting that they had been duped, damning the sheriff and his advisers for their cruelty in not telling Arnold of the reprieve until after his neck had felt the rope, the visitors who had swelled the number of Cooperstown's inhabitants to almost twenty times its usual size turned their faces toward home. They left behind a dazed group of villagers who did not know quite what to think. In a few days, however, they had made up their minds. The astute Elihu Phinney expressed their sentiments in the next issue of the Otsego *Herald or Western Advertiser:*

> The proceedings of the day were opened, progressed, and closed in a manner which reflected honor on the judiciary, the executive, the clergy, the military, and the citizens of the county.

❦ "O the Ee-rye-ee Was Risin'"

The saga of the Erie Canal, and of the boats and men
who made it the greatest man-made waterway of its time

Joining western waters, the Great Lakes long known as the "English Seas," with the Atlantic was not a new idea when the nineteenth century began. Elkanah Watson, originator of the county fair, had talked over such a plan with the distinguished soldier, ex-president, and agriculturist, George Washington. The idea had been earnestly recommended by the well-known patriot, Gouverneur Morris.

Opposition had developed. President Thomas Jefferson had expressed the gist of it when he said, "...talk of making a canal 350 miles through a wilderness is little short of madness at this day." President Madison had vetoed a bill that would have aided New York State in building a canal by federal land grants.

But the energetic, scientific mind of De Witt Clinton would not be denied. He saw the canal as a water link binding the productive West to the marketing East.

"As a bond of union between the Atlantic and the Western States," he said as the digging began on the long mid-levels of the tremendous project, "this canal may prevent the dismemberment of the American Empire."

That was on July Fourth, 1817. Long years of desperate, backbreaking, mind-paralyzing labor followed. "Clinton's Ditch" was the standard target for ridicule while the diggers sweated, sickened, died in the miasmic, mosquito-infested Montezuma swamps, or shivered through nights in country "so desolate it would make an owl weep to fly over it," while bosses without modern instruments of measure figured out ingenious locks "by guess and by God."

Stretch by stretch the channel was dug—forty feet wide and four feet deep—hardly enough draft for a vessel that would float on a heavy dew. Here and there, as a piece was completed, the waters were let in and jubilant "Yorkers," to quote a contemporary account, were "running across the fields, climbing on trees, and crowding the banks... to gaze upon the welcome sight."

At last the final day came. On October 25, 1825, the gleaming packet *Seneca Chief* entered the canal at its western end heading a long procession bound for New York Harbor's Atlantic waves. Cannoneers placed within earshot of each other all the way from Buffalo to Manhattan stood to their pieces and fired them as glad booming to the west announced that Erie water was on its way to the sea. In eighty-one minutes the people in the big city at the mouth of the Hudson knew that the limitless harvests of the western, lake-bordered states might now find market on the eastern seaboard or even in lands beyond the eastern ocean. Then began a celebration such as the state had never seen. Throughout the days and nights that followed there was marching and countermarching in the shore towns as the impressive fleet moved east, then south along the Hudson. Fireworks lit the skies, bonfires the shores, as the *Seneca Chief* moved at the head of the water parade. Behind her rode the *Young Lion of the West* (bearing a cargo of four raccoons, a fawn and a fox, two eagles and two wolves) and the *Noah's Ark* in which two Seneca Indian boys guarded a black bear.

The fleet reached New York on the sunny morning of November 4. Steamboats, white and gold "floating palaces," met it and came about to go down the bay. Near Sandy Hook there were solemn exercises topped off by a speech in which Dr. Samuel Latham Mitchill, emptying into the Atlantic phials containing the waters of the great rivers of the world, said he hoped that this action, symbolic of ultimate world peace, would have such effect "that at length even the sable and savage tribes dwelling in the tracts bordering on Senegal, the Gambia and the Congo shall lay aside their ferocity and enjoy, as we ourselves do, 'Liberty under the guidance of Law.'"

After that the canal went to work. Along the towpath the drivers ("hoggies" they called themselves) urged on their mules as they dragged western treasure eastward—grains and fruit and cattle. The packets were crowded with eager Americans bound for the fertile west. Many stopped off on the way, and in the first decade of the canal's history, the population of Rochester, Buffalo, Syracuse and Utica increased at a rough average by about 300 per cent. New towns grew up along the canal at a rapid rate, inland towns with watery names like Spencerport, Brockport, Middleport, Newport (now Albion), Adams Basin and Eagle Harbor. But there were many passengers who would not stop until they reached the shores of one of the great lakes. They were sturdy and optimistic and they sang as they went:

> Then there's the state of New York, where some are very rich,
> Themselves and a few others have dug a mighty ditch,
> To render it more easy for us to find a way,
> And sail upon the waters to Michigania—
> Yea, yea, yea, to Michigania.

The life of the "Canawler" was rough and tough. Saloons along the towpath found eager customers who, after a few samplings of York State distillings, were ready with songs and stories.

One of the latter told of a captain who stopped to mend a boiler plate in the Montezuma swamps and a swamp mosquito stuck his borer right through the plate. The captain made the mistake of splitting the borer and clinching it and the first thing he knew the mosquito flew away carrying the whole boiler off over the treetops.

There were songs, too, which the lonely hoggie howled into the night sky as his mules plodded beside the star-studded waters of the canal. There was "Low Bridge, Everybody Down" with its haunting refrain, "Fifteen years on the Erie Canal." There was the resounding chorus which ran:

> O the Ee-rye-ee was risin'
> The gin was gettin' low
> And I scarcelye think we'll git a drink
> Till we git to Buffalo-o-o
> Till we git to Buffalo.

There was *A Trip on the Erie* with its story of the cook so redheaded that the crew used her as a headlight at night on the deck.

And there was the song about tall fat red-haired Ezekiel Radford, manufacturer of liniment good for horse and mule alike. Ezekiel wore a bright blue shirt with its sleeves rolled up to the elbow displaying his red flannel underwear from elbow to wrist. In the cork of each of his liniment bottles stood a feather, ready for use in applying the magic remedy. I found the song about him written in the diary of a canawler captain and so far as I know it is here printed for the first time:

> We towed into Weedsport about ten o'clock
> And the first one I saw was Ezekiel on the dock
> Says Ezekiel to me "Who's driving this team?"
> Says I to Ezekiel "You're blowin' off steam."
> Ezekiel had come out and begun to bawl and shout
> Saying "Captain, are your horses galded any?
> I've a liniment to sell that will cure them up right well.
> I don't think I have ever sold you any."

With occasional improvements the Erie Canal did its work for seventy-five years. Then, at the turn of the century came the demand that it be supplanted by a deeper, wider channel. By popular vote three years later the people of the United States decided a modern Barge Canal should be built and in 1918 the job was completed. The towpath is no more and the dwellers by the widened stream no longer hear the old call "Look for a post!", prelude to a change of mules and drivers. Where once the wooden boxlike barges slowly met the ripples, seaworthy steel craft, propelled by Diesel engines, make better time. They breast the waters of lake, canal, river and ocean without interruptions for the transfer of cargoes. But Americans do not easily forget the pioneering that made the nation great. The Erie made its unique contribution to our heritage and we shall not cease to sing its songs and tell its tales though its old ways have been forsaken.

❦ Author's Note

Folklore is not only to be enjoyed for itself. It provides a never-ending stream of glittering stuff from which painters and sculptors and writers make pictures and statues, poems and stories.

Today as never before, Americans are aware of the joy that can come to them through understanding the minds of the people of the past. People feel that they know their forebears much better when they know what stories they made up, what songs they created and sang— in other words, what their minds found amusing and entertaining.

Folklore never stops flowing from the springs of the people's fancy, never stops changing as it flows.... Knowledge of a nation's folklore is knowledge of the creative workings of the minds of its folk. It is the key to a nation's values, a highway that leads into the hearts of its people.

❦ How John Darling Went Fishing and Caught a Bride

Upstaters are proud of John Darling and if you give them a chance like as not they will add a bit to the story of his surprising life. Although he was born down near the Susquehanna, in this story he gets as far west as Orleans County—a tolerable piece for a satisfied York State farmer to travel. You can hear about John in Adams Basin or Penn Yan, Bouquet or Nightingale, Limerick or Clove Valley.

John Augustus Caesar Darling—champion long-distance buckwheat pancake eater of the world, greatest sugarbush operator of the north, canal boatman superhuman and fisherman beyond all getout—is the favorite hero of many New York State stories.

Upstate folks tell so much about him it's a little hard to know where to begin, but aside from being born at Shandalee near Sand Pond and Livingston Manor, he got off to a slow start and never distinguished himself until he was about eleven. Then he was out plowing the lower forty one day when he drove his span of two pet steers right at a six-foot high stump. The plow split the stump, all right, and he got plumb through just in time, for the two halves sprang back together again so quick they tore his shirt right off his back. About a week later on a foggy morning John Darling's pa sent him up the ladder beside the house to shingle the roof. After John got through, the sun came out and showed him where he had laid the shingles on the fog twenty feet above the top of the chimney.

When he grew up John Darling had a long beard. Once a year, just before summer came, he would walk to town and get a shine, haircut, and shave. He always had the barber collect his whiskers into big gunny sacks and he took them home to his wife. She would throw them into the kettle and boil them and in that way she used to boil down seven or eight gallons of maple syrup that had got stuck on the beard during the buckwheat cake season.

As I've been telling you, John Augustus Caesar Darling was an A-1 sugarbush man. He never used a sap pan that weighed less than a ton. One morning he was out in the bush when he saw three mosquitoes as big as airplanes and singin' twice as loud making straight for him. He had just time to tip one of his ton sap pans over himself before they arrived. They started right in boring through the iron bottom of that sap pan with their bills and all three of them had got through and were prodding for him when John Darling got a good idea. He had his ax with him and he just split all three of those mosquito bills in two and then pressed each half back up against the iron surface over him. The result of that was that the last he saw of the mosquitoes they were heading off over the treetops toward Binghamton, and they were taking his sap pan with them. He never did get it back.

John Darling gave up working in the sugarbush after that and took

to drivin' on the Erie Canal. The cook on his boat, the *Erie Queen,*
was six foot tall and redheaded. Her hands were as big as elephant's
ears and her name was Sal. John fell in love with her at first sight.
He made up a poem about her but she didn't seem to like it much—
even though he recited it to her every moonlight evening. It went like
this:

> The cook she's a daisy,
> And dead gone on me;
> She has fiery red hair,
> And she's sweet twenty-three;
> She's cross-eyed and freckled,
> She's a darling and a pet,
> And we use her for a headlight
> At night on the deck.

The trouble was that Sal had too many other suitors to give John
Darling much of her time. But John wouldn't give Sal up. He just kept
pestering her to marry him, and she kept saying No. At last he thought
up a scheme for winning her. He knew Sal loved to cook and eat fish
more than any other food—and he pretty much fancied himself as a
fisherman. So he begged her to announce that she'd marry the man
who could catch the most fish in a single day—midnight to midnight.
Sal said she'd do that very thing and she told all her beaux about it.
Since there weren't enough fish in the canal for the contest, they all
tied up their canalboats at Albion and went over to Oak Orchard River
to try their luck. Folks came from all around—from Two Bridges and
Eagle Harbor and Pretty Girl's Crossing and Checkered Tavern—to
see the sport.

The whole lot of Sal's suitors started fishing promptly at midnight
and by noon every one of them had as nice a mess of black bass and
perch and pickerel and bullheads as ever a girl slipped into deep grease
—that is, everyone except John Darling. It just seemed as though he
couldn't get a single nibble. He fished and he fished and he rowed up
and down the river, and by suppertime he had less fish in the boat
than when he started, for he'd lost most of his bait. The sun set and
the river got dark and the rest of the boys rowed down to Point Breeze
to count their catch and see who'd won six-foot Sal—but still John
Darling kept on fishing. All of a sudden he saw a bright light on the

bank—it was Sal's red head. She had come to help him—because she didn't want him to lose.

"Get in this boat," said John Darling, and when she sat up in the bow he could see by the light of that red hair a school of black bass swimming along just ahead of the boat. He rowed up into them and then suddenly turned into the bank.

"Put your head down to the water," he shouted to Sal, and when she did, the whole school of bass, forced against the bank on one side and scared out of its scales by the blinding light on the other, jumped high out of the water. John Darling swung the boat under them as they came down. After he had dug Sal out from under the pile he counted the fish that had jumped into his boat. There were two hundred and thirty-three.

If you don't believe it, just ask any Orleans County fisherman about the fish jumpin' in the boat out of the Oak Orchard River.

John Darling had caught the biggest mess of fish and won himself a bride. He and Sal were married the next morning and set out for their honeymoon at Niagara Falls. When they got back from their honeymoon they found the *Erie Queen* all decorated up with new red geranium window boxes and a big shindig going on inside to celebrate the wedding. The party lasted all night long and then everybody hitched up and there were twenty canalboats in line on the water and twenty span of mules along the towpath with all the drivers joining together in a song as they moved along toward Rome.

✸ Philetus Bumpus

Philetus Bumpus in his fiery prime couldn't stay still long enough to receive visitors, and so he became captain of the prettiest canal-packet between Albany and Buffalo—the *Bathsheba C. Onderdonck*. Drivers who remembered him used to say that when the mules had plodded along the towpath until they had passed a wooden span across the Erie, Philetus never ducked his head at the cry of "Low Bridge! Everybody down!" He'd walk to the back of the boat and stand upright until it looked as if he was going to get his brains knocked out. Then he'd jump right over the bridge and come down up forward near the staple to which the towrope was hitched.

The event that made Philetus into a dignified and rest-loving citizen happened one day when he was about fifty and piloting a group of distinguished and refined ladies and gentlemen from Lockport to Rochester. It was a lovely day. White clouds drifted above green fields and the ladies and gentlemen seated on the deck exchanged polite remarks on the beauties of nature, as the mules dragged the big boat slowly eastward.

All would have been well if a Hudson River sturgeon on his way to visit cousins in Lake Erie had not noted in passing the anchor of the *Bathsheba C. Onderdonck* hanging neatly at her stern. Apparently the sturgeon was nearsighted and mistook the anchor either for an outsize angleworm or possibly one of those tangles of baked salt dough known as pretzels.

At any rate he made a grab for it and set out for Buffalo. Captain Bumpus and all his passengers felt a sudden jerk. The next thing they knew they were traveling back over the way they had come at a much faster speed than that to which they were accustomed, and the mules had developed with startling ease the ability to run backwards. The *Bathsheba C. Onderdonck* flashed through Rochester stern-first and by the time she reached Spencerport she was leaving so great a swell in her wake that the hired men working on the farms beside the canal later claimed they had seen a tidal wave.

The *Bathsheba C. Onderdonck* streaked it through Adam's Basin and Albion and Eagle Harbor, through Medina and Middleport. When the sturgeon reached Lockport the big locks had been filled to let a boat go through and the lockkeeper had just opened the doors to release the water. The big fish squirmed up that hill of water so fast it had no time to run out and the *Bathsheba C. Onderdonck* went right along.

All this time Captain Philetus Bumpus had been standing guard over the taut anchor rope, for indignant passengers were determined to cut it and this would make him lose his anchor. As the boat was backing through Buffalo, a frightened mother held up her little girl-baby to his stern gaze and begged him for the sake of the children aboard to cut the rope before they were all dragged into the depths of stormy Lake Erie. Only then, with a tear in his eye, did Philetus raise his axe and cut the rope.

The whole experience so unnerved him that he retired from following the canal and became a tavernkeeper at Albion. He sold his mules to a little traveling circus that came through Orleans County one day, and for many years they delighted circus crowds by galloping backwards as they learned to do when the sturgeon had them in tow.

❦ The Whooper Swan of Olivebridge

Collectors of regional lore seldom witness the beginning of a folk legend. No matter how sure their skill in recognizing the materials from which communal fancy builds, they will not often come upon an incident likely to stir the general imagination without discovering that those tireless co-authors, the people, have already begun their work of creative elaboration.

Because the origin of this narrative was observed by me when an occasional visitor to the community from which it emerged, and because the two main characters were my friends, here is a report of a story which the folk of a lonely mountain town have made, as most such tales are made, out of provable fact and their own fancying....

From the west bank of a northern reach of the Hudson, the Catskills roll back until they break around a circular plateau. There the flat highland becomes the bottom of a giant cup, its steep sides rising to a nicked rim against the sky.

In the center of the cup, haphazard as the mountain rocks, stand the houses of Olivebridge. The spire of the Methodist church is a neat white needle above the roofs of Boyce's General Store, the post office, and a few other business buildings. One dark and rutted road meets another in the huddle below, and each runs on through cleared meadow for some rods before it disappears into deep woods.

I used to turn left at an intersection in the meadowland after braking my car halfway down from the valley's rim. When my speedometer had measured six and six-tenths miles there would be a right turn into the rough and narrow approach to the low house where I would find Pierre Malakov.

I met Malakov first about 1940. My friend, the late Nikander Strelsky, professor of Russian at Vassar College, took me to Olivebridge to see him. As we drove north along the Hudson, Nik told me, in his shorthand, articleless English, the man's story.

Pierre, he said, was a younger son in a highly regarded Russian family. Soon after his graduation from the School of Imperial Theater he became a favored player of the royal court and married the lovely ballerina Nina Oginska. A captain in World War I, he was chosen to participate in the defense of Verdun when the French asked for Russian aid. His right shinbone was shattered by a bullet during the siege, and an ingenious surgeon fitted into its place a metal substitute which served well, though he still limped slightly.

When the war ended, Malakov stayed on in France, knowing that he would be executed by the Bolshevik revolutionaries if he went home. He had a hard time at first, but the arrival in Paris of the company of the famous Russian revue *Chauve-Souris,* directed by the genial dialectician Baliev, improved his circumstances temporarily. Malakov was soon appearing nightly as the expressionless drummer in the show's most memorable act, "The March of the Wooden Soldiers." His quest of escape from memory of his early stage successes led him to drink, however, and the exacting Baliev, fearing profanation of the robot perfection of his manikins, discharged him.

Without rancor, and with high hopes of better things, Malakov then set out for the United States of America. He wrote Nik of his coming and said that Nina, then dancing in Constantinople, would soon join him. Perhaps he and she would found a school of the theater arts in New York and be rich and fashionable again.

"He will tell you about Nina," said Nik. "She is ideal of his dreams. He will say she was greatest ballerina. And when she dance *Dying Swan*"—he waved a hand—"she was making Pavlova novice."

"Was?" I said. "Has she stopped dancing?"

"Yes," said Nik, "under wheels of Paris metro last year."

We had made our left turn in Olivebridge, and Nik excitedly counted off the decimals of the miles as they clicked into sight on the instrument panel.

"Why is he way out here?" I said.

"He is caretaker of summer shack," said Nik, "only no longer summer shack. I have good friends who ask him to live here. They think he will not drink so much here. Ha! He drinks more, but he has made shack into fine Russian house. You will see."

We made the second turn, crossed a dilapidated bridge, and stopped at the edge of a black-amber pond. Dark water was pouring over a dam, and beside it stood the weathered ruin of a mill. We heard a door close and looked across the pond, where, on a rising bank, stood a long, one-story house. Pierre Malakov limped toward us. He was of medium height, slim and erect. His features were strong and regular, and his deep-set eyes were a clear blue.

Nik introduced me, and Malakov was politely formal. He led us to the house and became more cordial as I exclaimed over it. It had been little more than a boxlike hunting-shack, he said, but he had enlarged it and built a fieldstone chimney at each end. He had artist friends among the White Russian refugees in New York. One was a mural-painter, another a wood-carver, and so it went. Each had chosen to leave behind a sample of his skill.

We spent the late afternoon drinking vodka and eating black bread. Nik, a fascinating talker, was in good form. I listened, but Pierre seemed restless. He drank steadily, and I was not surprised when he rose from the floor where he had been sitting cross-legged near the fireplace and walked to the center of the wide room. There he began to speak in Russian, and the only word I could understand was "Nina," which seemed the emphatic end of every sentence.

"Now he tells how she danced *Dying Swan,*" said Nik suddenly, and was glared at for interrupting. Pierre did not exactly imitate the ballet, but his gestures were so full of meaning that he somehow conjured up for each of us in his separate mind's eye the sighing of the music, the pool of light, and the piteous, ever-weakening flutters of a slim white creature sinking into stillness.

Then he said in English: "Man dances this dance—and never ceases. The swan is spirit. It dies each hour—each hour until—" He wavered and, abruptly but not without grace, slid to the floor, then stretched out with his forehead down upon the arc of his arms.

"Let us leave him," said Nik. "We must go back now to Poughkeepsie." He grinned at me. "He is very Russian."

In the next two years I saw Pierre occasionally, both at Nik's in Poughkeepsie and at Olivebridge. In the latter place he was already becoming a kind of legend. Perhaps because of his previous prowess with vodka, applejack had no terrors for him. He loved it, and the hill men who lived round about and sold him the distilled liquor without benefit of revenue stamps circulated tales of his ability to down incredible amounts and still stay conscious and "a gentleman." The hill women knew him to be the latter and learned to accept his bowing over their hands and his heel-clicking compliments without self-consciousness. Nik, gay and friendly, was happy to be accepted among the mountaineers as Pierre's best friend.

There were ducks on the pond the last time Nik and I went to see him, and Pierre cared for them with affection. "I love ducks," he said, "but I wish swan. They will not give me swan."

Nik explained patiently that swans were expensive, that they did not like ducks, that they were quarrelsome and sometimes dangerous. The owners of the place, he said, were entirely justified in refusing to buy a swan.

Then Pierre grew morose and said that it was just as well that there was to be no swan, for he had little time left in which to enjoy it. Nik and I laughed and reminded him of his boasts of the longevity of the Malakovs, but he remained gloomy and said that he would soon be dead. He began again on his memories of Nina and her dancing, and he said again: "Swan is spirit." Then he quoted a short poem by Rainer Rilke. The German words and rhythms were beautiful, and I gathered that the poet was saying that life is heavy and ungainly—like the awkward walking of a swan—and death is like the swan's fearful leaving of the element of earth, where he fares badly, to be borne on the unfamiliar element of water, and what comes after is the contentment and majestic serenity of the swan as he moves at last and ever more happily on the liquid surface.

That was in April, early spring in those parts, of the year 1942. On the night of May 11 the Russian house blazed fiercely in the mountain dark. Neighbors telephoned for aid, but when it came only smoldering embers remained. The heat had been so intense that the windows were blobs of molten glass, the stones of the two great fireplaces had been blunted, the silverware with which Pierre had eaten his supper had been melted. Pierre's body lay among the ashes of his bed. It was recognizable only by the metal shinbone, which heat had rendered shapeless.

Standing together, the mountain people who came to Pierre's funeral whispered that he might have been murdered. There had been rough strangers in town, they said, and Pierre had quarreled with two of them in a barroom. The gossipers stared curiously at the people who had come to the Catskills to attend the service—the grieving owners of the place, Vassar professors, a distinguished Russian scientist, a once-famous military officer who had a job as a uniformed doorman in New York. As the Reverend Mr. William Barringer, pastor of the little church, said what needed to be said, the motorcycles of the state police were roaring up and down the hill roads, but no evidence that Pierre died from criminal violence has been found.

After the benediction, the owners made arrangements for Mr. Barringer to feed the ducks, look after the old mill, and keep the lawn mowed. Then we all went home.

A few weeks later the owners received a letter from the Olivebridge preacher. He wrote that he had seen a white bird "of enormous size" fly in from the south on a clear afternoon and settle on the pond. He had walked over to see it. It was a swan. The bird had immediately made friends with the ducks, though they were nesting, and it had not left the pond since its arrival.

When this news got about among Pierre's friends, a few of them went to Olivebridge. Mr. Barringer had been feeding the swan white bread and corn, the customary food of the ducks. One of the women of the party, remembering Pierre's love of black bread, had brought a loaf of it. The ducks would not touch it when it was offered them, but the swan had no sooner taken some into its scarlet bill than it refused white bread altogether and would eat none but the black. The group were nervous and annoyed when they saw that the swan limped as if its right leg were injured. "That's a little too much," said one of the men angrily.

The hill people had heard about the swan, too, and they came to look.

"Remember how he went on about swans?" they said. "It's him, all right. Never seen a bird like that in these parts—and I reckon nobody'll see another."

A scientist who had been fond of Pierre wrote an inquiry to the State Conservation Commission at Albany, and soon an ornithologist came to Olivebridge. He said that the bird belonged to the genus known as whooper, whistling, or wild swan (*cygnus musicas*), native of Iceland, eastern Lapland, and northern Russia. He added that it was a very rare species of the genus, identifiable by its scarlet beak. He would not venture even a guess as to how it happened to be circling the millpond in the woods outside Olivebridge. A migratory wild bird with a song sometimes compared to the tootling of a flageolet, it was accustomed in autumn to fly from the northern arctic, at a great height and far out to sea, to distant southern waters. Why it had come out of the south to this spot, he did not know. It would fly back again in the fall.

But the swan did not leave. On fall mornings when a thin ice cover made passage for the ducks impossible, it broke way for its quacking companions to the little rock island where they had built their nest. When winter came, ducks and swan lived amicably in Mr. Barringer's barnyard. The preacher insisted to his congregation that the coming of the big bird had been a strange but not inexplicable coincidence. But the hill people, even some of his own congregation, said that they knew better; there was no denying to them that, by some supernatural process, something of Pierre had its identity in the swan. Their simple belief was less disturbing to them than were puzzlement and doubt to Pierre's close friends, who in the next four years made many trips to the Barringer farm, took snapshots, and talked much.

In the spring of 1946 Nik Strelsky died. In their grief over losing him, his friends forgot for some time his fascinated interest in the swan, his many visits to it, his poetic surmises about it. But last fall I made one more pilgrimage to Olivebridge. Mr. Barringer had moved away, neighbors reported, and the swan had stayed on for a while after his departure. A friendly man who keeps a small summer hotel nearby said, "The swan used to drop into my little lake here sometimes, but he always went back to his own water. Last time I saw him, though, was—let me see—spring of 'forty-six—little over a year ago."

"So you've been up to the old millpond," said an old lady who stopped to chat. "I don't go there no more. Them burned-black stone chimneys look sad standin' there. Cold, too. It's lonesome since they left."

"Who?"

Her candid blue eyes were suddenly wary. "You know." She shrugged her bent shoulders and walked away.

This conversation led me to pay a visit to an elderly man who lives alone in a shack near the headwaters of Jake Dubois's Creek. Braced by a pull or two on a flask filled with genuine Catskill applejack, we made a slow and friendly approach to the story. At length he said:

"I ain't sayin' that another swan showed up, but I ain't sayin' he didn't. Course, word got around that Pierre's friend had died. Then we began to hear things. Some folks who don't lie much said they seen the two of 'em. There's a kind of noise the first one used to make when he wasn't whoopin'. Reverend Barringer used to say that it sounded like laffin'. Well, the two of 'em was makin' that noise— accordin' to the tell of these folks. Then one day they was gone."

"And that's the story that's going around in these hills?"

"Rickashayin'," he said, "sort of rickashayin'."

❦ Cupola Song

When my tower darkens
Climb it slow,
Hear the hounds of Hastings
Give tongue below,

Hear miles upriver,
Swift antiphony,
Echoing choirs at Tarrytown
In full cry:

Black George to Silver Duchess,
And that impetuous pet
Jiggsy belling bald desire
To Yvette.

Then a timeless instant,
Silence—near and far—
Howling hounds soundless,
Stunned by a star!

Hudson River Aesthete

Old Baron de Liderer, wandering the Hudson's banks on a summer day, came upon a tall thin boy whose brown eyes were deep and full of light and whose glinting dark hair tumbled about his collar. Before they had returned to Newburgh in the evening—the baron, Austrian consul general to his summer residence; the boy to a red cottage in the Highlands—they had talked about many things and they knew that they would walk together again. Andrew Jackson Downing, a good name for a boy born in the autumn of 1815, had found a friend whose mind was stored with knowledge of stones and flowers and trees. The baron had found that treasure to the experienced, an eager listener.

The old man and the young one explored the river country often after that. Andrew's schoolmates at Montgomery Academy and his four older brothers and sisters would have been surprised at the animated face, the quick tongue of the dark boy whom they knew to be usually silent and expressionless.

It was not long before the baron had walked his protégé up the river to the flat rock, which has been called "Danskammer" ever since Henry Hudson saw savages prancing there, and had presented him to Edward Armstrong, beau idéal of the west bank, deity of a granite temple of his own devising which was the wonder of the near-by countryside. Puffing steamers had dragged barge after barge up to the Armstrong wharf, all loaded to the water line with slabs of dark-gray Breakneck Mountain granite from downriver and of pearly granite brought over from Quincy for the trim of the columns. As for the big columns themselves, yokes of oxen in long double line had strained and heaved at the sharp cries of the teamsters but no column had moved, until someone had the idea of making each into a roller with holes at the ends

to receive an impromptu axle so that it might be revolved slowly up
the bank.

Inside the granite temple all was black walnut, for mahogany was
"out" now. There were a billiard room, a gun room, and many nurseries, because billiards, shooting, and the begetting of large families
were activities that current fashion approved, and handsome Edward
Armstrong was current fashion's darling. With his vivacious wife, who
could be fluent in both Italian and French and painted in water colors
the fruits and flowers he gathered for her, he lived the life of a cultured
American country gentleman as he and many of his fellow countrymen conceived it. He wrote poetry and he played upon the violin and
he danced "better than any young gentleman between New York and
Albany," cutting perfect double pigeonwings. Southdown sheep nib-
bled his meadow grasses, thoroughbred horses neighed in his stables,
his wharf ran out into deep water where even the biggest of river
steamboats might stop, his shore line was a wide crescent of white and
shining sand.

Young Andrew Jackson Downing's visits to Danskammer set the
current of his life. Sensitive and lonely, child of a poor nurseryman-
gardener who had died when he was seven, he found in the river
temple a life more perfect than he could have dreamed. Edward Armstrong affected him profoundly. Many years later an intimate wrote
of Downing: "The workman, the author, the artist were entirely sub-
jugated in him to the gentleman. That was his favorite idea. The *gentleman* was the full flower of which all others were suggestions or parts.
...His social tendency was constantly toward those to whom great
wealth had given opportunity of ameliorating culture."

The young man's progress toward this sort of snobbishness was
hardly delayed by Mrs. Armstrong's eager acceptance of his suggestion
that she plant a double row of locusts along the "avenue" leading to
the door or by the attentions of Charles Augustus Murray, English
travel writer, and Raphael Hoyle, English landscape painter, who
found their visits to Danskammer the more pleasant for his company.
Impatiently he put aside his mother's insensitive request that he become an apprentice-clerk in a dry goods store and announced that he

would be a horticulturist like his brother Charles, who had inherited their father's nursery. His new friends understood and valued such a profession.

Charles made him a partner when he was nineteen and Andrew went to work. Soon he had visited every estate for miles up and down the river to study its planting and arrangement. He had put aside now the cabinet of mineral specimens which he and the old baron had gathered in their walks in the Highlands. And, since college was financially impossible, he would try to educate himself by reading and by observation of the manner of life of cultured people.

Nowhere on the Hudson, not even at the Armstrongs', was there a greater emphasis on the joys of the cultured life than across the river in Fishkill Landing at "Locust Grove," the low, many-gabled Dutch homestead of the De Windts. The old trees that gave the place its name interlaced above the approach in fan vaulting so perfect that the "avenue" was called the "Cathedral"; creepers and roses and honeysuckle clambered over the long piazza; horse chestnuts and weeping willows shaded the big garden. John Peter De Windt had married Caroline, daughter of that Abigail Smith Adams who had been born of Abigail Smith Adams and John Adams, second president of the United States. Eleven children were born to John Peter De Windt and his delicate spouse, and the eldest of these was birdlike Caroline.

It was inevitable that Andrew Jackson Downing should find his way to Locust Grove, that the De Windts, living gaily in an atmosphere of luxurious decay, their house a rendezvous for all the young people of the neighborhood, for West Point officers, for lovers of the arts, should be impressed by his dark, glamorous person and by the quiet, polished manner learned at Danskammer. As for Downing, he must have been pleased by a home where guests and the family sat on the veranda and "listened to the tale of fiction." This habit was expressed in the hostess's own rhythms:

> By Dryden and Pope the breakfast is graced
> At the close of the meal to the garden they haste,
> And with congenial powers
> Beguile the fleeting hours.

He was even more delighted with piquant daughter Caroline. There was many a chaperoned row on the moonlit Hudson, many a piazza promenade, many a visit to a near-by river estate where, again to resort to his future mother-in-law's inimitable verses:

> Statues and paintings, Dianas and fauns
> Embellished with flowers, and garnished the lawns;
> The mansion displayed with delicate skill,
> Refreshed by the fountain and cooled by the rill.

On June 7, 1838, Andrew Jackson Downing and Caroline De Windt were married. "It was a grand affair, a dance and supper," wrote Rose Armstrong in a letter from Danskammer. Andrew had bought his brother's interest in the nursery now, business was prospering. He began to build a dwelling for his bride among the Downing Botanic Gardens and Nurseries. From Locust Grove through a long telescope Caroline watched her new home across the river grow stone by stone. She saw no pillared shrine. It was a "Tudor Gothic villa" of sepia-colored sandstone with two small towers projecting high above the roof just over the wide entrance, and it was designed to prove "that a beautiful and durable and convenient mansion could be built as cheaply as a poor and tasteless temple." Despite his happy memories of Danskammer, Downing had concluded that a copy of a place of worship was unsuitable for human living.

"Highland Gardens," as they called their new home, lay above the water and looked out over strange treetops. The Hudson River whalers and traders had been bringing green booty home and Downing had profited by their voyages and those of many another American ship. Sophora, Deodar and Gingko, Jezo and Judas and Tree of Heaven, Nezo, Nana and Incense Cedar, Weeping Cypress and Stinking Yew were neighbors of Baffin's Bay Borealis, Patagonian Fitzroya, African Tamaris and Taurian Pine. In the greenhouses down below, Chinese Rice Ropes, New Zealand flax, aloes, palms and Arundo made the Hudson's bank seem the edge of a tropic river. Just above the water a path went past rockwork covered with alpine plants and a pond filled with water flowers. And at one end of the velvet lawn before the house stood a great Warwick vase, rich arabesques looping the bowl in fantastic design.

The interior of the house was dark. The woodwork and furniture were heavy and deep brown. A visitor wrote: "Even the daylight is dusk—or, more properly speaking, pregnant with light...a sort of imprisoned sunshine, something warm and deep like a reflection of the man's brown eyes." In Downing's library, on small bookcases shaped like Gothic windows, white busts of Linnaeus, Franklin, Newton, and other scientists were ghost-heads in the gloom.

Among these plaster portraits Downing sat down to write a book which would tell what he had been thinking about building and planting in America. The earliest professors of landscape gardening were correct, he wrote, in dividing the art into two variations—the Beautiful and the Picturesque. The first of these was marked by undulations of turf melting into each other, gently flowing brooks, smooth-stemmed trees with full round heads, walks and roads that bent in easy arcs, smooth still lakes with flowered margins widely curving. Only houses of classical mode—Italian, Tuscan, or Venetian that would "readily admit of the graceful accompaniment of urns"—should stand in such surroundings. And "such a scene should be of the most polished kind— grass mown into a softness like velvet, gravel walks...firm, dry and clean...the most perfect order and neatness should reign throughout."

If the reader would discover in the fine arts an artist who epitomized in his paintings the Beautiful, let him look upon the graceful and flowing forms, the noble and chaste qualities in the pictures of Claude Lorrain.

As for the Picturesque in landscape gardening, Downing said that it aimed at "a certain spirited irregularity." Surfaces should be comparatively abrupt and broken with growth of a "somewhat wild and bold character." The trees should have rough bark and be planted close together as in thickets of undisciplined nature. "Against the sky outline breaks the wild irregular form of some old half-decayed tree.... If water enlivens the scene...let the stream turn the ancient and well-worn wheel of the old mill in the middle ground and we shall have an example of the picturesque."

The house suitable to such a background would be a Gothic man-

sion, an old English or a Swiss cottage. Nowhere in the field of painting would one find so many of the elements of the Picturesque as
among the bold rocks and wild passes, the vigorous rugged scenes—
robbers, banditti and all—that came from the brush of Salvator Rosa.
The romanticism of Sir Walter Scott and of the Gothic novel had
struck deep into Andrew Jackson Downing. With his arbitrary theory
as a basis, throughout the rest of his book he showed how building and
planting might be made to conform to it. Prejudiced in favor of the
Picturesque, possibly by the fact of his own residence in the wild Hudson uplands, he told how deciduous and evergreen trees might be
planted to give free natural effects, how walks should be formed, how
water should be treated. Then he was ready for "rural architecture."
"But how shall we designate that singular perversity of taste, or rather
that total want of it, which prompts the man, who, under the name of
a villa residence, piles up in the free open country ... a stiff modern
three-story brick which ... only served to call up the exclamation

> 'Avaunt stiff pile! Why didst thou stray
> From blocks congenial to Broadway!' "

Objecting strenuously to "stables built after the models of Greek
temple and barns with elegant Venetian shutters," mansions with concealed chimneys and "without porches or appendages of any kind to
give the least hint to the mind of the doubting spectator whether the
edifice is a chapel, a bank, a hospital, or the private dwelling of a man
of wealth and opulence," he admitted to favorable consideration Gothic
castles in romantic scenery or "where the neighboring mountains or
wild passes are sufficiently near to give that character to the landscape."
This approval apparently led to such a plethora of castles on the moun-
tainous shores of the Hudson that he was obliged to reprove their
builders in a later book for the use of inappropriate materials. "We
could point to two or three of these imitation Gothic castles with
towers and battlements built of wood. ... If a man is ambitious of
attracting attention by his house and can only afford wood, let him
(if he can content himself with nothing appropriate) build a gigantic
wigwam of logs and bark ... but not attempt mock battlements of pine
boards, and strong towers of thin plank." And he added a further

word of warning to the castle-dweller: "Unless there is something of the castle in the man, it is very likely, if it [his home] be like a real castle, to dwarf him to the stature of a mouse."

Further approving villas in the Italian style and in the varied Gothic styles of England, Downing moved on to a concluding chapter recommending "embellishments." In this category he included urns, conservatories, covered seats, summerhouses, weeping fountains, prospect towers, pavilion bridges, and rockwork. Most curious of these were a moss house, an octagonal gatehouse, a rustic seat in which the central structure was circular and intended for a collection of minerals, shells, and geological specimens of the immediate neighborhood, a prospect tower three stories in height with a double thatched roof and a spiral staircase leading up to a platform "whence a charming *coup d'oeil* or bird's-eye view of the surrounding country is obtained."

Downing had written truly when in the Preface to his first book—*A Treatise on the Theory and Practice of Landscape Gardening Adapted to North America*—he had said: "A taste for rural improvements of every description is advancing silently but with great rapidity in this country." No sooner was his book off the presses than the culture-hungry East pounced upon it. It went through edition after edition. While western pioneers were building their cabins out of logs cut to make a clearing, the prosperous merchants of the Hudson River country talked learnedly of Tuscan villas, Tudor mansions, Mansard dwellings, Gothic cottages, always referring to *Landscape Gardening* as authority. The book became a favorite wedding gift and no young couple thought of planning a home without thoroughly perusing it. Horticultural societies elected the author to honorary membership. Letters came from European enthusiasts. The big estates on the Hudson and in Connecticut and Massachusetts bulged with full-rounded curves or took on the rough defiant angularities of a scene from *Marmion*.

It was all very heartwarming, and Downing was so pleased by his recognition that he retired at once to the little dark room with the bookcases and the busts to compose a companion volume, *Rural Cottages,* in which he showed how his ideas could be applied on a less expensive scale. In this book he added to his list of acceptable architectural styles America's one contribution, "Hudson River Bracketed," a mode that met with such general response that the Hudson is still lined with cottages, mostly yellow (for he disliked white houses and green surroundings), their gables trimmed with vergeboards cut in mad scroll-saw patterns, poetic fancies of thousands of carpenters let loose in an orgy of quick carving, their sidewalls battened, their roofs set on brackets visible from without and within, brackets that offered a gentle compromise between the sharp upward angle of the pointed Gothic and the flatness of the Italian mode.

In two years Andrew Jackson Downing, twenty-six years old, had achieved fame. Now rich man and peasant sought his advice either in person or through his books. The Hudson River folk were proud of him. They pointed out that he gave fine proof of the opportunities the young democratic republic offered to the humble poor. He was "self-made," he had overcome his lack of formal education, he had leaped social barriers to marry a girl who was both great-granddaughter of one President Adams and niece of another. But no one would have dared suggest these things to the tall Spanish-looking young man who walked slowly and spoke with easy elegance, whose "perfect *savoir faire* would have adorned the Escurial," who seemed to be watching his companions constantly and keenly from behind the pleasant mask that was his face.

Now that Downing's success had given him more opportunity to do what he wanted, it was at once noticeable that there was an objective he more ardently wished to achieve than fame as a landscape gardener. It was a way of life. The yearning that beset the poor gardener's son when he had first visited Edward Armstrong in his granite temple would not be stifled.

But he wanted something better than the empty catering to fashion he had seen at Danskammer. The new way of life was to be aristocratic and at the same time worth while. It would be such a life as went on at his father-in-law's home across the river—carried to a higher degree of intellectuality and with much of the frivolity left out. All about him on the Hudson he saw gropings toward this kind of living, in Edward Armstrong's poetry and his wife's painting, in the verses of his mother-in-law whose mother and grandmother had written poetry before her. It was a logical development and carrying out of the nation's new

cultural ideal. Now that he had time for leisure, like his neighbors in
the river estates, now that he was recognized as one of the country's
most gifted men of art, he wanted to live as America's men of means
and background should live.

It did not take Andrew Jackson Downing long to make his idea
into a reality. In proper living there must be no evidence of anything
so distasteful as work. His library seemed "the retreat of an elegantly
cultivated gentleman." There were pens, portfolio, a desk—but no evidences of labor. Though he constantly produced more written work,
it was impossible, said his friends, to believe him a diligent worker.
The attitude that work was unpleasant and should be withdrawn from
attention was carried so far by Downing and his friends and pupils
that they urged keeping the entire machinery of an estate out of sight
so that flowers might bloom, lawns be mowed, walks swept, "by invisible hands," at night or "at such hours as the family is supposed not
to come out."

The hours at Highland Gardens passed in a synthetic haze as real
in its artificial way as that which lay along the river on the summer
mornings or shrouded the blue Catskills at twilight. Life was a planned
idyl. To Caroline Downing's younger sister Elizabeth the villa was "a
paradise where friends met congenial friends and where the feast of
reason and flow of soul mingled with delicately seasoned meats, fruits
and wines." Elizabeth's fiancé—young Christopher Pearce Cranch, who
had come to Fishkill as minister—was persuaded to give up preaching
for writing verses and painting pictures.

There were always guests at Highland Gardens, and more and more
distinguished ones as time went on. Downing became known as the
most perfect host in the river country—where hospitality was studied
as an especial art. By day there was boating, botanizing, archery, painting, reading, conversation, lying on the lawn—with an occasional excursion into the mountains across the Hudson or a visit to a neighbor's
highly decorated estate. In the evening by the lamplight in the bust-
studded library Andrew and Caroline Downing took turns in reading
aloud to the guests Lowell's new "Vision of Sir Launfal" and other
poems which they liked.

In the mild twilights of summer there were charades on the lawn beside the Warwick vase, but the taciturn host who kept them going, directing them delicately, did not laugh at the antics of the players, and no one could guess the syllables he enacted because he performed so self-consciously and with such forbidding reserve. There was music —fine playing and fine singing of "Oh, Fly to the Prairie" and, for the baritones, "Rocked in the Cradle of the Deep." There was even a male trio, of which the distinguished writer George William Curtis was a member, who "made music in the moonlight on the lawn." Inevitably there was "some slight violation of the Maine law," a tasting of the soft sweet wines of the Ohio valley sent to Mr. Downing by his friend Nicholas Longworth, in Cincinnati.

At breakfast each guest at Highland Gardens saw beside his plate a blossom, a flower he was known to love or one his host had judged most fitting to his character. The tenderhearted found tea roses and honeysuckle; the modest and shy, violets and pansies; the brilliant and gay, marigolds, asters, or carnations.

Time seemed to stand still in the ordered world that Andrew Downing had created. When he was thirty-five he looked but thirty, and Caroline seemed younger and prettier with the passing of the years. In 1845 Andrew was editing the American edition of Mrs. Loudon's *Gardening for Ladies*. In 1846 he had accepted the editorship of the *Horticulturist* and soon thereafter he had begun to write articles and editorials urging that New York City provide itself with a large central park.

In 1849 came the greatest triumph of the career of living which seemed so much more important to him than professional success— the visit of Sweden's famous novelist, little gray, blue-eyed, red-nosed Fredrika Bremer, whom Hawthorne called "maiden aunt to the human race." She came directly from her ocean voyage by the river steamer *New World,* "a little floating palace, splendid and glittering with white and gold on the outside and splendid and elegant within."

Now all the machinery was put in operation and it all worked. By the library fireplace on the first evening Andrew and Caroline wooed their distinguished visitor with readings from the most esteemed American poets. Miss Bremer's incorrigible sentimentalism was encouraged by the opportunity of seeing a morning wedding in the neighborhood.

Catherine Sedgwick, best known American woman novelist of the age, came over from Connecticut bringing her niece Susan to join the house party. A picnic was arranged, the spot to be the top of South Beacon Mountain. Downing, Miss Bremer, and Miss Sedgwick were to ride together, but the vigorous fifty-three-year-old American woman walked "as usual" and played havoc with the capon and champagne, while the Swedish guest of honor thought the party "too large and too merry for me." Later she wrote in her journal: "One little moment partly alone and partly with Mr. Downing, who knows how to be gay and jocular with the gay, and silent with the silent was to me the crowning luxury of the excursion."

To make matters even more perfect, invitations began to come in from neighboring villas. The very rich Mrs. Donaldson, whose grounds at her estate "Blithewood" Downing thought the best example of his landscaping ability, asked them over for a day. It was misty Indian summer, October on the river, when they set out. "The Indians are smoking their pipes in their great powwows," said Caroline Downing. There were sixty or seventy neighbors for breakfast at Blithewood. The meal ended with a dance, and Miss Bremer could observe that the American young girls were lovely and lively with "delicate figures though deficient in strength," and she complained of their lack of facial expression.

In the evening the gracious Mrs. Donaldson, for whose silken gowns three hundred silkworms were spinning their cocoons upon the Donaldson mulberry trees, played upon the harp in the darkly lustrous parlor. Then all of them went for a night stroll beside the river. Fortunately Mr. John Church Cruger's estate bordered on Blithewood. Mrs. Donaldson's guests were rowed out to look upon its recently built ruins from the shimmering water that they might grow silent in sadly ecstatic reverie. On the farthest point of land stood the huddle of tumble-down stone arches, dark and beautiful beneath the moon. Miss Bremer was amazed at the resemblance between the Mayan figures among them and Egyptian statues she remembered. One had a sphinxlike countenance and head like that of a priest of Isis. "The ruin and its ornaments," she confided to her journal, "in the midst of a wild, romantic rocky and wooded promontory was a design in the best of taste."

From Blithewood, Downing and Miss Bremer took a railroad coach down the river. A rough young man spat on the floor in front of them and Fredrika, remembering Dickens's comments on American boors, said, "That gentleman needs a Dickens."

"Dickens would have mistaken him for a gentleman," said the elegant Mr. Downing with hauteur.

They paid a visit to another river house before Miss Bremer set out on a long tour of America. It was to the home of Mr. Hamilton, "the son of the general of that name, the contemporary and friend of Washington." There Fredrika was triumphant because elderly Washington Irving sat next to her at dinner and did not fall asleep as was his custom. After dinner she and one of the young ladies played duets on the piano and had just finished an overture for four hands—"which we played so that they who heard us cried 'bravo!'"—when Downing said it was time to go. Fredrika would have liked to continue but was compensated later: "I sat silent in the railway carriage beside my silent friend, the music of whose soul I am always conscious of though he speak not a word, so that after all there was no interruption of the music."

From her journal it would appear that the middle-aged Swedish virgin had quite unconsciously fallen in love with the brown-eyed, long-haired haughty young man. She longed to see him again and after nearly two years of travel in America, she eagerly awaited their reunion. Meanwhile, in 1850, Downing's growing interest in building expressed itself in a volume entitled *The Architecture of Country Houses* in which he divided all rural dwellings into three categories: cottages, farmhouses, and villas. He defined a cottage as a small dwelling in which the family might employ at most two servants, stated that a farmhouse should not be expected to display architectural ornaments any more than the farmer himself would be expected to wear "garments made by the most fashionable tailor in Broadway or to drive to his market town in one of Lawrence and Collis's most modish carriages," and described a villa as a house requiring a staff of three or more. In the same year he went to England, where he was flattered and feasted by a British society which saw in him its own champion in the States.

He returned to add a few perfecting Anglophile touches to his precious way of life which, more than any of his writings, he had come to look upon as his masterpiece. That Christmas, to the singing of fiddles, Downing and all his guests danced on the marble pavement of the great hall at Highland Gardens. Antlers and pikes, helmets and breastplates gave back the yellow light from rustic chandeliers wreathed with holly and the dancers were the gayer for looking upon the plumed hats of cavaliers hung on the walls.

"He seemed to me handsomer, more manly," wrote Fredrika Bremer when she was allowed the boon of seeing Downing again. "His beautiful eyes beamed with self-conscious power."

She was delighted with his material progress. "He works as Jenny Lind seems to sing," she said. President Fillmore had appointed him to lay out the grounds for the Capitol, the White House, and the Smithsonian Institution in Washington. He was carrying on a voluminous correspondence. Presently he urged the establishment of a great park in New York, the park which his young pupil and assistant, Calvert Vaux, was eventually to plan and achieve. Indeed, the idea had caused some wavering in his attitude toward society, much to Fredrika Bremer's delight for she had often playfully rebuked him for being more exclusive and aristocratic in his beautifying activity than became an honest downright republican.

"It is indeed both curious and amusing," he wrote, "to see the stand taken on the one hand by the million that the park is made for the 'upper ten' who ride in fine carriages, and on the other hand by the wealthy and refined that a park in this country will be 'usurped by the rowdies and low people.' Shame upon our republican compatriots who so little understand the elevating influences of the beautiful in nature and art."

Though admitting the improving influence of landscape gardening on people of the class into which he was born, Downing still wanted it clearly understood that he was no believer in complete democracy, for a few months later he wrote pompously of the "inextinguishable rights of superior organization in certain men and races of men which Nature every day reaffirms, notwithstanding the socialistic and democratic theories of our politicians." He undertook at about this time a campaign against men of inferior organization in Newburgh who were allowing their pigs to wander the public streets and, despite threats and appeals for pity on the poor pig-owners, succeeded in having the pigs banned. Nathaniel Willis, dude poet and neighbor in the town of Canterbury, wrote, "Now *we* want such a pig-apostle."

Fredrika Bremer said good-bye to Downing at the Astor House, where she had first met him. "I felt that we parted forever on earth." And on the last day of the following June, in 1852, Highland Gardens opened its doors to a gay company as its owner prepared what was to be his final tribute to the ideal of perfect living. It was a festival of roses. Music drifted above the exotic greenery that lined the lawn, filtered out over the moonlit water. Melodious voices sounded in the regular rhythms of Lowell and Longfellow. There was discreet giggling in the games beside the great Warwick vase. The Ohio wines were sweet and clear. The perfume of the roses seemed to thicken the air. When the moon was high the host and all his guests rowed across the river to the Verplanck house to see the room in which officers of the Revolution had formed the Society of the Cincinnati. Downing spoke of swimming across the river and back when he was a boy and said he believed he could do it again. If one had to leave life, he said, he would rather drown than die in any other way.

A month later he and Caroline and their lovely young friend—the widowed Matilda Wadsworth—Mrs. William De Windt and two of her children, stood on the dock at Newburgh in the sunny heat of early afternoon awaiting the arrival of the steamer *Henry Clay*. The boat swung sharply in to the pier and the passengers hurried aboard. A few hours later the *Henry Clay* was a smoldering wreck on the bank at Riverdale, and of the little party only Caroline and the De Windt children were alive. Downing had been drowned.

The news of the great gardener's death filled all lovers of homes and flowers and all his fellow worshipers at the shrine of aristocratic living with deep and genuine mourning. They made word-laments for him. One said: "There lay the lifeless form of Nature's own gardener, protected from the burning sun only by leaves and shrubbery gathered from the banks of that river which, in the words of another, 'had he lived he would have made a river Rhine.'" Another wrote: "His name shall be perpetuated by fragrant flowers and delicious fruits, by gushing fountains and murmuring streams." From Sweden came a cry of anguish for "My American brother ... whose image is forever pictured on my soul along with its most beautiful scenes, its romantic life, its Indian summer, and, above all, its highland scenery on that magnificent river where he had built his home and now—has his grave."

In Washington some of his friends erected a monument to his memory—a vase like the great Warwick vase at Highland Gardens, its base decorated with acanthus leaves. On one side the first lettering of the tribute reads: "He was born and lived and died upon the Hudson River." On another is a quotation from one of his essays: "The taste of an individual as well as that of a nation will be in direct proportion to the profound sensibility with which he perceives the beautiful in natural scenery.

"Open wide, therefore, the doors of your libraries and picture galleries, all ye true republicans! Build halls where Knowledge shall be freely diffused among men and not shut up within the narrow walls of narrow institutions.

"Plant spacious parks in your cities, and unclose their gates as wide as the gates of the morning to the whole people."

The dwellers in the Beautiful and in the Picturesque villas along that stream, those who understood Andrew Jackson Downing best and shared his love of ordered, artificial, luxurious living, felt a chill about their hearts. It was as if the rumble of an upriver thunderstorm had silenced for a moment the festival of roses and all the guests knew they would be scattered soon. Only for a little while longer the ladies of the river houses looked out from the belvederes and gazebos that crowned their undulant acres of lawn and trees and sighed for the proud dark man who had made them beautiful. A little while longer they played sad songs upon their harps, remembering him in their moonlit pavilions.

❦ America's Victorian Homes

In 1837 when young Victoria succeeded to the British throne, forerunners of the architectural period which was to bear her name both in England and America were already observable. Pillared Greek temples adapted by such architects as Benjamin Latrobe and William Thornton to the requirements of luxurious habitation were appearing in New England and the Deep South and had already begun their march westward through Ohio. A house of six oddly angled walls and more oddly dubbed "Octagon House" had served as a temporary residence for President James Madison and his charming Dolley just after a British army had captured Washington and burned the White House. Memories of cathedrals had been translated here and there throughout the new republic into private houses of the "pointed style."

Two influences toward the birth of an architectural age were very strong in America. One was prosperity (jealous Europeans were already calling us "moneygrubbers") and the other was a plenitude of nature-decorated land. The hills of New England and that magnificent "River of the Mountains"—the Hudson—cried out for castles. The riches of New York City commerce replied with many replicas of distant European fortresses and other dream bastions designed by American architects. Some still stand high above Hudson water, moated, battlemented, crenelated, frowning down upon foes who have never advanced to storm up the river slopes.

The most influential architect of the early Victorian days along the Hudson, Andrew Jackson Downing of Newburgh, encouraged the building of castles. During the mid-Victorian years no less than fifty turreted fortresses (some made of wood) adorned the wild and forested banks of the river.

Near Lynchburg, Virginia, Thomas Jefferson built in the first decade of the nineteenth century an octagonal home called Poplar Forest to which he meant to retire when his beloved Monticello might prove burdensome. The idea of building such polygonal dwellings, however, did not take hold of the popular fancy for another forty years. Then the immensely successful American phrenologist, Orson Fowler, began to recommend the circled-cross floor plan as more functional than any other. Fowler's textbook on phrenology had gone through sixty-two editions, and the legion of his followers were so influenced by his book *A Home for All or the Octagon-Gravel Wall Mode of Building* that many of them immediately set about surrounding themselves by eight neatly oblique walls. The arguments for "more surfaces to the sun," central heating (thus avoiding the nuisance of fireplaces), shorter distances between focal points, the supplementing of outdoor toilet facilities by others under the central staircase, won literally thousands of converts across the nation. Fowler's description of his own octagon house at Fishkill on the Hudson helped mightily to encourage an architectural fad that assumed major proportions. One of its five stories opened up into a huge lecture hall where he might address audiences on the validity of judging character by feeling cranial bumps, and the house held eighty rooms including a gymnasium.

Enthusiasm for octagons reached its peak just before the Civil War. By then, eight-sided dwellings had marched from the east coast to the west. Utah had an octagon log cabin and San Francisco, always welcoming the outré and avant garde, boasted two elegant octagonal mansions.

In the 1860s, toward the end of the popularity of this form, two octagons were built which combined the period's love of decoration with simple functionalism. One now belongs to the author of this book and is unique in its use of Chinese motifs. (The second owner, who spent several years in completing the house, was an importer of Oriental teas.) The other is in Natchez, Mississippi, where it is known as Longwood or, less formally, as Nutt's Folly. Three porches or, to use the Deep South vernacular, "galleries" encompass it, and its cupola is of the Turkish or "onion" variety.

As business prospered and leisure grew, the American housebuilders, embarrassed by the condescension of visitors from other lands, were increasingly impressed by classic influences, by ideas developed in foreign lands, and by cultural ambitions. The architects they employed responded by offering their clients large residences which were free adaptations of dwellings in the traditions of older nations. These compositions and improvisations were at once adopted by the nation as a whole.

After Downing's death by drowning in a steamboat accident in 1852, one of his assistants, Calvert Vaux, carried on his projects (including New York City's Central Park).

Downing had begun an era in which taste would eventually change for the worse. Queen Victoria lived for another half century, and during its years came other periods to which Americans have attached names indicative of their date and quality—French Mansard with its flat roofs and its extra story where those roofs began, Italianate with its intricate ironwork decorating its central towers, Neo-Jacobean with its tumbled short roof angles above its almost hidden porches. Though these are usually included under the comprehensive term "Victorian" they have had few champions and are not often regarded with pride.

Historians of our architectural past now find in their appraisals of the Victorian period much to praise. Though often (and sometimes justifiably) criticized for inhibitions and overgenteel conventions our Victorian years produced more architectural "follies" and individualistic do-it-yourself oddities than may be found in the records of any period before or since. It was also a time of free and imaginative adaptation, of spacious comfort, of efforts toward elegance that often succeeded.

While it has been derogated for its lack of light, it contributed the octagons, some of which give the impression of being enlarged glass-walled lanterns. While it was accused of overdecoration, some of its creative designs are today more admired than the glass-box products of a "modernistic" functionalism which are now regarded as clichés.

In recent years, as loss of bachelorhood often precedes the college president's grant of a bachelor's hood, as more and more babies are distributed in university circles before the doling out of diplomas, rambling many-chambered Victorian piles have once more come into their own. The luckiest of the younger married couples have been those who have been able to make the jump from the unicellular campus trailer to the "monstrosities" their grandfathers lived in. The house that only yesterday was regarded as a horror such as cartoonist Charles Addams might caricature, is today a priceless treasure to the young couple whose increasing family is a status symbol.

The prolific father smirks as he looks down the aisle of the upturned faces of his children seated at a long table in a real dining room (not an "area"), and his girl wife repeats the oft-told incident of a neighbor's saying "We would have bought your property if it hadn't been for the expense of tearing the house down." The occupants of bassinets, cribs, nurseries, and playrooms have crowded ghosts and bats out of attics, cupolas, parlors and "reception rooms," and the old mansions serenely shelter the "heap of living" that converts them once more into happy homes.

Real estate agents (now called "realtors") are hastily turning their price listings upside down as properties, once given up as hopeless, turn into gold mines "good for another hundred years." Perhaps as a result of this fact real estate salesmen have found the good taste of their clients must be reckoned with and that tiny hodgepodges of architectural design remain unpurchased too long for their satisfaction. (Last year's directional sign in a Hudson River suburb—"To the ranch-type, split-level Cape Cods"—has been taken down.)

The owners of ornamented Victorian homes claim their smugness is justified. They say their dwellings are admired conversation pieces. They have proved, they believe, the soundness of their economic judgments and the distinction of their minds. They blandly proclaim they are the squires of a new and youthful society, and they find humility difficult as they observe about them the look-alike regiments of already dated houses where picture-window eyeballs stare blankly into picture-window eyeballs with never a blink from a Victorian pull-down roller shade.

Architects, who, a score of years ago, abandoned their aims toward beauty-through-decoration for functionalism and the happy juxtaposition of geometric forms, are at last admitting that their Victorian predecessors possessed elements of virtue. American architects Edward Stone and Minoru Yamasaki, who have consistently recognized decorative elements (held within bounds) as part of our national tradition, have won great honor.

Gradually the valuable aesthetic qualities of America's Victorian period are recognized. Museums of Victoriana have begun to appear. People of taste buy Victorian residences and provide them with "good Victorian" furniture. As our own architectural period takes on identity it turns away from the condescension with which the Victorian was once regarded and gives it the respect it has long deserved.

✾ The Fowlers, Practical Phrenologists

The birth in 1809 of the first white child in the village of Cohocton, New York, which had been settled by Vermont farmers, was a matter for rejoicing. It gave the settlers a sense of permanence and dignity, and they prophesied great things for the little boy, Orson Squire Fowler, whose parents, the Horace Fowlers, were in moderate circumstances but were well thought of in Cohocton. They and their friends instilled in the boy, as soon as he was old enough to understand them, a respect for religion and education. Like many an eldest son of his time, he decided to be a preacher, and he prepared himself, under ministerial instruction and at Ashfield Academy, to enter Amherst College, where courses leading to the ministry were particularly emphasized. When he was ready to matriculate, he realized that his parents could ill afford to send him to college while supporting his brother Lorenzo, two years younger than he, and his sister Charlotte, who was five years younger. So for two years he worked his way in Amherst—chiefly by carpentering, sawing wood, and doing other handy-man jobs about the college.

Then occurred an event which was to set the current not only of his entire life but of the lives of his brother and sister as well. Dr. Johann Spurzheim delivered in Boston a series of lectures on the new science of phrenology, first expounded by Franz Josef Gall some thirty-five years before. Orson Fowler heard Spurzheim talk and became tremendously excited over a teaching which denied Calvin's gloomy creed of man's innate sinfulness and proclaimed each individual endowed with certain qualities, some good, some bad, which made themselves known in the shape of his head. Fowler was no more excited, however, than his handsome classmate, Henry Ward Beecher. He and Beecher immediately plunged into the reading of all that they could find on the subject of phrenology, exhibiting an energy and attentiveness which had not previously been noticeable in their studies. They learned to classify man's faculties phrenologically and to be able to tell where in the human head each was located. They spoke learnedly of the contours which indicated Ideality, Veneration, Eventuality, Amativeness, Philoprogenitiveness. It was not long, according to a contemporary account, before young Beecher was delivering to the Amherst Society of Natural History "an able address upon the subject of phrenology expressing the futility of objections offered ... and exhibiting and defending its fundamental principles," and young Fowler was running his hands over the heads of his college-mates—at two cents a head—and telling them what vocations they were best fitted to follow.

Beecher was so earnest that he scolded the lovely Eunice, whom he was later to marry, for wearing golden-brown ringlets in a bobbing fringe about her face. "A good-shaped head is a greater beauty than a wig any time," he told her, and the abashed maiden thereupon brushed out the curls and wore her hair folded close.

The new science became more than a study with these two young men. They announced that in order to give themselves practice in the art of preaching, they had arranged a number of visits to nearby towns to explain and demonstrate phrenology. Ignoring the jibes of their classmates at "the religion of bumps," they made their tour, and Beecher's golden words and Fowler's sensitive interpretations convinced many a New England skeptic. The lectures also brought in dollars—so many that as graduation approached, the call of the Christian ministry grew dimmer and dimmer in Fowler's ears. Beecher could not be persuaded

to join him in refusing it. The spellbinder already knew his destiny—
at least enough of it to keep him firm on the evangelistic path. But
Fowler had found his profession. His first solo appearance as a practical phrenologist had brought him forty dollars. He would not be a
preacher.

When he had received his diploma, the young enthusiast sought out
his brother Lorenzo, instructed him, and took him to New York City,
where in 1835, at 135 Nassau Street, the two opened offices for the practice of phrenology and for the arrangement of lectures on the science
throughout the United States. Then Orson Fowler began a career
which was to make its influence felt throughout the English-speaking
world. In 1835 he wrote, between lectures, the first edition of a book,
Phrenology Proved, Illustrated and Applied, which was to sell by the
tens of thousands and to have such wide popularity that in the next
twenty years it ran through sixty-two editions. I do not know that
Fowler planned to write nonfictional best-sellers, but if he did not,
he must have had a subconscious feeling for the selection of those subjects in which the credulous are always interested. The most intriguing
of these being sex, he followed his first great success with a volume
entitled *Love and Parentage; Applied to the Improvement of Offspring, Including Important Directions and Instructions to Lovers and
the Married Concerning the Strongest Ties and Most Sacred Momen-
tous Relations of Life.* This he dedicated:

"To all who have ever tasted the sweets of love; or felt its sting; or
consummated its delightful union; or who anticipated its hallowed cup
of tenderness; or expect to enfold its dear pledges in parental arms—
or more especially to women, the very embodiment of this angelic
emotion—to all who would enjoy its heavenly embrace, avoid its pangs
or render their prospective children healthy, and talented, and lovely."

Almost a century before the American censor's banning of Dr. Marie
Stopes' *Married Love* ran that book into the best-seller class, Fowler's
Love and Parentage, unaided by censor, reached two-score editions, of
which none was less than a thousand copies. In it, for full measure,
he added to his "Directions to Lovers and the Married" a eugenic pro-

gram which advocated the ascendancy of spiritual love over sensual and advised that prospective parents should develop the phrenological qualities evidenced in such protuberances as those labeled Marvelousness, Ideality, and Approbativeness.

The rush to the bookshops for this book must have prompted its immediate sequel, *Amativeness or, Evils and Remedies of Excessive and Perverted Sexuality; Including Warning and Advice to the Married and Single,* which was soon running neck and neck with its predecessor, at forty editions, in 1844. Meanwhile the business had been so brisk for the Fowler brothers, who now called themselves "practical phrenologists," that they had summoned their sister from Cohocton, where she had been preparing herself by giving talks about the new science. She helped Lorenzo with the lecturing and the head-reading, while Orson dashed off *Intemperance and Tight Lacing Considered in Relation to the Laws of Life, Fowler on Memory and Intellectual Improvement,* and *Fowler on Matrimony, or Phrenology and Physiology Applied to the Selection of Congenial Companions for Life Including Directions to the Married for Living Together Affectionately and Happily.*

In these three volumes he succeeded in anticipating modern dress reform, modern popular memory courses of the "Addison Sims of Seattle" type, and many a modern psychologist's treatise on how to live happily though married. On the title page of *Fowler on Matrimony* he took a further fling at what he considered one of the crowning evils of the age with a slogan, printed in capitals, "Natural Waists or No Wives," and he continued the argument a few pages later with the statement that "The object of the ladies in padding some parts and compressing others is to make themselves not better but more handsome.... Tight lacing is gradual suicide...besides exciting impure feelings." These attacks led to the formation of many antilacing groups throughout the United States, a fact that must have given Fowler a sense of his increasing influence.

I have put together a few of Mr. Fowler's maxims on marriage into which he launched after a description of "How to get in love" and "How to know the character of your intended," the answer to the latter being to have the head of your intended read by a good phrenologist. They seem to be quite as modern and quite as futile as advice on the subject from any contemporary specialist:

A man should first make his selection intellectually, and love afterward.

Let courting be done in the daytime...in your everyday clothes.

Marry your first love.

Do not marry for a home merely.

Marry to please no one but yourself; not even your parents.

Do not marry an intemperate companion.

In expansion of this last precept, Fowler echoed his eloquent appeal in his earlier volume, *Amativeness:* "Ye daughters of loveliness... who would return again to purity, health, and happiness, sip no more of the beverage of China; no more of the drinks of Java." In the same passage he reported the case of a man who, "professor though he is," was carried away to excesses after a few cups of strong coffee, "returning to the straight and narrow path only when he finds himself debilitated, penniless, having squandered the savings of months, perhaps years of industry."

The response to such popularizations of pseudo-scientific theory must have outdone the most optimistic dreams of the Fowler family. Hundreds of thousands of Americans were going phrenology-mad. The Fowlers took larger offices at 308 Broadway. These were crowded daily. The trio were swamped by the demands of the public, and they needed help. Fortunately, that was obtainable within the family. Though Orson had put his matrimonial theories to work as early as 1835 by marrying the young widow Martha Chevalier, daughter of Elias Brevoort of New York, apparently that lady took little interest in the business. Not so with Lorenzo's choice, Lydia Folger of Nantucket. Lydia went to work as a "practical phrenologist" as soon as she married Lorenzo, in 1844. Five years later, at the age of twenty-seven, well known as a lecturer and author, she entered the Central Medical College of Syracuse, New York, and emerged from it in 1850 with the degree of Doctor of Medicine, the second ever given a woman in the United States. The school was so pleased with her that it gave her the first professorship ever granted a woman by an American medical college. Throughout her career, she proved herself a most valuable addition to the Fowler ménage.

One more member was needed to make this little monopolistic family group complete. The Fowlers had not been slow to see that with the tremendous popularity of Orson's books, the ownership of a publishing house would be a distinct financial advantage. So in 1844 the brothers formed a partnership with twenty-four-year-old Samuel Roberts Wells, graduate of a medical school and believer in phrenology, and established the publishing house of Fowlers & Wells. At about the same moment Charlotte Fowler married Mr. Wells.

Now the Fowlers were phrenology and phrenology was the Fowlers. With the exception of Mrs. Orson Fowler, they all wrote books, they all delivered lectures. Horace Mann wrote treatises on phrenology, and Fowlers & Wells published them. Advertisements for employees in the daily newspapers stipulated "It will be necessary to bring a recommendation (a chart showing properly developed bumps) ... from Messrs. Fowlers and Wells, 131 Nassau Street, New York." Horace Greeley was converted to phrenology; so was Walt Whitman. Emerson listed Spurzheim as one of the world's great minds. In England, Albert and Victoria had the head of the Prince of Wales examined by a phrenologist. One by one the Fowler books covered the entire field of human thought from the phrenological point of view. They were bought by the millions.

Through the late forties and the fifties, the Fowler alliance continued their rushing business. They took up the water-cure fad as an adjunct to their phrenological activities and published tracts on hydropathy. With their rare genius for selecting popular subject matter, they added such titles as *Should Women Obey?*, *How to Behave*, *A Pocket Manual of Republican Etiquette* (forerunner of Emily Post), *The Family Gymnasium*, *How to Write*, and *A Home for All*, of which more will be said later.

Though their publications did not have the wide sale of popular novels such as *The Wide, Wide World*, and though their prices for their wares were comparatively low, the Fowlers prospered. They even dreamed of expanding their business to other cities, and having for four years trained a young protégé, Nelson Sizer, as a "phrenological examiner" (head-reader), they sent him in 1853 to open a branch office of Fowlers & Wells in Philadelphia. At the end of two more years, however, the Fowler brothers tired of the grind of publishing. Orson wanted to get away from office work, and his interest by now was the building of a great new house on his Hudson Valley farm in the country near Fishkill, New York. Lorenzo preferred to spend his time lecturing. Therefore in 1855 the two of them sold their interests in the publishing house to Charlotte and Samuel Wells, who had been the business pillars of the firm from its beginning. That necessitated bringing Nelson Sizer back from Philadelphia to read heads in the bust-decorated Examining Room of the Fowlers & Wells Phrenological Museum at 308 Broadway. There, for eleven years, and in successive locations at 389, 737, 753, and 775, as business slowly climbed up Broadway, Sizer read the heads of thousands of New Yorkers, a few of whom are alive today. Of those who are not, the three most distinguished met violent deaths. Blindfolded, Sizer read the head of John Brown in 1858 and said "This man has firmness and energy enough to swim up the Niagara River and tow a seventy-four-gun ship, holding the towline in his teeth." Not recognizing the head of General George A. Custer, because it had been shorn of its yellow curls, he made to that soldier the statement, tragically ironic now, that he was "inclined to overdo." He told a gangling youth that he had all the combativeness of a Stephen A. Douglas and that with proper development he could someday be a Chief Justice, without any prophetic knowledge that the young man, James A. Garfield, would aspire to a higher office.

While Orson Fowler was busy rearing his architectural monument at Fishkill, the Lorenzo Fowlers and the Wellses were living in the gracious, high-ceilinged, elegantly adorned residence, still standing, at 233 East Broadway. Lydia Fowler's personal charm, her unusual education, her experience as a lecturer, combined with her husband's dignity and scientific prestige to make them one of the most prominent couples in the city's intelligentsia. When the first Woman's Temperance Meeting was held in Metropolitan Hall on February 7, 1853, the Lorenzo Fowlers entertained the Bloomers of Seneca Falls, New York, as their guests. On that historic night, while Amelia Bloomer and Susan B. Anthony, clad in knee-length silk tunics and pants of the same material, waited their turns to harangue an audience which, according to the press, was "almost as large and fully as respectable as that which nightly greeted Jenny Lind," Lydia Fowler, in a "sky-blue delaine, with open corsage, not differing from the ordinary attire of women," was elected chairman, and she opened the first meeting at which women addressed an audience of New Yorkers from the public platform. Mrs. Fowler "came forward with a pleasing girlish manner," said the New York *Daily Times* on the following day, "became flushed, and was evidently not so well trained to self-command as her more 'strong-minded' companions. She, however, acquitted herself very creditably in repeating a pretty little set speech...."

Amelia Bloomer's autobiography tells of this visit and of a second one, which she made at the East Broadway home of Lorenzo Fowler, and speaks of meeting their friends, Horace Greeley, Charles A. Dana, Lucy Stone, the Reverend Antoinette Brown, and other notables. She describes a big vegetarian banquet, during which she sat on the speakers' table near Mrs. Fowler, who had helped to arrange the affair. Newspapers of the day, she wrote proudly, recorded that at this board "were gathered all the reformers of every description in the city."

A few years later, in 1860, Lydia and Lorenzo Fowler made a lecture tour through England, and the revenue from it was so great that they moved with their little daughter to London, where they lived the rest of their lives, lecturing on "laws of life, physical culture, moral duty, and social reform." Lydia wrote a "temperance novel," published in England under the title *Nora, the Lost and Redeemed,* and in her later years composed a book of verses called *Heart Melodies.* She and Lorenzo, Fowlerlike, brought up their daughter Jessie to help in the phrenology business. Lydia Fowler died in 1879, and Jessie, at the age of twenty-three, was called on to take her mother's place in the work her father was carrying on. This she did so successfully that in ten years she was editor of the London *Phrenological Magazine.* In 1896, however, Lorenzo Fowler having just died at the age of eighty-five, she returned to her native America.

In the meantime, Orson Fowler, with distinguished, flowing beard, high forehead, strong nose, and piercing blue eyes, was not only building his house but was also continuing to expound his phrenological and moral ideas from the lecture platform. A contemporary account states, "There is hardly a town of any importance from ocean to ocean or between Nova Scotia and the Gulf in which his voice has not been heard."

Orson had first become interested in building when, on a lecture tour through the West, he had been impressed by the building material of a house known as Goodrich's Folly, at Janesville, Wisconsin. It was made of lime, small stones, and sand, looked like modern concrete, and was called "gravel wall" or "grout." In his book *A Home for All,* he describes his theories on housing, advises the use of grout, and also advocates an octagonal building form, which last idea, he states, was "wholly original with the author." The phrenologist began his book and his house at the age of forty. The book appeared in the same year; the building of the house took nearly a decade.

A Home for All or The Gravel Wall and Octagon Mode of Building was published in 1849. The more modernist of contemporary architects may well blush a little, when they read it, to discover some of their favorite arguments pre-empted eighty-seven years ago. The spherical form, Fowler stated, is the most beautiful, and it encloses the most space in the least compass. The octagonal, therefore, being the nearest practical building form to spherical, is by the far the best. With gravel-wall material, he claimed, the objection to the construction of angles, difficult with brick, stone, or wood, was obviated. He emphasized the gain in sunlight obtained by having eight outside surfaces, and pointed out that the corners of square rooms are dark and useless for furniture. Moreover, he added, the distance traversed by "a weakly woman" in bringing up wood from the basement to the parlor (he assumed this to be one of her duties) will be in a square house nearly double that in an octagonal.

Fowler's plans for his ideal house included the main entrance on the basement floor and a first floor which would contain four large rooms —the parlor, drawing room, dining room, and amusement room— arranged around the central stair well and all capable, through wide, double doorways, of being opened together to form a large room out of two small ones, or one huge hall out of four rooms, which could receive as many as a hundred guests. His third floor would contain a number of small rooms, those on the inside about the stair well being lighted from the central glass dome of a cupola and from skylights, made of Crystal Palace glass, strong enough to bear a man's weight. Fowler would have, rising above the flat roof of his house, the glassed-in cupola surrounded by a balustraded balcony where clothes might be hung to dry or guests and their host might promenade.

A Home for All caused an immediate reaction among the people of New York State and its environs. Long before Fowler's own huge residence was completed, octagonal houses dotted the valleys of the Hudson and the Mohawk. At Red Hook and Stockport and Millbrook, at Madison and Sherburne and Geneva and Akron, and in dozens of other New York towns, these witnesses to Orson Fowler's reputation for wisdom still stand.

Fowler chose an oval knoll just north of Fishkill on the Albany Post Road for his residence. People who watched it in the building thought it would never be done. They said work would go on for a while and then cease while Fowler went away on a lecture tour to gain money enough to continue the building. When it was finally completed in 1858, however, it was even grander than the plans he had detailed for it in *A Home for All*. It had four stories and a basement, and since the basement was more than half above ground, it gave the effect of five stories. From its twenty-foot square, glass-roofed cupola that stood eighty feet above the basement floor, crowning the well of the stair, sixteen towns could be seen. Its nearly a hundred rooms included, besides the rooms suggested in *A Home for All,* a playroom for children, a "gymnastic room for females," and a dancing room.

No sooner had Orson Fowler and his wife gone to live in Fowler's Folly, as the house was inevitably to be called, than a constant stream of clients began to pour in. From all over the state, and particularly from the Hudson Valley, came hordes of people asking that the great scientist feel the curves of their craniums and advise them about their lives. Hundreds of children were brought to sit beneath the prophet's hands and hear what professions they had best prepare themselves to adopt. Fowler announced lectures for certain evenings, and the four big rooms of his main floor were made into a big auditorium by opening the double doors which joined them.

But just at the height of Orson Fowler's personal success—when at least one follower in almost every New York State community was building an octagonal home, when he was spending his mornings dictating (to two secretaries) books for his brother-in-law Wells to publish, when his big residence, already the most talked about in the Hudson Valley, sheltered a large group of distinguished visitors— tragedy came. A plague raged through Fowler's Folly, bringing death to many guests. Those who escaped fled in terror. For some time no one understood the cause of the mysterious malady. At last an investigation proved that one of the gravel walls, whose impermeability Fowler had praised, had allowed seepage from the cesspool into the well. Typhoid had done the rest.

Discouraged, Fowler rented the huge place to a Professor Andrus Cassard, who established in it a military school for Spanish and Cuban boys. When Cassard disappeared in 1865, leaving behind him many unpaid bills, a Mrs. Cunningham leased the place and made it into a boardinghouse. The rumor that she was the same Mrs. Cunningham who eight years before had been indicted and tried for the shocking knife butchery of a New York City dentist, Dr. Harvey Burdell, led to an exodus more hasty even than that caused by typhoid, though the lady denied, with truth, that she was the notorious suspect. After that, though the house changed ownership thirty-three more times and was in 1880 restored for the purpose of occupancy, no one lived in it again. A Poughkeepsie newspaper account states that Fowler sold the house for $150,000. The last price paid for it was $800. In 1897 it had become unsafe, a menace to the many sightseers who still visited it annually, and it was razed with dynamite by order of the Fishkill town authorities.

The coming of the plague to his dwelling seems to have marked a definite turning point in the career of Orson Fowler. Gradually, in the succeeding years, phrenology was discredited. Still believing, still its itinerant apostle, he continued his lectures and demonstrations, before ever-dwindling audiences, and offered readings at cut-rate prices. In 1865, after his first wife died, he married another widow, Mrs. Mary Poole, daughter of William Aiken of Gloucester, Massachusetts. After her death, he at last risked wedlock with a lady of no experience of that state, and at the age of seventy-three married a forty-two-year-old maiden, Abbie Ayres of Osceola, Wisconsin. She bore him three children and must have had a well-developed bump of Amativeness, for thirteen years after Fowler's death, when she was sixty, she secretly married her twenty-nine-year-old private secretary.

From 1863 to 1880, Orson Fowler lived in Manchester, Massachusetts, writing books with titles and contents similar to those he had produced in his youth, lecturing occasionally, interpreting the bumps on people's heads for modest fees. Then he moved to a little farm near Sharon Station, Connecticut, where he died in August, 1887.

As for Charlotte Fowler Wells, she had taken over the business of running the publishing house when her husband, Samuel, died in 1875. She ran it for nine years unaided, for a dozen years more as president of the stock company known as the Fowlers & Wells Company. Its ownership, but not its name, was changed in 1896. The last time a Fowlers & Wells advertisement appeared in *Publishers' Weekly* was in 1904.

America had not heard the last of phrenology and the Fowlers, however. Nine years after Orson's death, his niece Jessie, Lorenzo's daughter, returned, as I have said before, to America. She at once became editor-in-chief of the *Phrenological Journal*. Like her mother, Lydia, Jessie was strong in her desire for education. While in London, she had studied brain dissection at the School of Medicine for Women. In America, she took the time to enter New York University Law School, from which she graduated in 1901 at the age of forty-five. She was for many years vice-president of the American Institute of Phrenology and she wrote several books on phrenology, of which *Brain Roofs and Porticoes* provides the most intriguing title. She died at her New York City residence, 843 West 179th Street, on October 16, 1932. So far as I know, she was the last of the phrenological Fowlers.

❧ O Ye Great Waters!

Niagara Falls is a tall story come true. It is not believable but we must believe it. From the days of my early youth (spent in a Victorian cupolaed house beside the "Honeymoon Trail"), I have been aware of the stimulating effect of the thundering waters on our arts. Even before I had seen them, I had beheld depictions of them on boxes containing my breakfast food.

It is a known truism that tall stories beget tall stories and the first of these children of the incredible cataract was fittingly enough concerned with height. So bemused were the earliest white observers of the current's long drop that they reckoned it as eight hundred feet—well, seven hundred—well, not an inch under six hundred feet. The lowest of these estimates being more than three times the height of the falls, it is not surprising that the French explorer, the Jesuit Father Hennepin, suggested the absence of Indians in the vicinity was attributable to their being constantly deafened by the "vast and prodigious cadence of water" and frightened by an assembly, behind the running waters, of black rattlesnakes six or seven feet long and as thick as a man's arm. Having gone this far, the usually reliable missionary added that the area the snakes inhabited was wide enough to allow the passage of "four coaches abreast!"

It may be that years later Benjamin Franklin, in England as an emissary, felt that Hennepin's disquisition on the natural history of

Reprinted from a catalogue of paintings of Niagara Falls by permission of The Buffalo Fine Arts Academy.

Western New York gave sufficient basis for writing a letter of protest to the London *Times*. Scientist Franklin complained in it that subjects of the British Crown traveling in Western New York had not commented on the cod fisheries in the Great Lakes. He anticipated the argument that the cod is a salt-water fish by claiming that fish will swim anywhere when pursued. The hungry whales of the Atlantic, he added, had driven the cod up the Niagara River into Lake Erie without being noticed by English visitors. "But let them know, sir," he wrote, "the grand leap of the whale in the chase up the falls of Niagara is esteemed by all who have seen it as one of the finest spectacles in nature."

The use of the fanciful untruth that the resistless waters could not only be resisted but overcome continued in America well into the nineteenth century. A publication in praise of David Crockett, half the Congressman of history, half the folk-hero, listed among his wild assortment of pets a huge alligator named "Long Mississip" astride which he "once rode up Niagara Falls."

Besides exaggerative folk tales there were Niagara Falls jokes, too—thousands of them—and they were so widely distributed that they became a part of our developing national consciousness. Said the housewife on her first glimpse of the falls, "That reminds me, I left the kitchen water faucet running." Said the tailor, "What a location for sponging coats." Said the Irishman, "Hell, there ain't no such place." A popular song of the mid-nineteenth century set to music the most worn jape of all in its beginning stanza:

> Oh the lovers come a thousand miles
> They leave their home and mother
> Yet when they reach Niagara Falls
> They only see each other.

Being the most advertised feature of a boundary river, Niagara Falls has played an important role not only in folklore and humor but in documented history, both political and social. Here again, perhaps because of the extraordinary phenomenon's awesome power and grandeur, fact seems to have imitated fancy, and true annals to have taken on the semblance of tall-tale fiction. In 1829, before numberless spectators, the two incredible jumps from a hundred-foot platform into the gorge at the base of the Falls by the celebrated "leaper," Sam Patch, were surely much more important to the disparate histories of society and of athletics than Sam's solemn contribution to philosophy uttered before each take-off: "Some things can be done as well as others."

Even more unbelievable were the feats of the little French tightrope walker, Blondin: Blondin who paused midway on his narrow path above watery death to hold out a hat through which a passenger marksman on the little ship *Maid o' the Mist* below pumped a bullet from his rifle; Blondin who carried his terrified manager pickaback to Canada and back on a suspension bridge no wider than a rope strong enough to bear the weight of two men.

As for political history, the most pictorial of happenings that troubled diplomats on both sides of the unfortified border was the burning by loyal Canadians of the good ship *Caroline* which was engaged in giving transportation to rebels against the dominion government in a conflict referred to by historians as "The Patriots' War." Set afire and committed to the current of the Niagara River on the night of December 29, 1837, the *Caroline* went blazing over the brink of the falls but was entrapped by rocks a short distance below. There the flames died out and what was left of her stayed until the pounding of the water gradually demolished her.

In the mid-nineteenth century American poets, essayists and historians gradually came to regard the great water-drop as a challenge matched only by the view of the Hudson River from the templelike Greek Revival "Mountain House" in the Catskills, and the seemingly endless land-waves of the prairies. Literary efforts to inspire devout readers who could be impressed by the landscape miracles performed by the Almighty resulted in a fever of poetic apostrophes best described as the "O ye's" and usually beginning with such lines as: O ye great waters tumbling from on high.

In this same period of the "Sublime Subject," painters, including those of the Hudson River School, joined their author confreres in tributes to the Lord for having created Niagara Falls. Fortunately, however, their paintings were of a much more impressive quality than the essays, poems and songs of the same epoch.

Parallels between the products of American artists in all separate media can still be found. In the light of the preceding notes, however, it would seem that in neither of the two fields of creative endeavor allied to painting—writing and music—did American artists equal the imaginative and moving pictorial interpretations with which their painter contemporaries paid homage to the great cataract.

❦ The Ghost of the River Octagon

High on the east bank of the Hudson River, and only twenty miles from New York City, stands a strange eight-sided gray house. It seems to have a park of its own, for it is surrounded by a high hedge in which the bushes were so planted that a number of them bloom in each month from March to October. The park has a unique atmosphere, and anyone who enters it through the winding driveway becomes aware that the trees are of unusual varieties and were planted long ago. Here stand tulip trees, magnolias, maples of Norway and Japan, and a tremendous giant called a "Kentucky Coffee Tree" of a sort which was popular among Hudson Valley residents a hundred years ago. Perhaps the strangest of the trees are the Chinese gingkos, whose leaves in sunlight throw intricate shadows on the green lawn. Since the largest of these stands near the old well-house, which was made in the shape of a Chinese pagoda, the visitor gets a sense of Chinese influence before he reaches the end of the drive. The house, which is painted in two shades of gray and decorated with white trim, rises five stories high, the last one being a many-windowed cupola which is higher than even the tallest trees. It surmounts a slate-roofed two-storied dome which curves upward from the walls of the second floor. The first floor is circled by a wide veranda bordered by an elaborately designed white wrought-iron railing from which white pillars in groups of three rise to flowered capitals beneath the eaves.

The prosperous merchant to whom this mansion belonged completed it almost a century ago. He was an importer of Chinese teas, and he had recognized in a number of octagon houses then being built (for the building of eight-sided houses was an architectural fad at the time) a similarity to Oriental "summerhouses" which he had seen in his travels beside the lakes and rivers of China. Consequently, many of the designs of the decorations within the house are of Chinese origin, giving it an atmosphere not to be found in any other American dwelling.

The whole place looks as if it had been the scene of a mysterious story. It has been! And it is this story I am about to tell.

When his wife died, the merchant was heartbroken and left the house, which held many happy memories for him. He sold it to a French lady of noble family who, after her husband's death, had brought her only daughter to America. The girl had inherited from her mother great charm and a lively temperament. She was darkly beautiful with black hair and even blacker eyes, and her form was slim and exquisitely modeled.

On a great estate near by lived a rich and aristocratic American family whose ancestors of English blood had lived for several generations in feudal splendor among the "Sugar Islands" off the southern coast of eastern North America. The eldest son of this family had no sooner seen his lovely young neighbor than he fell desperately in love with her. His parents soon discovered that he was making daily visits to the octagonal house whose cupola they could see rising above the hills and trees to the north of their home. Since they had already planned for his marriage to the daughter of another of the great-estate families of the valley, they disapproved of his interest in the French girl and forbade him to see her again.

Though he continued his visits secretly, the girl's mother soon became aware of the situation and, being a person of great family pride herself, ordered her daughter not to see her ardent wooer again. The young couple then took to meeting in a lonely spot on the bank of the river. They soon felt that the restrictions put upon them were intolerable and they planned to run away to New York and be married.

One morning in the spring of the year they met again by the river and hastened to Tarrytown to embark on a steamboat for New York, where they intended to be married. Unhappily for them, a servant of the young man's family saw them hurrying along the riverbank and reported the fact to his employers. At once the father set out in hot pursuit on a spirited horse. In the meantime, his wife ordered her carriage and went to the octagon house, where she upbraided the girl's mother and accused her of conspiring with the lovers.

The pursuing horseman galloped onto the Tarrytown dock just after the gangplank of the steamboat had been drawn aboard.

The steamboat, it developed, was racing against a competitor owned by a rival line. As it entered the shadow of the Palisades, the boiler, which had been subjected to terrific pressure, burst, killing the young man instantly. The steamboat caught fire, and the remaining passengers were soon confronted with the choice of burning to death or attempting to swim from midstream to the shore. That evening when the bodies of the drowned lay upon the river's bank, the corpse of the girl was among them.

The next day a farmer's wagon approached the octagon house bearing a pine box. To the consternation of the driver, however, he was met by an angry woman who bitterly refused to accept his cargo. Eventually the girl was buried in a potter's field near the river.

This should end the story of the fated lovers. Nevertheless, a happenstance—possibly an unrelated coincidence—could be considered by the romantic-minded as having a later bearing upon it.

My wife and I now live in the old octagon house. Twice in recent successive springs my wife has wakened at the end of a strange dream. In it she stands on the moonlit veranda and sees a young girl walking up the drive. She seems to be surrounded by a mellow golden light. Suddenly from the shadows of the veranda darts an older woman, who bars the path of the girl and by stern gestures bids her be gone. The girl wrings her hands and weeps, but her companion is obdurate. At last the girl turns about and, still weeping, walks back whence she came. As she reaches the pagoda-like well-house, she turns about for one last look. As she does so, the other woman beckons to her and opens her arms. The girl begins to run toward her—and the dream ends!

It seems to the present occupants of the house that the two have
been reconciled, because whenever we have a visitor who claims to
have psychic powers and to understand ghosts, we hear that Octagon
House has a special feeling about it—a kind of aura from the past
which bears with it a sense of happiness.

ʚ   Three Crops

Though Will Christman was for about five sixths of his
long life a typical, not very successful York State farmer on a rocky
hill farm (he was in a good company, and a big one, as many a Yorker
family can testify), he turned out to be worth his salt after all because
he spent his last decade writing true and beautiful things about the
sixty years of living that had gone before it. Many farmers with about
the same experience have sat out their last weary days damning the
fickle soil and the more fickle weather that brought them so little return in this world's goods. This world had other "goods" for Will,
and he spent ten years listing them and discussing them. Other farmers
have shared and still share his point of view but as a rule they have
not had Will's knack for communicating it or they have taken it out
in talk instead of setting it down on paper as Will did.

Will Christman wrote poems when he saw life coming to its even-
tual and inevitable close. Only a few lines of them can be repeated
here as "come-on" samples. The rest can be found in libraries. They
were fine poems but that is not the point. The point is that Will was
an honest-to-God upstate farmer and, when the time came when he
could do it, he did some thinking on what he and his like had been
through. Then he told what he had been thinking in language as simple as his work, and his work, take it by and large all his life through,
was to make things grow—food plants, children, poems—three crops.

Drive west from Albany twenty miles and the Helderhills will be rising and falling about you in lyric rhythms. In summer long rectangles of snowy buckwheat will tilt toward you, and the dwellings of the bees, like architect's models of modernist houses, will gleam white from the deep-green shade of apple trees. Find the old Schoharie Turnpike and follow it over a roller-coaster trail to William's Hollow. A square weathered farmhouse fronts the road, and behind its honest façade older graying timbers tell a story of plodding generations.

The legend on the mailbox reads "W. W. Christman" and, though Will Christman died in 1937, Lansing Christman has preferred to leave his father's name there. The farm does not need those letters to distinguish it but they are symbols, a summing up of the identity of a unit of acres.

Lansing works at a radio station in Schenectady but he and Lucille, his South Carolina wife, have planted enough of a vegetable garden to tell the truth about this farm as a farm. If the pebble-spattered soil does not give immediate answer, look beyond the dark stone fence behind the house and see the Bozenkill—the Drunkard Creek—tipsily careening down a flight of stone steps longer and higher than the stairway of the Albany Capitol building. "Untillable Hills" Will called these slopes, and he knew them as such from the day he began helping his father at the plow and harrow.

Will was born in the midsection of what is now the barn of the William's Hollow farm. Like many of the families that lived on the Schoharie Turnpike, the Christmans had been Palatine German in the old country. They came to the Hudson Valley in the early eighteenth century, then moved west along the Mohawk and south toward the clovered flats that line Schoharie Creek. One of them aimed his musket at the British at Oriskany and another a generation later came safe home from the fight at Sackets Harbor.

Will's father was an uneducated, quiet farmer who worked hard and hated weeds. His son helped him with the chores, building wall, plowing, harvesting. The boy inherited from him a love of soil, even of the rock-bound recalcitrant ground that defied the work a man put into it. Will knew as soon as he knew anything that he would be a farmer all his days and he knew there was nothing better.

Three winters in a one-room "academy" was the best schooling the Helderhill country offered. Will took it, and never forgave its shortcomings. Thanks to a grandmother with a love of words, the boy had read all of Shakespeare by the time he was twelve and he was reading everything else he could get his hands on—especially poetry.

If his formal education was scanty, there was learning to be had from stony acres and the struggle of living things to grow there. Wildflowers blossomed in the wild valley, bird song threaded the air above it. The seasons repeated his lessons to him until they became a part of him.

"When I was about twelve years old I heard a bird singing in a swamp near a field where my father was sowing oats while I followed with the team and harrow covering the seeds...I knew the bird then only as a thrush.

"About two years later...I read John Burroughs' description of the song of the hermit. I recognized the bird more readily from Burroughs' interpretation of its song than I would from an ornithologist's description of its color and size."

Burroughs and Walt Whitman followed after Shakespeare. Will Christman rejoiced in the lucid prose of the naturalist who lived only a few miles away and described natural images no different from those visible in the valley of the Bozenkill. He found ecstasy in the verses of big, bearded Walt praising companionship and freedom. "Stick to Whitman," Burroughs wrote back to young farmer Christman, who had dared to write him a letter both admiring and confiding. "He can do you good."

Men's voices lifted old songs as the pickers set out along the turnpike for the hop fields beside the Schoharie and Will's tenor was one of them. From the mows of big red barns bouncing rhythm of fiddles rained on dancers below. Floors shook to their stomping, rafters echoed. "Swing her, swing her!" Skirts whirled upward, and screams wove into laughter. Girls were willing beside Schoharie water under the hop pickers' moon.

There was a girl at home—Catherine Bradt—an old Palatine surname that her grandfather two generations before had given to a Mohawk woman. Will was a wild blade but something told him she would give him as much of peace as a woman can give a passionate and moody man. Her family lived on the next farm, he had drawn her to school on his sled, she had come to William's Hollow when she was

seventeen to help his mother at her work. Night after night she and
Will spent reading aloud the poetry of Byron, Tennyson, Shakespeare,
the prose of Thoreau and Burroughs. The girl must have had many
heartaches then, for the son of the house was again and again in love
but even as many times he returned to her and to the interests that
bound them together—verses, wildflowers, birds, the shy animals of the
Bozenkill valley.

They were married when Will was twenty-two and she was twenty
and the banks of the Bozenkill were blazing with October yellows and
crimsons. They lived on in the Christman house while father and son
kept on working the family's unfertile soil. For forty years, while the
nine children—seven sons and two daughters—were being born and
growing up to help in the battle with the land, Will was a dirt farmer
on a York State rocky farm. He burned stumps and pulled them,
plowed, hoed and harrowed. He hitched up the long market wagon,
filled it with beets and beans, peas and potatoes, and drove to the surrounding towns to sell—Quaker Street and Delanson and Duanesburg.
On days of the Schoharie Fair he filled the wagon box with his children—three each to the three spring seats they kept in the front parlor
—and made triumphant laughing entry to the fairgrounds: "Special
Rates for Large Families."

While the children were young he fought for better schooling for
them and for all children in the state—denouncing in strongly phrased
letters to the Albany and New York papers the inefficiencies and inade-
quacies of the one-room schoolhouse.

> I grieve a little every year when the 5,000 or 6,000 one-room schools
> in the Empire State re-open to receive their quota of two, three or
> four or more unfortunate pupils; too few for a game unless it is soli-
> taire, and too few to stir impressionable youth to friendly rivalry.
>
> I visualize the cheap bare buildings toeing the road just as they did
> 60 years ago ... many without a playground or even a tree on which
> the forlorn and discouraged teacher may hang herself.

One day he did some figuring and sent out a letter for publication.
His children, he said, had traveled a total of 129,460 miles for their
education, 92,820 by train to high school and 36,640 by foot to a "typical
meagerly equipped rural school." Railroad fares had cost him over a

thousand dollars. "No consolidation, no centralization, no union free schools." Before his plain farmer's common sense the arguments of the sentimentalist advocates of the "little red schoolhouse" wilted like uprooted weeds.

Will Christman was nearly sixty when the children had got their schooling, married, found homes. "My farm stood on edge and I tilled both sides," he said. From then on he decided to till only one side and write poetry. He cut down to about twenty-five the number of acres he worked. "I'm not doing any more farming than I have to these days. I sort of like weeds and I let 'em grow in a good many places where I used to help my father dig them up and burn them. And I'm planting pines on the slopes I helped him clear. He'd be shocked if he knew." He alternated planting pines and writing verses.

His poems found an immediate market in the York State journals he sent them to—the *American Agriculturist,* the Syracuse *Post-Standard,* the Albany *Knickerbocker Press,* the Altamont *Enterprise,* the Cobleskill *Index.* They were like their author—simple, direct, observant, wise. Farmers who read them recognized their own daily doings. This was York State farming put into words, rhythmic words that reminded knowing readers of Whitman and Housman, and Hodgson, that reminded knowing farmers of birds and flowers, and plants that were around them as they worked. He wrote about his creek and his plowing, his family and his harvest, the wings and songs that flitted through his woods, his neighbors, his dogs, the wild flowers his wife had collected and transplanted to a patch beside the farmhouse door, and his memories—memories of old friends, and especially of old loves, yearnings

> To hear the love drum of the grouse throbbing
>   like thunder in the wild valley ...
> To think of love without regret.

After Will Christman's death the woman he loved best and longest, "First Reader, Critic and Wife," wrote with objective tenderness: "Will was very fond of the girls and he had many love affairs which helped to make material for many of his poems." One of these was his first love—the petal-smooth Belle Williamson who lived across the hill, drawing his long steps thither on many a windy, moony night in the old wild times before her death:

> The dear glad ways are over that were ours;
> She is a shade, past age and discontent,
> And this her clay beneath the wreaths and flowers;
> This is a cup from which the wine is spilled,
> An empty cup that cannot be refilled.

One girl was Margaret and one Elizabeth and others were Seraphine and Gladys and Helena and the hop-field girls of Blenheim.

> Hop fields are in clover,
>   Corn, and pasture grass;
> Dancing days are over
>   For each youth and lass.
> But one that was in denim
>   Wishes he were still
> Picking hops in Blenheim
>   By Schoharie Kill.

Will Christman did not write really great poetry. It was remarkable poetry for a York State farmer because this kind of man is not usually so simply expressive as Will. If the average York State farmer could sit down and become by quick and strange magic poetically articulate, Will Christman's poetry would be the kind he would write. It would have the compressed dry humor of men who are used to getting little cider from their apples, as in Will's remarks about his neighbors, Mrs. Jeremiah Saddlemire for instance:

> When Mrs. S. from worship came
>   The good old man would say:
> "Be keerful, little children,
>   Run out o'doors and play,—
> Your mother's been to church ag'in,
>   She's full of hell today."

Or his poem about the Quaker wife whose husband asked her where he would find a rope to hang himself:

"Thee'll find it on a nail out in the shed;
Thee'd better double it," his good wife said.

Or his report on "The Cider Hound," an alcoholic relative (by marriage), perhaps a victim of the ancestral Mohawk yearning for fire-
water:

Poor Will would stop and drop a hint to me:
"I'm dry," he'd say, "as a woodpecker's hole!"
Or digging ginseng, cutting a bee tree:
"A drink of cider would restore my soul."
"Wine is for boys," he said; "or ale, or Bock,
Hard cider is the draft that men demand."
Will's jug was like the shadow of the rock
That saved the Psalmist in a weary land.
Full of old Ira's cider, home he'd come
Like a sandpiper teetering up the creek;
"I'll draw my load," he'd say, "though I'm rum-dumb;
My soul is willing but my legs are weak."
So with his burden quite content, poor Will,
Down on all fours, would draw it up the hill.

"I raise pigs so I can live near hummingbirds," said Will Christman,
and he sat down at sixty and wrote four books of poems: *Songs of the
Helderhills, Songs of the Western Gateway, Wild Pasture Pine,* and
The Untillable Hills. He wrote about the white-throated sparrow, the
hermit thrust, the nuthatch, flicker, snow bunting, mourning dove,
goldfinch, shrike, and rose-breasted grosbeak. He helped Wife Catherine collect her wildflower garden and he wrote about the jack-in-
the-pulpit, wild clematis, the lady-slipper, the pinxter, bloodroot. He
planted trees and wrote about wild apple, basswood, oak, hemlock and
elm, and most of all about his pines. "I'm like an old tree," he said.
"My roots have grown so deeply in this hill-land soil, it would be hard
to transplant me now," but in the last decade of his life, the "and ten"
of his allotment, he began to think of the inevitable transplanting:

I leave my harvest and good will
To red poll, siskin and cross-bill:
To every singing soul good cheer:
Some walker of the snow may hear

The ringing carol of the shrike
Where the first shafts of sunrise strike.

I give, bequeath, devote, devise
Shelter to every bird that flies;
Harbor to all that walk or creep;
To the red fox a bed for sleep;
Table and roof for every guest
And place for dove and thrush to nest.

Years hence, some boy driving tranquil,
Slow cattle up the pasture hill,
In a spring morning dewy and sweet
When field sparrows stay his loitering feet
Shall see my pine spires tipped with sun
And hear the thrushes carillon.

Men of letters, many of them distinguished and famous, came to see
him at his farm and he made them welcome with no fuss and feathers,
striding in from the barn in his khaki wool shirt and wrinkled pants
held up by galluses. He was awarded the John Burroughs Medal for
nature writing in 1934. It had gone to professional writers and scholarly naturalists before—never to a working farmer. His living friends
remember him sitting at the head of a long table, lined with children
and guests (there were always extra places set for droppers-in), a pencil
in his hand, a sheet of paper below it, jotting down lines of verse while
good talk and laughter flowed about him. There were dances at the
house sometimes and the fiddlers sat on chairs on top of the long
dining-room table and the gnarled face of the farmer-poet was joyful
at the swing of their rhythms and the sight of dancing boys and girls.

When the last allotted decade had passed he walked, in the May
morning before his seventy-first birthday, twenty miles to Albany to
see his son Henry Esmond. "I get tired behind a harrow," he said, "and
this is the way I rest—I walk."

Will Christman's heart stopped beating in late February of the next
year—1937. He had prayed "to die in silence like a tree" and his peti-

tion had been granted. In wordless grief the family went mechanically about the task in which his talk and his verses had long instructed them. The ashes of the strong-sinewed body that had planted the pines were strewn at their roots. Far below their pointed tops a slanting brook tumbles past a granite boulder toward the Bozenkill. A bronze plaque on the boulder tells his name and the dates of his birth and death. Two days before he died he had sent to his publisher a poem for inclusion in a new volume. Its beginning read:

> The gift of rest be with you where you lie
> Under the weeds and grass and the wild rose
> Or where steep acres run to meet the sky.

The family had its ending engraved on the plaque:

> ...when you went
> We grieved, we felt the bitterness, the lack,
> Then softly fell the evening of content—
> The world had changed, we would not wish you back.

To the memorial services beside the stone on the late May birthday that would have been his seventy-second came a man from the State Education Department in Albany, "speaking for the boys and girls on the farms and in the villages and hamlets of rural New York," to say that "he lives in buildings, in courses of study, in better educational opportunity which he helped to create for rural children." Came a poet to say: "Those who come here in later times will find in the spot he loved something of the man himself and remember him as he would like to be remembered."

The later visitors of whom he spoke now know he told the truth. As soon as they arrive and see the slanting acres of the old farm they remember Will's words about them:

> My hill land is so cold and lean
> It is the last to put on green
> In winter first to put on snow
> In spring the last to let it go.

It would be difficult to see his son Lansing getting the earth of the garden behind the house ready for planting without recalling:

> Here I labored, here I delved,
> Swung the ax-blade, hickory-helved;
> Here I drove the walking plow,
> Sweated here and wiped my brow;
> Where my father earned his bread,
> Planted, sowed and harvested.
>
> On these hills, the God I saw
> Laid the tables of His Law;
> I, like the philosophers,
> Viewed His glory in the stars;
> Found no footprints save His own
> Stamped in earth's foundation stone;
> Heard the Voice that Moses heard
> Uttering a final word
> On the cloudy mountain-head;
> "I am all that is!" it said.

The other children, all but William, the eldest, who died young, drop in on the Lansing Christmans whenever they feel like it—they all live within not too many miles of the homestead. That was a good crop. Nancy and Emily are busy, successful housewives and mothers and they bring their children by to see the old place where their fathers used to come courting the Christman girls. Tall, lean, earnest Philip— mail carrier and fisherman and father and deacon—comes often with his two children. Less frequently comes Spencer—plumber, trapper, best shot at a moving target in the Helderhills. Neighbors say Spencer knows the wild animals of the Helderhills so well that when he sits by a foxhole the little ones come out and play fearlessly about him. Duane drives over from Schenectady. He inherited an interest in civic improvement and last election he made the best run against a long-entrenched Republican opponent machine ever yet made. Tell him so and he laughs ruefully and says his father used to tell of the time when folks said, "In Schoharie County everybody is a Democrat or a horse thief." "Times have changed," he says. Each of the remaining three, 50 per cent of the lot, is making part of his living from writing.

Walden (named for Thoreau's pond) is a patient, sure automobile mechanic, a good gardener, a rattling good columnist for the Altamont *Enterprise*. Henry Esmond, distinguished historian, author of *Tin Horns and Calico,* definitive and charmingly written history of the York State Rent Wars, loves every inch of this land and talks of building a house on the hill someday if Lansing and Lucille will let him.

Finally, there is Lansing. He talks about his father a good deal and of the many younger poets who used to come to see Will Christman and were influenced by him. There are at least five who have published volumes of verse or achieved a considerable amount of published work in magazines and anthologies. Sometimes, he says, they call themselves jokingly "The Helderberg School." Three are from Esperance, a few miles away, and one is a Massachusetts Yankee who spends his summers in Duanesburg. The fifth, he admits shyly, is himself. Though the old farm produces less vegetables from its rocky soil than it used to, the verse crop is still abundant. Bring up that subject and Lansing laughs and says that his verses help out more than you'd think in a lean season, total receipts from his sales of poems have passed the thousand-dollar mark.

The farm has kept on saying things to the man in the house. Lansing has listened to many that his father did not hear. His verses tell of "Sorting Apples," "Fixing Fence in August," "Going after Wintergreens," "Picking Wild Blackberries." They report purple finches singing in the rain, song sparrows feeding in his snow-covered garden, the first hepatica, shadbush blooms which "all in a day scatter their pyramids of white over the wild side hills," buttercups and marigolds blowing beside his roadside spring:

> Rain sings on the roof, and the horses,
> Temples throbbing, munch on the new mown hay.

He rarely writes on subjects that Will Christman chose, but, though he drives to Schenectady to work in a radio studio, he shares his father's distaste for the city. Will wrote in his "Spring Thoughts in Town":

> Here's dust and roar and men in throngs
> But never roses or bird songs
> I must go back to the wild rose
> And pasture where the black haw blows...

and Lansing speaks his pity of the metropolis in his "They Too Were Meadows":

> The boulders will press themselves firmly
> Into the snugness and the warmth of grass,
> In the peacefulness of the old meadow
> Worlds away from the acres of steel and smoke.
> They too were meadows once, with grass,
> And lichened stones, and wild deer loping.

Three crops grew on the William's Hollow farm that Will Christman's father chose for a home because a splashing creek raced from the hills there. The first was soil-born green things, the second was men, the third was songs. A stony section of York State did better than you might expect with all of them, and there are many Yorker farmers who feel that these are not unusual or not-to-be-expected products. They say if centuries hence a farmer digging in long-uncultivated ground should find a moldy, musty volume of Will Christman's verse he would discover much that would tell him how things were with us. He would find in them our stony acres, the birds and streams and winds that sang to us, the things we felt when we were plowing. That distant fellow down the future years would understand, they say, because after all, as Lansing says his brother Henry tells him, "You have to be something of a poet to be a farmer and like it."

> A chant for the birds and trees,
> For the flowers and fragrance of youth,
> For the rooftree over the weather-strained house
> And for its topmost twig where the robin swung to the
>   rhythm of his evening carol,
> For dark, hill pines that almost touched the stars.

> From *The Basswood,* by W. W. Christman

> ...There was a picture of an old blocked quilt:
> The white of the open fields; the woods, dark.

> From *Snow on an October Night,* by Lansing Christman

Woods Secret

The sun was mighty hot and John and I
Had come in early and were at the pump
When Aunt May screamed for us to come right quick.
We ran outside and there she stood
A-pointin' down beyond the valley hill.
We stopped and looked but all that we could see
Was tops of trees, of pines and beech and oak,
All still beneath the hazy heat of noon.
And then we heard it awful loud and clear—
A man's voice calling. "Help!" he yelled. "Oh, help!
For God's sake won't somebody come to me?"
Out of that valley filled with leaves it came,
From somewhere under all those sunny limbs.
We grabbed our rifles off the chimney shelf
And started down the slope into the woods,
And every time he'd shout we'd run like hell
Toward where it seemed he was, until at last
John stopped and said, "We're comin' mighty close.
Get ready, for you can't tell what could be."
And then he called right loud, "Where are you now?"
The fellow couldn't help but hear, for he
Must not have been more'n twenty yards away,
At least, that's how it seemed, but when John quit
We couldn't hear a sound in all those woods.
We called and called but no one answered us,
And walked and walked but didn't find a thing—
Until a red-faced man came puffin' up;
He said he'd heard the shouts from Foster's pool
Where he'd been workin' and he'd run four miles;
And pretty soon a boy came in from Vance
Who'd heard it too, and we all looked for hours,
But never to this day has any trace
Been found. And so we'll never know who 'twas,
Or what strange terror came to him that noon
When shade of trees hid him from human sight.

❦ "I Am a Cayuga"

The old chief, Clinton Rickard, lives in a little house near the Niagara County town of Sanborn on the reservation of his tribe, the Tuscaroras. York State Indians and those of the Iroquois Federation who dwell in Canada will always remember that house— not merely because Clinton Rickard, now white haired and nearly blind, has done many good things for his people in his long lifetime, but because, at his invitation, another fine man, a homeless exile, lived out his last days there. Though his name is known to few white people, no loyal eastern Indian will forget Deskaheh, chief of the Young Bear Clan of the Cayuga Nation.

Deskaheh was a descendant of Mary Jemison and he was born in Grand River Land, a reservation of the Six Nations people who fled or were driven to Canada from York State after the American Revolution. They chose these acres gratefully ceded to them by Canadian Governor Haldimand, because the Grand with its level flats reminded them of their beloved Mohawk valley which they had tried to preserve for the English king.

After his years of grammar school, Deskaheh, like many other Grand River Indians, exercised his treaty right to cross the United States boundary to become a lumberjack among the lower York State and upper Pennsylvania Alleghenies, but after an accident he returned to Grand River and took up farming. He married the daughter of a Cayuga mother and white father and she bore him four daughters and five sons, most of whom live today in western York State.

By 1914 Deskaheh had reached the middle period of what white neighbors called a successful reservation-Indian life. His honesty, his sincerity, and his ability as an orator in the Cayuga language had brought him deserved election as head chief when the Canadian government, satisfied until the beginning of World War I to allow the

Iroquois the status of a separate nation, decided on grounds of expediency to disregard old treaties and assimilate the Indians, by force if necessary. Deskaheh was the leader of the delegation that patiently explained in Ottawa, first, that the Canadian government had no jurisdiction over the little nation they represented, second, that, since the Indians had already volunteered in proportionately greater numbers than the people of any other nation in the world, enforced draft of its young men by a foreign ally would seem silly.

They won this argument but the end of the war brought other attempted encroachments and the red men soon knew that the majority in the legislative halls of the Canadian capital planned further inroads on their rights as citizens of the separate country known as Grand River Land. In 1921, to thwart the purposes of these schemers, Deskaheh, appointed "Speaker of the Six Nations Council," presented as travel credentials a passport authorized by his nation and crossed the Atlantic to seek British aid. Since, as he pointed out, the treaty on which his people based their claims had been made with George III he asked its confirmation by George V.

The English authorities refused his request, saying that they would not deal with a Canadian domestic problem and the Indian returned, defeated. Then the Canadian enemies grew bolder. The creating of a fifth-column party through persuasion, promises, and payments was easy, easier still to get the new minority to ask for protection, easiest of all to order a detail of the red-jacketed Royal Mounted Police to ride into the Grand River country to protect the "loyalist" Indians and "to keep the peace." So obvious was this procedure that Deskaheh, who had strongly opposed it, pleading earnestly for arbitration, won many white sympathizers among his neighbors and through them news of the coming raid reached him in time for a hasty flight across the border of the United States to the city of Rochester in western York State.

The raiders arrested and jailed a number of Indians and, though Deskaheh was known to abstain from alcoholic liquors, they searched his house on the pretext of looking for illegal beverages. The Canadian government then ordered barracks built for the housing of their police and Grand River was suddenly an occupied nation.

Deskaheh now began to fight back desperately. With the Six Nations' counsel, George P. Decker, a white Rochester lawyer, as his companion, he again used his passport, this time to travel to Geneva to bring his people's case before the League of Nations. He arrived in September of 1923, took lodging in the Hotel des Familles, and began to work toward presenting personally to the Council of the League the petition of his people. Though he met with no success, he fought doggedly. Winter came and went and in mid-April he wrote to his wife and his sons and daughters:

> I have no time to go anywhere only setting on the chair from morning till night copying and answering letter as they come and copying the documents and I have many things to do.

May came to the city by beautiful Lake Leman but his thoughts were with his people beside the Grand River and like a good believer in the religion of the Long House he was seeking aid through the prayers of his people to their God. To his brother, Alex General, he wrote:

> I believe it will be a good thing to have a meeting in one of the long house, but you must be combined all the good people and the children of the long house, only those that are faithful believers in our religion and no other, and it must be very early in the morning to have this, so that our God may hear you and the children, and ask him to help us in our distress at this moment and you must use Indian tobacco in our usual way when we ask help to our Great Spirit ... and you must have a uniform on ... and also ask God you wish the religion will keep up for a great many years to come and the Indian race also ...

By June he had obtained the services of a Swiss lawyer who was preparing a statement of the case of the Six Nations Indians in French. The money the Indians and their friends had raised in America was almost gone and some means of replenishing it was necessary.

Again he wrote Brother Alex from Geneva:

> And we had a meeting of the Iroquois of the Six Nations of the Grand River Land [really the committee devoted to the interests of the Six Nations] on the 27th of June and the meeting decided to raffal off the two portrait pictures which they made, and just think

of it, these two pictures of myself with my costume on it, and it is finished and it is very good pictures ... and decided to set the price for the two pictures for a small sum of money only 6,000 Swiss francs ... the rich lady she said at the meeting we must win no matter it takes ten years because our case is so clear and just and I may mention to you this 6,000 francs it means a little over 1,000 dollars of our money ... and it gives me very great lift to our fight ... very strong committee all big people of high class people, when the meeting takes place everybody looks decent of their suit and dress very well.

If these informal reports written to his loved family in an unfamiliar language seem naïve, the campaign Deskaheh and his good friend, George Decker, were waging was not. It was hard hitting, simple, direct. Continually put off by officials who found it embarrassing to deny this representative of a small nation the right to speak before the League Council, committed to the Wilsonian doctrine of autonomy for small nations, these two made the situation more awkward for the British interests by getting into the public prints distributed in Geneva quotations from treaties and documents that Canada had decided to abrogate as "scraps of paper."

The Indian was also attracting much favorable attention as a person. To the Irish woman correspondent of the *Freeman's Journal* of Dublin, who "felt as excited as a little girl of twelve at the thought of meeting face to face a real live hero of my childish dreams," he seemed "a good looking, broad-shouldered man, about 40 years of age [he was really 54] wearing ordinary dark clothes ... and presenting every appearance of a well-to-do Canadian farmer with the one exception of his beautiful moccasins...." She commented on the penetrating, searching glance of his dark eyes, his kindly smile disclosing remarkably white teeth, and finished her description with the sentence: "His beautifully-shaped but stern mouth, firm chin and heavy jaw-bones are those of the born fighter, the strong man who knows his strength and believes in it, whilst his shining eyes speak of enthusiasm and idealism." But in the middle of this enthusiastic and sentimentally feminine interview the chief had persuaded her to quote from the text of a memorial addressed to the Grand River Indians, dated as late as December 4, 1912, and filed by Great Britain:

The Documents, Records and Treaties between the British Governors in former times, and your wise Forefathers, of which, in consequence of your request, authentic copies are now transmitted to you, all establish the Freedom and Independency of your Nations.

Time wore on and though a few Englishmen and Canadians spoke up for the Six Nations Indians, though the representatives of the Netherlands and Albania listened sympathetically and spoke of supporting his petition, Deskaheh began to suspect that his cause was lost. News from his homeland was bad. The Canadian government had announced a "free election," which would in effect determine whether or not the Six Nations government of Grand River Land should be dissolved. For this vote the Canadian government agent had taken possession of the Six Nations Council House, surrounding it with a guard of twenty police. In protest, the Indians favoring their nation's continuance did not vote. The Canadian authorities then broke open the safe holding the records of the Six Nations and took therefrom a number of wampum belts, revered as sacred by the tribes, refusing, on demand, to return them.

In November, 1924, Deskaheh wrote to the editor of a Swiss journal:

It is the heart broken that I must affirm that since several months I am against the most cruel indifference ... My appeal to the Society of Nations has not been heard, and nothing in the attitude of Governments does not leave me any hope.

It is in this dreadful agony that I take the advantage to cry out that injustice, by the mean of your free Review to my brothers from all races and all religions ... Too long we have suffered from the tyrany of our neighbors who tread under feet our Right and laugh at the Pact which binds them ... Our appeal is for all those which are animated by the spirit of justice and we ask them their benevolent help.

As if to seal its own lack of interest, the Secretariat of the League which had notified Deskaheh of the refusal to allow him to appear as a petitioner before a plenary session, aware of the embarrassment he had caused, now denied both the Indian and George Decker seats in the gallery to observe deliberations.

Despairing, the two friends struck their last brave blow. They hired the Salle Centrale and advertised in the press their own meeting at which Deskaheh would present the case of his nation to those who would come to listen. The response was amazing. The American Indian had been a popular figure in Europe since the time of Columbus and the populace, the vast majority of whom had never seen an example of the noble savage as popularized by translations of the works of James Fenimore Cooper and other romanticists, attended in thousands. All the Geneva Boy Scouts were present, but not a single League of Nations official. Members of the press of many nations, sensing possibilities of stories about a picturesque if not politically important character, were at their reserved tables, among them the distinguished Hungarian journalist Aloys Derso, now resident of New York State, who tells amusing and movingly pathetic incidents of the occasion.

"I went to the evening to see my first American Indian. He was in the dressing room already in full regalia. I drew a few sketches of him and he was a good model, sitting immobile. He had not the typical Indian profile, the nose not the aquiline nose I expected. His eyes were tired and there was a great melancholy in his expression."

When Deskaheh appeared before the great audience he walked in dignity and with no self-consciousness. There were giggles because, though in the elaborate dress of the chief of the Cayuga Nation, he carried an enormous yellow suitcase which he placed carefully on a table in front of him. Says Derso:

"One of my neighbors turned to another—'Why the hell brought he this suitcase?'"

"'Most probably,' said the other, 'he did not trust the garde-robe.'"

Smiles soon ceased, however, for Deskaheh related his story simply and sincerely. His people had heard in 1915, he said, of a repulsively homely white chief with a frightening mustache who had made war on their ally, the good bearded chief of the British people. The young Indian braves had swiftly formed a regiment and gone across the big water to fight for the government that had once so gratefully given his nation its land. Here he repeated a passage from the treaty of 1784 as worded by Sir Frederick Haldimand, governor in chief of Quebec and territories depending thereon:

"I do hereby in His Majesty's name, authorize and permit the said Mohawk Nation and such other of the Six Nations Indians as wish to settle in that quarter to take possession of and settle upon the banks of the river commonly called Ouse or Grand River ... which them and their posterity are to enjoy forever."

Then he recited the tale of the broken pledge—the raid of the Royal Mounted, the rummaging of his own house, the building of the police barracks, the seizure of the sacred wampum. The story would be incredible without evidence, he said, but he had foreseen this and had the proofs with him.

Then he lifted the lid of the suitcase and with care and reverence drew from within the old beaded wampum on which might be read the sworn agreements of white governments with his people. Speaking with deep feeling, translating these documents slowly and impressively, stopping now and then to make clear the meanings of the bead colors and of the representations of wild animals, he made his entranced hearers feel that this was not the narration of the grievances of a small racial unit, but the story of all minority peoples—the tragedy of every small nation that is neighbor to a large one.

When he had finished there was a moment of silence—then the roar of a tremendous ovation. Thousands rose to their feet to cheer him and the great hall echoed and re-echoed with their applause. Straight, unsmiling, impassive, he waited until after many minutes the sound began to wane. Then, still expressionless, he left the platform.

As Derso was leaving the Salle Centrale a friend, whom he describes as an antiquaire and art dealer, approached him.

"Derso, have you see those Indian embroideries?"

"Of course I saw them."

"*Combien ça vaut?*" said the antiquaire.

"It is very difficult, my friend," said Derso, "to estimate the value of these things. For *me,* for instance, they have the same value as all other treaties registered in the League offices. For *you,* their value may be from 50 to 150 Swiss francs, because you expect to sell them to a connoisseur for 1,000 to 5,000. But I would advise you to leave this Indian alone with his beads."

Before the end of 1924 the Speaker of the Six Nations Council had returned to America, a beaten and discouraged man. An exile from Canada and from the nation he thought he had failed, he found refuge with Clinton Rickard in the house where the benign old chief of the Tuscaroras still lives. There, by the Niagara River, which marks the Canadian boundary, he found that the people for whom he had fought did not think him a failure. From their northern homes in Grand River Land they journeyed here to see him and assure him of their loyalty. Though his disheartening experience had weakened him physically, his spirit took fire from their words and with never-ending courage he kept up his battle.

On the evening of March 10, 1925, suffering from a serious attack of pleurisy and pneumonia, he made his last speech. It was before a radio microphone in Rochester. Once more, and more forcefully than ever, he hurled defiance at the big nations that had disregarded the claims of the Six Nations people.

> We call the little ten miles square we have left the "Grand River Country"...it is just enough to live and die on. Don't you think your governments ought to be ashamed to take that away from us pretending that it is part of theirs? The governments at Washington and Ottawa have a silent partnership of policy. It is aimed to break up every tribe of red men so as to dominate every acre of their territory...over in Ottawa they call that policy "Indian Advancement." Over in Washington they call it "Assimilation." We, who would be the helpless victims, say it is tyranny. If this must go on to the bitter end, we would rather that you come with your guns and poison gases and get rid of us—do it openly and aboveboard—do away with the pretense that you have the right to subjugate us to your will...
>
> Ottawa officials under pretense of a friendly visit asked to inspect our precious wampum belts...seized and carried away those belts as bandits...our aged wampum-keeper did not put up his hands. Our hands go up only when we address the Great Spirit.

One by one Deskaheh told of the agreements solemnly made on the sworn good faith of each of the two big governments that had guaranteed the Indian his own land, fair treatment, independence.

> If you are bound to treat us as though we were citizens under your government, then those of your people who are land-hungry will get

our farms away from us ... We would then be homeless and have to drift to your big cities to work for wages to buy bread, and have to pay rent, as you call it, to live on this earth and to live in little rooms in which we would suffocate.

Sick, fever-ridden, despairing, Deskaheh raised his voice to speak his proud last message.

This is the story of the Mohawks, the story of the Oneidas, of the Cayugas—I am a Cayuga—of the Onondagas, the Senecas, and the Tuscaroras. They are the Iroquois.

This story comes straight from Deskaheh, one of the chiefs ... I am the Speaker of the Council of the Six Nations, the oldest League of Nations now existing. It was founded by Hiawatha. It is a league which is still alive and intends as best it can to defend the rights of the Iroquois to live under their own laws in their own little countries now left to them; to worship their Great Spirit in their own way and to enjoy the rights which are as surely theirs as the white man's rights are his own.

The next morning Deskaheh was in a Rochester hospital. Eight weeks later he knew he was dying and asked to be taken back to Clinton Rickard's home on the Tuscarora Reservation.

While he made ready for his journey along the Milky Way to the land of Happy Hunting, his brother, wife, and children tried to cross the border at Niagara Falls to be with him and were refused permission to do so. On June 27, 1925, alone and with his eyes set toward the Six Nations Land he had tried to serve, he died.

White Americans and white Canadians have done little to keep the story of Deskaheh alive. Few have seen the small stone that marks his grave in the burial grounds of the Cayuga long house. Fewer still care to remember his words. They make the white man uncomfortable because they bear so emphatically on contemporary thinking about the Indian, on proposed laws in the legislative bodies of states and the nation that would still, despite our agreements to (in Deskaheh's words) "protect little peoples and to enforce respect for treaties," regard Indians as incompetents to be governed for their own good by wiser neighbors. But the Iroquois remember. And when they speak of

Deskaheh the white men who know his story grow troubled, wondering if they and their governments could by some unlikely chance have dealt unjustly with a great man.

❦ Budgets as Death Warrants

It is now clear that the tragic plight of the American Indians, riddled with disease, weakened by malnutrition, plagued with ignorance, is not the result of casual mischance or more casual inefficiency. The accusing finger points to those who, year after year, recommend budgets which perpetuate these festering conditions.

"If you happen to know a Papago Indian boy living on the Sells Indian Reservation near Tucson," writes Herb Nelson in the Phoenix, Arizona, *Gazette,* "be good to him: the chances are only 50-50 that he will survive his 18th birthday.

"If you have a Montana Indian friend living on one of that state's seven reservations, write him a letter: the chances of his dying from tuberculosis is 14 times greater than that of your white neighbor next door."

The death rate from tuberculosis in the nation is 40.1 per 100,000. For Indians it is 211.9. Less than 42 American babies in every 100,000 die during or immediately after birth. For children of Indian parents the figure is over 135. The rate of death from pneumonia in the nation approaches 52 in 100,000. For Indians it is over 123. Conditions among Alaskan Indians, under federal jurisdiction, grow steadily worse!

Why? As a nation we pride ourselves on disease prevention through sanitation, adequate feeding, medical care, in our own country and in those occupied areas where our recent enemies live. Yet that minority which gave a higher percentage of volunteers to our military service in the last war than any other has been left to become, through no

From *The American Indian,* Volume V, Number 1, 1949. Written by Carl Carmer when editor of the magazine.

fault of its own, a disease-breeding foe of national security, a source of deadly infection that recognizes no racial barriers. Yet, the men whose duty it is to know this and take precautionary measures are significantly mute.

Is the answer as simple as this, that nothing is being done, and that doing nothing in the face of rising costs and a desperate situation steadily growing more desperate is the policy written into the annual budget? "The Bureau of Indian Affairs is providing no preventive medicine program organized for service to the Indians on an Agency or area basis, and no such service has ever been provided," writes Dr. Fred T. Foard, now Health Director of the Bureau of Indian Affairs, in a letter to the Association on American Indian Affairs. According to the *Washington Post* on January 14, 1949, this disregard of the welfare of American citizens is perforce continued by the current budget now under consideration in the Congress. The *Post* reports Dr. Foard asked one and one-half million dollars for "procedures of preventive medicine among the Indians" which would be "at least...a start... toward cutting into the appalling death rate," and this request "was disallowed by the Federal budget makers."

Is this the simple truth—that the same expenditures which were grossly and ridiculously inadequate when first adopted are still recommended to our legislators: That those who administer Federal Indian services (many guaranteed by the sacred word of the United States in treaty agreements) are even asked to "get along with less," forced to stand helplessly by while death takes its toll?

It is to be hoped that those responsible for the cut in the asked appropriations are not sleeping well these nights while Indians are dying from want of the proper medical care which has been promised them. If the facts are as reported, the current niggardly budgets are equivalent to death warrants for thousands of doomed Indian citizens. How long must it be before those men who reckon and recommend the budgets for Congressional approval become aware that budgets are made by human minds and hearts to serve the human needs of all the citizens of the United States? If they cannot respond to the plea of sick and dying citizens for succor, then we must take the call for action to the people of the nation and the peoples of the world. These are outrages to which mankind will not be an accomplice. There are ways of saving money other than those which require the sacrifice of human lives.

ぴ The Big Party

Most everybody in these parts'll go to a party sooner'n they'll spit. They've had some high times off 'n' on. Ever since a year ago last May, though, it ain't been quite the same. Folks go but they don't put no life into it. Seems like they feel they wa'n't no use tryin' to come up to the Big Party. Like that little dog o' mine that's part fox terrier, part Boston. Ever since he mounted Jim Massey's collie bitch he ain't been interested in nothin'. He's done the best he *can* an' so he's takin' it easy.

Nobody expected the Big Party to turn out the way it did when they give out word t' come t' the summer openin' o' Henry Mastin's beer place down in Tiny Town. Course folks said they was goin' an' when the day come an' it was hot fer the first time that spring ye could see they was gettin' a little excited. More'n you'd think quit plow' 'fore sundown, 'n' chores got a lick 'n' a promise. By eight o'clock buggies an' autos was linin' up in the lot behind Henry's place. Quite a crowd was around outside waitin' fer the fiddler to show up when the Raders drew in. They couldn't get their Model T started so they jest hitched it up to the sorrel team an' Joe sat on the top an' drove the horses while Jule steered inside. Some o' the boys had brought jugs along an' they sure whooped t' beat hell when Joe an' Jule rolled up. They had Herb Gulick, the fiddler, in the back an' so everybody whooped again an' went inside an' ordered beer though it didn't set so good on top o' what was in the jugs. Vi Harley, Henry's housekeeper, was sellin' tickets for the dancin' an' she says, anybody that don't buy no ticket gits throwed out but before I throw 'em I'm layin' 'em on the floor an' settin' on 'em. Vi'd run to about three hundred without no extrys an' it ain't all fat neither, so folks laughed but they bought tickets.

Henry had cleared away all the tables so they was room to dance but all the drinkin' had to be done at the bar, less'n you had a jug. Herb set his chair up on top o' one end o' the bar, spit in the cuspidor over by the mirror an' let fly on *Yankee Twostep*.

Well, sir, from that minute y'could tell things was goin' t' happen. 'Twa'n't no time at all 'fore George Smith got lickered an' when Herb hollers "Swing Your Partners" George swung Abbie Barkeley so hard he couldn't hang onto her an' she went through one of Henry and Vi's big glass windows right into the junk yard. Didn't hurt her none but it made Vi so mad she grabbed George by the seat o' the pants and throwed him like a bowlin' ball right through the hole Abbie had made. George landed smack on top o' blacksmith Jackson's old anvil an' it broke his leg an' he had to go home.

By that time Vi'd had as much beer as she could hold an' a lot more. She didn't want to go out back 'cause somebody might get in without buyin' a ticket so she fetched a tall tin pail from behind the bar an' goes about halfway up the stairs with it. Well, she sort o' overbalanced an' the first thing anybody knows they hear a crash and Vi turns a complete somerset down the stairs and lands, forty acres o' bare bottom up, on the dance floor, with the tin pail a-clatterin' and bangin' behind her. You could 'a' heard folks laughin' from here to West Bloomfield.

But what made the Big Party was the woman-fight. They was a feller named Ryan lived over Baptist Hill way with his housekeeper. One day he come back from Rochester with another woman an' when folks asked him about it he said, "They ain't no law against a man havin' two housekeepers, is they?" He was a pretty mean cuss an' nobody said much to him nor him to them. So everybody was surprised when he drove up to the party bringin' both women. They got there late an' went inside an' first Ryan'd dance with one of 'em while the other took a suck at his jug an' then they switched around. You could see them gals didn't like each other none from the start. One of 'em was a big woman with black hair an' looked sort of like a fat Indian.

The other was sandy-haired an' tall and scrawny an' she had a lot o' gold teeth.

Toward the end of the evenin' when folks was all pretty lickered Ryan finished up one dance with the sandy-haired woman an' when the fiddlin' started again he went right on with her. The big black-haired one stepped up to the two of 'em an' says, "It's my turn." "The hell it is," says the other one.

"You give up that man," says the black-haired one, "or I'll kill you. I was his housekeeper 'fore you an' I know where he got you in Rochester."

"Git away from here," says the tall one, "or I'll tear you apart."

"Quit your talkin'," says Ryan all of a sudden. "You're always sayin' what you're goin' to do to each other. Why don't you do it?"

At that the fat one grabs the scrawny one by the throat an' starts to tear at her hair.

"Wait!" yells Ryan, grabbin' 'em both. "This has got to be a fair fight an' we're goin' outside where we won't hurt nothin'."

Everybody made a rush for the door an' when they got outside Ryan began orderin' folks to make a circle with their autos. They did a lot o' backin' an' turnin' and pretty soon they had a circle o' headlights around a little plot o' ground an' all of 'em was turned on. All the time the two women was screamin' an' cursin' an' tellin' what they were goin' to do to each other. Then Ryan had a couple men take the fat one to the other side o' the circle while he held the scrawny one. "Ready," he shouts. "Let's go!"

The women started runnin' toward each other an' they come together in the middle of the circle. They was scratchin' an' screamin' and clawin' at each other an' their hair come down an' their faces were bleedin'. Then their clothes began to tear an' come off like feathers at a cockfight. First thing you know they was both stark naked an' still goin' at each other. They was game all right, them two. Sometimes they'd get tired an' just glare at each other not sayin' or doin' nothin' an' the next minute they'd both be screamin' an' tearin' handfuls o' hair out by the roots. First one'd fall down an' then the other, but they'd get up an' keep right at it. Their hair was all streaked with blood, blood was pourin' from scratches on their sides and backs. They was nasty teeth marks on their shoulders an' breasts where they'd bit each other. I never seen a worse mess.

I dunno how it would have come out if Henry hadn't heard his phone ringin' an' answered it. He come runnin' out in a minute hollerin' that the state troopers had seen the circle o' headlights an' wanted to know what the hell was goin' on out there an' said they was on their way to find out. At that Ryan says the fight's over an' walks between the two women.

"Ye better git into my Ford," he says, "or they'll run ye in sure."

The women just stood there for a minute lookin' at each other.

"Go on," says Ryan, "or I'll belt hell out of ye."

But they wasn't payin' him no mind. They jest stood there—all mud an' blood an' hair. Then all of a sudden they tipped forwards, throwed their arms around each other's necks and begun cryin' and kissin' each other.

"Here, what the hell is this?" says Ryan, and he grabs 'em and shoves 'em both in the back seat of his sedan, naked as the day they was born, an' druv off with 'em.

Folks've called it the Big Party ever since. They jest don't expect they'll have a time like that again.

❦ The Champlain Valley

In the summer of 1916 at Plattsburg's Civilian Officers' Training Camp I was a timorous sentry on my first tour of guard duty one shivery dawn before the sun's rising. Below me, slatelike and rippleless, lay Lake Champlain and above the upslanting fringe of trees on its far shore there was a blaze in the sky as if a Vermont barn was burning. The patch of crimson spread swiftly and soon silhouetted three giant forms, black and hooded, that stood like blanketed Indians against the horizon. Even after the sun rolled above the flaming clouds, the towering trio stood lightless, but an hour after I was relieved of duty I looked across glinting waters toward rounded mountains splotched with a garish green.

Twenty years would pass before I would visit among those hills and, looking back from the lake's eastern edge, catch glimpses of other mountains, notching the western sky. Standing on the jagged rocks of Oakledge—a quiet Burlington resort—I could see on a clear day the "uphisted" lands, as natives call them, the craggy Adirondacks rising from the "Dark Country"—their slopes clothed in a hemlock green so deep it is almost black. The sun was well up then, but even as I looked the high-tossed rocky peaks faded—like visions that had come and gone as if summoned by a secret incantation.

From a plane bound south from Montreal some years ago I was able to see at last the whole panorama of the Champlain Country—the Richelieu River, north-running outlet to the narrow, one-hundred-and-seven-mile-long blue lake, the narrows at its southern end which connect it with smaller Lake George, and far beyond, the rippling bright current of the Hudson moving southwest toward the wide, deep channel that guides it to the Atlantic.

History can be absorbed sometimes in a moment and by a glance— and no one with an inkling of the American past could fail to see why the French believed the waterways of the St. Lawrence River and of Lake Champlain would lead them to dominance of the eastern seaboard, why the Dutch and the British decided to oppose them by pushing straight up the line of the Hudson, and finally why the British during the American Revolution saw this great north-south aisle as a water barrier, control of which would prevent the rebels of New England from supporting their comrades to the west and south.

Champlain lies south-to-north along the western side of Vermont in the shape of a slim, gently belling clarinet. At its thin throat (on the New York side) is Whitehall and here on a barn, once the shelter of mules that towed the canalboats of Champlain Canal, you may behold a sign reading "The Liberty Eatery" which should in no way deter a gourmet from entering.

Follow the water north to Ticonderoga where Mount Defiance stares across the narrows toward Mount Independence. Already this lake will have made its individuality clear. It has no concentration of hotels, restorations, motels, camps, frozen custard drive-ins, hot-dog stands, such as maddens motorists passing through the town of Lake George, nor are its banks crowded with resorts and estates that shoulder each other. Champlain is quieter, lonelier, more open. It is dotted by dozens of rocky little islands which have no official listing—though some go by many different names, conferred by residents of various sections of the lake shore.

Once luxury hotels stood among clusters of outbuildings—boathouses, summerhouses, belvederes—on these banks. Most of them have disappeared and more popular now are hotels consisting of a low main building (dining hall and living room), circled by family-unit cabins, with basketball and tennis courts, golf courses, docks and canoe shelters nearby. Life in these functional buildings through the years has become simpler, more wholesome, more comfortable. Resort existence on Lake Champlain now resembles camp living more than the dressy, overfed, concert-ridden formality of early twentieth century hotels. A number of the less ostentatious hostelries, however, have endeared themselves to succeeding generations and are now receiving the adult grandchildren of earlier patrons. At Basin Harbor, still reserved, still accustomed to polite behavior, a member of long ago can tell the names of some of the youngsters by the familiar features of their ancestors.

Farther down the lake (and remember this water is flowing north, hence "down" is "up" on the map) lies Charlotte on the eastern shore where high Mount Philo gives breath-taking views of higher Adirondacks in the western sky. Beyond the hill city of Burlington, the many-windowed factories of Winooski catch the sun and the splashing river of the same name loses itself in the lake's deeper water.

Champlain widens here, and there are a series of small bays on either side. North of these the lake is split by three island areas—South Hero and North Hero (named for the Allen brothers, Ethan and Ira) and between them, Grand Isle—from which the spires and towers of Plattsburg, rising from green trees, make distant patterns. The lake flows on past Highgate Springs in an eastern fork, where at a picturesque inn, the Tyler Place, visitors may muse upon the old-time splendors of this early watering place. The waters roll by Rouses Point to the west and beyond the border is French Canada—whitewashed farmhouses, little churches with golden crosses above them, road signs in French.

The Richelieu River receives the flood. It is sure and smooth, broad and bountiful and for a time flows easily toward its goal. It waters farm country that raises harvests to be carried to Montreal. There are factories at St. Johns, a mill or two, and then at Chambly the bottom seems to drop from the channel and the water races into foam. A canal skirts this hurly-burly of rapids to allow peaceful navigation as the water sweeps on to meet the St. Lawrence at Sorel.

In early July of 1609 a war fleet of twenty-four canoes moved up the Richelieu into Lake Champlain, beginning there two centuries of deadly water pageantry. They carried sixty Indians—Algonquins, Hurons, and Montagnais—two Frenchmen (their names unknown to history) and their commander, a sturdy captain in his early forties, Samuel de Champlain, already a veteran of many an exploring expedition in the New World.

For two weeks and more this flotilla moved steadily southward. The lake looked then much as it does now—a goodly portion of its shores barren and rocky or lined by woods. Champlain delighted in the grove of chestnuts (where Burlington now lies) whence he could look west to blue mountains, east to green.

Soon the Indians told the white men they had come into hostile Iroquois country and must travel by night and hide in the woods by day. Champlain liked the change. The mountain masses took strange shapes in moonlight, filling the valley in between with mystery.

Near the end of the lake, as the canoes silently rounded a little cape, their occupants heard sharp cries from the blackness near the western shore. A war party of Mohawks, bound north on a raid, had come upon enemies sooner than they had expected and had started driving their canoes ashore. Almost immediately the Hurons and their companions heard the sound of axes felling trees so that makeshift fortifications could be built. Champlain and his two men watched as the Indians in their own party lashed their canoes to long poles to create a compact floating raft.

Out of the darkness near the shore sped two canoes bearing Mohawk warriors, bent on conference. Did the invaders from the north wish to fight? Yes, said the chiefs of the flotilla; that was why they were there, but it was too dark now to see their enemies and this would hamper their slaughter. It would be necessary to wait for daylight.

All night the Mohawks danced and sang around their fires on the shore, stopping only to shout scorn of their enemies. All night the Hurons and their friends sang insulting songs in reply.

At dawn, the Hurons landed on the western shore and dashed toward the barricade of tree trunks. Already the Mohawks were coming toward them—big men and strong, two hundred of them—walking "with gravity and calm" behind three chieftains wearing huge plumes. At sight of them the Hurons and their allies suddenly slowed down, and separated to the right and left to form an aisle, down which marched the white warrior in shining corselet, armed with an arquebus. He was twenty yards ahead of his companions and thirty from the plumed Mohawk chiefs. Amazed by this ominous shining being before them, the Mohawk chieftains stopped abruptly and reached for their bows. As they did so the French captain halted, aimed his arquebus and fired.

"...with this shot," his own report reads, "two [of the chieftains] fell to the ground, and one...was wounded, who died thereof a little later."

Stunned by the explosion of gunpowder and the sudden death of two of their three leaders, the Mohawks stood motionless. At this moment one of the two other white men, who had been concealed off to the side, fired his arquebus. It is not known whether his shot hit anyone but the noise of the explosion started a terror-stricken rout and the sixty northern Indians raced after the fleeing Mohawks, capturing, slaying, scalping. The first battle of Ticonderoga was at an end and the Mohawks, one of the five tribes of the Iroquois confederacy, strongest of all tribal unions, had learned to hate the French. One shot from Champlain's arquebus had influenced the history of the world.

Champlain moved south a few miles to the end of the lake but could not persuade his victorious friends to continue to Lake George. He turned back and before he had reached the Richelieu River on his return to Canada he had named for himself the lake which he had discovered and explored.

Morris Bishop, biographer of Champlain, wrote, "Some spots on this earth seemed destined to be battlefields; they smell of blood." Almost a century and a half after Champlain had discovered the lake which bears his name the French had built Fort Carillon, a safeguard against invasion from the south, and British General James Abercrombie was seeking to take the fort with a force of nine thousand Americans and sixty-four hundred English. Behind the walls a French army of only thirty-two hundred under the command of General Montcalm awaited the attack. It seems incredible that an officer of Abercrombie's rank could have been so stupid as to order a closed-rank frontal assault. Nevertheless, he did, and the British casualties that fateful July eighth numbered two thousand before Abercrombie ordered his men to retire to Lake George.

In 1759 Lord Jeffrey Amherst captured Fort Carillon. The British restored its old Indian name and held it for sixteen years.

In darkness and blowing rain on the night of May 9, 1775, big, blustery, rhetorical Ethan Allen and eighty-five volunteers from his private army, the Green Mountain Boys, crossed the lake to the New York side. Colonel Benedict Arnold was with them; he had attempted to claim command, but the Boys would obey orders only from Ethan. If dawn could have been postponed, the shivering band doubtless would have been treated to a longer speech on the shore, but light from the uncontrollable sun forced Ethan into unaccustomed brevity. "Friends and fellow soldiers," he said, "you have, for a number of years past, been a scourge and terror to arbitrary power. Your valor has been famed abroad....I now propose to advance before you and in person conduct you through the wicket gate; for we must this morning either quit our pretensions to valor or possess ourselves of this fortress in a few minutes; and inasmuch as it is a desperate attempt (which none but the bravest men dare undertake) I do not urge it on any contrary to his will. You that will undertake voluntarily, poise your firelocks."

A few moments later the courageous band (all having again volunteered by poising their firelocks) were following big Ethan Allen and much smaller Benedict Arnold through the wicket gate that allowed entrance through the main gate of the fort. As they poured into the parade ground they saw that Allen and Arnold had, in a sense, already engaged the enemy. They stood halfway up an outside stair of the barracks gazing upward at Jocelyn Feltham, a lieutenant of His Majesty's 26th Foot Regiment, who had, at a sentry's alarm, clad himself in white waistcoat, silver gorget and his short scarlet coat with yellow facing, but had failed to jump into his pants, the usual masculine gesture in such crises. From the waist down he was most noticeably naked.

"Come out of that, you damned old rat," yelled Ethan Allen but Feltham, not quite understanding, stood irresolute. Then, according to the Lieutenant's report, the American demanded "immediate possession of the fort and all the effects of George the Third."

At this moment the British commander of Ticonderoga appeared, fully clothed, and inquired in whose name surrender was demanded.

Allen bellowed, according to his own tell, "In the name of the Great Jehovah and the Continental Congress!" Cynics have doubted this, since no eyewitness ever affirmed it. But no one who was present ever denied it. And there are historians who not only believe that he said it but, being an imaginative literary man, had been rehearsing it for hours.

There would be other important events of the Revolution on Lake Champlain. Arnold—before his betrayal—commanded a rickety fleet at Skenesborough (now Whitehall) and, on October 11, 1776, challenged a British fleet, almost as impotent, near Valcour Island in the northern waters of the lake. The Americans were defeated. At the end of the day, of sixteen craft Arnold had left only six.

The parade of General Johnny Burgoyne's army, bound for Saratoga and ignominious defeat, on October 17, 1777, in a battle that has been called the turning point of the war, was picturesque beyond anything the area had ever seen. Barges carrying shining English and Hessian cannon and transports loaded with supplies splashed down the center of the lake. On the west shore marched the red-coated regiments of the British Advanced Corps; down the east trudged the hireling Germans—sweating in the Indian-summer weather under their long coats, their heavy queues of powder-whitened hair, their towering feathered hats made weightier by brass insignia.

The last of the spectacular battles on the lake began in a flurry of sail and a crashing of cannon on September 11, 1814. Thomas Macdonough, young American commandant of a fleet that had been built hastily at Vergennes in Vermont, set out to smash the superior British fleet that awaited him. In the hours that followed, the Americans destroyed the threat of British dominance of the Champlain region. Their deadly marksmanship at close range overcame the enemy's longer-range cannon and frighteningly large frigate, the *Confiance*. As the sea battle progressed, invading ground forces had compelled the defenders of Plattsburg under General Macomb to fall back through the town, but the silence from the lake gave news of Macdonough's success, and the resistance of Macomb's troops caused the British to retreat.

At the beginning of the naval battle one of the first shots from the enemy brig *Linnet* struck the American flagship *Saratoga,* smashing a crate from which a gamecock, suddenly freed, flew to the rails and uttered a defiant crow. Regarding him as an omen of victory, Macdonough's men gave him spirited support. For months after that significant victory the brave rooster was so popular a symbol throughout the country that he even threatened the pre-eminence of the American eagle, and citizens sang a topical minstrel song which told the progress of the battle in an infinite number of stanzas. Here are two samples:

> On Lake Champlain Uncle Sam set his boats,
> With Captain Macdonough to sail 'em,
> And General Macomb, he made Plattsburg his home,
> With the army whose courage never fails 'em.

> Now General Macomb, he was setting there at home
> And he looked out through the winder...
> He see Governor Prevost's Britishers a-comin'
> And it made him as mad as tinder...

The Battle of Plattsburg ended international warfare in the lake country as suddenly as Champlain's arquebus had started it. After more than two centuries of bloody, selfish battling, the lake again became a peaceful and lovely body of water over which vessels hauled their cargoes. The citizens of the Eastern states sought its curving shores for rest and recreation. Steam packets bore thousands of passengers to its quiet woods, its rocky shores, its picturesque islands. Competition grew as bitter and violent as that prevailing on the packet-ridden Hudson. The *Vermont,* built at Burlington, was on regular schedule less than a year after Fulton's *Clermont* had made its first famous voyage. And the lake produced its share of the elegant and luxurious "floating palaces" that European visitors praised and envied. Richard ("Dandy Dick") Sherman, after supervising its building, became captain of the *Burlington,* a craft so superlative that even Charles Dickens, far from enthusiastic about *anything* American, waxed lyric over it, and President Van Buren, ever the politician, won popular acclaim by "taking down" her stuck-up commanding officer with the dry judgment, "He thinks the world is a steamboat and he the captain."

It is an easy jump in history from the nineteenth century to the present on the waters and along the shores of Lake Champlain. From the time Samuel de Champlain named the lake, the east and the west shores have developed in different directions. No other border between states in this nation separates such differing populations. The Yankees of the Vermont shore are a quite different breed from the Yorkers across the narrow lake. Place a blindfolded visitor without warning in the midst of Burlington, Vermont, and he can tell you simply by listening that he is not in Plattsburg, New York. The short vowels of New England talk will inform him at once. So will the understatement and the shortness of sentences. In Plattsburg vowels are more generous, r's more pronounced, conversation more Western in its general atmosphere.

It hardly seems possible that Vermonters, because they are a few miles nearer the Atlantic, are therefore more concerned with life on the water. Nevertheless, the lake serves as an ocean for them and seamanship seems to be inherited. In a small community on the Vermont shore the town's fattest man died and his funeral was set for the succeeding day. Then it was discovered that no available coffin would contain him. The town fathers met over this crisis and one of them suggested that a carpenter down the lake road a piece could make a satisfactory container overnight.

"Just give him three dollars and a quart of whisky," he said, "and the funeral services can be held tomorrow as planned." The next day a committee waited upon their obliging neighbor. "There she is," said the carpenter, patting his handiwork, "but somehow or other I got a centerboard in her."

Yorkers have teased Vermonters for generations by claiming that the state has more cow residents than people. ("We like 'em better," has been the standard Yankee retort.) The statement used to be true and the percentage of cattle in relation to humans is still very high. The green of the meadow pastures along the lake front is still spattered with cows—mostly black-and-white Holsteins which give more milk, though it contains less butterfat than the milk of Guernseys and Jerseys. Some farmers keep a Jersey or two for luxurious family use and sell the thinner Holstein milk in York State where, say the Yankee dairymen, "they won't know the difference."

The French-Canadians who live by Champlain's northernmost water provide strong contrast with Yorkers and Yankees. The cold weather of their home country has not cooled their Gallic blood. There is Latin intensity in them and neither breed of their fellow lake-shore dwellers would embarrass themselves by expressing their emotions so strongly. I found this out when, returning from Montreal to Plattsburg, I told a French-speaking officer of the Canadian customs that I had bought a tweed jacket in Montreal and left it there to be altered. This so shocked his thrifty soul that he berated me hotly for not wearing my purchase across the border, to save paying duty, and having the alterations attended to in my native New York State.

Most trotting-horse records are now held by standard-bred racers of breeds other than Morgan, but it is impossible to convince a Vermonter that this is a situation that won't change tomorrow. In 1795 Justin Morgan, a Massachusetts singing teacher, received a small two-year-old colt in payment for a debt, and took him to Vermont. There the man died, but the colt, named for him, started a royal dynasty that will never die. The typical Morgan, pound for pound, has more pull in him than any other horse. He is small but intelligent, healthy, fast and gentle. Few Vermonter owners of trotting horses would care to own a string that did not include at least one Morgan.

There are many tales of Morgan strength. One tells of a Champlain country farmer who wagered with a neighbor that his team could start and pull a load of logs of great weight for twenty yards on the frozen surface of the lake. On the day of the test the Morgans failed on the first try. Their owner looked over the horses, harness and load, then said sharply to the man who had wagered against him, "Take them mittens o' yourn off that top log." The order was obeyed and the team started off with the logs at once.

Both the York State towns on the west shore and the Vermont lake towns are proud of their past and have constantly given evidence of this. Since most of the battles of the region—from Champlain's day on —have been fought on the York State side, it is natural that those who would memorialize them have done so where they occurred. Most important of the west-shore activities has been the restoration of Fort Ticonderoga, the site of which was leased in 1816 by William Ferris Pell and later bought by him from Columbia and Union Colleges. Ever since then the Pell family has made a continuous effort to restore the fort and improve the museum that has been established there. Now it is considered by most experts to have the most important of all displays in America of Revolutionary guns, uniforms and equipment. More poetic, and poignant, is the walled enclosure behind the home of John Pell, which in summer presents in pastel profusion a replica of the garden planted in the mid-eighteenth century by the French officers of Fort Carillon.

At Shelburne, a few miles south of Burlington, Mrs. J. Watson Webb has restored a typical old Vermont village and has placed on exhibition several important collections of antique objects. Marked by imagination and utter sincerity, this is a contribution to Americana that enchants every visitor. It is based not on newly acquired interests but on a lifetime of activity as a collector of carriages, hats, dolls and other treasures of early America. Few restorations and museums so effectively emphasize the continuance of our national life.

In her lake-shore home nearby, dynamic, witty, white-haired Electra Webb is always dreaming up new educational enterprises. A few years ago, encouraged by the enthusiasm of Burlington's Ralph Hill, Jr., author of many a book on Vermont, she acquired the last of Champlain's passenger packets, the *Ticonderoga,* built a lock from which it was lowered to flatcars, and launched it on an overland rail voyage of more than two miles. Moored on solid ground at the edge of her restoration, it now serves as a steamboat museum.

Perhaps the best-defined differences between the two sides of Lake Champlain lie within the fields of human communication. Burlington, called the "Queen City" by Vermonters, has a truly royal air. It is dignified by aristocratic old houses, wide, tree-shaded streets, a magnificent Unitarian Church—which unites the talents of Bullfinch in its architecture and Paul Revere in its bell—and it gives an impression of security and polite aloofness.

The University of Vermont looks out across Champlain's waters from the top of a hill, and yet I have never heard anyone call Burlington a "college town." The city minds its own business calmly and with a set of unwritten rules made rigid over centuries of use. The college fulfills its ambitions surely and without the irrelevant frills and the unnecessary fuss that tend to characterize state universities in the Midwest where the institutions have swallowed the towns.

Both Burlington and the university seem to ignore the manufacturing town of Winooski.

Across the lake in New York State's Plattsburg, there are also rambling old houses that satisfy the heart with the sense of having been lived in with affection, but the town seems to feel its college more. It joins gratefully in the intellectual activities provided by an alert faculty and eager students at the Plattsburg State Teachers College. Meetings of Plattsburg's men's clubs are less inhibited than those in Burlington.

"We're not strong on 'bonhomie,'" said a merchant of the Vermont city. "I think we have a good time but it's a quieter enjoyment of our association with each other." The "old families" of Burlington are reserved and are not likely to welcome newcomers until they have survived a long period of cool examination. Plattsburg "society" for the most part is hearty and trusting. Its families still share a sense of pioneering in a border city.

Cities, however, are not the major influences on living in the Champlain area. The lake and its long stretches of lonely shore are what matter. There is a stillness about this land-encircled water where summer noons are hot in sunlight and summer evenings cold beneath the moon. The feel of the Champlain country was described long ago by its favorite author, Rowland Robinson, whose untutored but poetic hunter, Sam Lovel, said:

"It comes natural for me to run in the woods. If I do get more game to show for it than some does I get something besides that I can't show ... I get lots of things a-hunting that I can't tell you about and a fellow that don't, don't get the best of hunting according to my idea!"

The Climber

Out of a world whose beauty is desire
A twisting flux where nothing is complete
And life's one hope is hope's eternal fire
He strives with aching arms and weary feet.
Undaunted by the dizzy height before him,
Leaving behind him all his sires called light,
And heedless of the jeering age that bore him
Alone he climbs into the starless night

Almost a song whose echoes never ended
Almost a poem telling all he meant
Almost a poem ultimate and splendid
Almost a love whose first dream never went

Upward he yearns, heartsick and vision blurred,
To read in that black sky one finite word.

❧ The Years of Grace

The Sexton Magnificent

Among those stone memorials to good and faithful servants of Grace Church which are set in Gothic architectural panels along the north wall, there is one tablet made of brass. It reads:

> To the memory of Isaac Hull Brown. Born Dec. 4, 1812. Died Aug. 21, 1880. For thirty-five years the faithful Sexton of Grace Church. This tablet is erected by members of the Congregation who gladly recall his Fidelity, his Generosity, and his Stainless Integrity.

To the stranger unfamiliar with the history of the church this legend might seem a touching commemoration of the usually unrecognized duties of an obscure servant, a faithful performer of menial churchly duties. Actually few, if any, members of Grace Church were as well known throughout Manhattan as this remarkable character. Brown the illustrious, Brown the incredible, is still an important figure to the social history of New York.

Though he had been in the employ of the vestry as sexton since 1845, it was not until the new church gave him a fitting grandeur of background that Isaac Brown attracted general attention. Then the usual congregation and the visitors alike were amazed by the appearance and manner of the sexton-usher. Brown was six feet tall and straight as a ramrod. His walk down the aisle, swinging before him one of the most reputable paunches of the well-fed populace, had an élan and a swagger that could be described only as the very essence of the "grand manner." The effect was heightened by his swallow-tailed coat, the blinding whiteness of his tentlike linen shirt above his low-cut waistcoat, the black contrast of the bow tie that circled his collar. His manner was at the same time so proud and so courteous that, as Nathanial Parker Willis (editor of the *Home Journal,* now the *Ladies Home Journal*) once remarked, it "would well become the nobleman who is Gold Stick in Waiting at the Court of Her Majesty."

Though Brown was not included in New York society, he was very proud that "his" church contained so many of its members. He had no fear of rector or vestry or the leaders of the *bon ton* and there were times when he took emphatic issue with them. He was not unaware, moreover, of the commercial advantages of his position and he was able to win monetary profits from them. He was the city's most prominent undertaker and his knowledge of proper ritual at funerals made him much in demand. He was also intimately conversant with the formal practices of parties and weddings among New York's "first families," and few housewives in this group ever thought of entertaining at receptions, large dinners, or cotillions without obtaining the services of the "glorious Brown." His knowledge of town gossip was prodigious, and he was an authority on who should be omitted from invitation lists and who should be added to them. His presence, whistle in hand, at a social function was a guarantee that all events of the evening would be run on time and with authority.

Since Brown was not one of the social group which he nevertheless controlled, he was the butt of many good-natured jibes on the part of those who looked upon themselves as his social superiors.

> *Where Brown is found,*
> *To Fashion's eye is hallowed ground*

went a popular passage of *vers de societé.*

When a section of the flooring gave way at the ball for the Prince of Wales given in October of 1860 at the Academy of Music, George Templeton Strong reported to his diary "A score of carpenters and policemen and the illustrious Brown were energetically repairing the damage within fifteen minutes after the accident," and added with grim irony, "Brown peering down into the oblong hole looked as if engaged in his sextonical duties at an interment."

Another parishioner reported that on a certain Sunday a quartette of distinguished singers employed by the church were rendering a familiar hymn for the delectation of the congregation when a visitor who knew the hymn and thought all were to join in sang out loudly. At once Brown moved up the aisle, nudged the stranger, and announced, "We hire the choir to do the singing in this church."

As was befitting "the most famous man connected with New York high life," Brown had a wit of his own and could easily compete with those who offended him. Once when a rude *nouveau riche* young man scolded him for not having his carriage at the entrance of Grace Church after a society wedding, Brown waited until the young man was seated, slammed the door, and then said to the coachman in a voice that was heard by many of New York's elite, "Drive the gentleman to Pat Hern's," naming a notorious gambling house.

One of Brown's most repeated remarks he made in sorrowful tones a few days before Ash Wednesday: "The Lenten season is a horridly dull season but we manage to make our funerals as entertaining as possible."

The sexton *extraordinaire* died during the rectorate of Bishop H. C. Potter, who used to report many of his astonishing remarks. The last of these Brown made shortly before his death, when the residences of society were continuing their northward march up Manhattan Island. "I cannot undertake," he said firmly, "to control Society above Fiftieth Street."

"A Love of a Man"

In William Rhinelander Stewart's comprehensive *Grace Church and Old New York,* published in 1924, the author expresses his regret that the parish records of the thirty-three-year rectorate of Thomas House Taylor "are so meager that little of interest has been gleaned from them." In the last thirty years, however, historians have come upon documents relating incidents in the life of Rector Taylor so significant as to allow some deductions as to that gentleman's active and at times peppery career.

One of these, which delighted the soul of the temperamental and indefatigable diarist George Templeton Strong, was regarded worthy of inclusion in his daily journal in early 1859, when the rector was sixty years old:

"The Rev. T. H. Taylor of Grace Church fights a good fight, not only of faith (in the way of his profession) but also pugilistically." The rector had received, Strong goes on to say, a lawyer's communication asking him to settle a note which he had endorsed. Dr. Taylor forthwith called at the attorney's office to pay the amount, but was affronted with a demand that he pay also the costs of the judgment which had been obtained against the maker of the note. This the rector refused to do, and a squabble developed in which, to quote from Strong, "The presbyter forgot the lesson of meekness and lowliness he inculcates on Sundays, like a love of a man, as he is. He let his angry passions rise and called the attorney a pettifogger and a swindler. The attorney replied by an averment that the presbyter lied, whereupon the latter proceeded to a laying on of hands—uncanonical but worthy of the best days of Ecclesiastical Discipline and gave the lawyer an emphatic shaking and cuffing."

The Marriage of Tom Thumb

Most trying to Dr. Taylor of the events during his rectorate was the wedding at Grace Church in February of 1863 of the famous midgets known as Lavinia Warren (her true name was Lavinia Warren Bumpus) and Tom Thumb (christened Charles Sherwood Stratton). These two tiny people had been appearing at P. T. Barnum's Museum in New York with tremendous success. Tom Thumb had won worldwide interest when, during visits to England and France, he had won invitations to appear before Queen Victoria and King Louis Philippe. When these two midgets fell in love and announced that they wished to be married, showman Barnum had at first considered a wedding at the Academy of Music to which he would charge admission. The tiny couple were truly in love, however, and desired that their marriage be celebrated in a solemn, dignified, and impressive manner. Barnum agreed, and the request was made that they be allowed to be wed at the most fashionable of all Manhattan's churches. The storm that rose then within the church membership reached proportions that threatened a split in its ranks. To many of the city's elite the idea of allowing professional "mountebanks" the use of Grace Church was unthinkable.

Thomas House Taylor, however, stood firm for the rights of "little people" to be married where they wished.

The circumstances of this wedding are too numerous and elaborate to be detailed here. Suffice it to say that admission was obtained by invitation only, and the demand was so great that some of the not-invited offered to pay sixty dollars apiece for the precious requests to be present. Though Horatio Potter, Bishop of New York, at first agreed (when asked) to conduct the service and then refused, Rector Taylor never retreated an inch from his stand. Though one vestryman resigned and many influential members of his parish protested violently, he co-operated in every possible way. A platform was built before the chancel in order that the ceremony might be seen, though many of the most distinguished members of New York Society ruined the pillows of the pews by standing on them anyway. Twenty-four-year-old Tom Thumb was less than a yard high and weighed a scant fifty-four pounds at the time of the wedding. Commodore Nutt, his best man (also a midget in the employ of Barnum), weighed about half as much and was a head shorter. The bride was thirty-two inches high and weighed twenty-nine pounds. She was attended by her midget thirteen-year-old sister, then much smaller than herself.

The ceremony was performed by the Reverend Junius M. Willey, the Episcopal rector of St. John's of Bridgeport, Connecticut, Tom Thumb's home town, and Dr. Taylor, standing beside him, uttered the benediction. Among those who rose from their seats at the end of the service that day were Mrs. Cornelius Vanderbilt, Mrs. August Belmont, Mrs. Astor, General Ambrose E. Burnside, and hundreds of other prominent New Yorkers.

Thirty-four years later Bishop Henry Codman Potter, fifth rector of Grace Church and nephew of the bishop who had refused to conduct this marriage, discovered a letter from an outraged parishioner to Rector Taylor and that South Carolinian's spirited reply. Bishop Potter sent the letters, along with his own comment, to his successor, Rector William Reed Huntington.

The three missives tell their own story too well for anyone to alter them, and since they give a further impression of Thomas House Taylor, here they are:

10 Washington Square
October 7, 1896

My dear Dr. Huntington:

One of the privileges of invalidism is to rummage in old drawers;
—and while engaged in this process last evening I turned out the
enclosed which ought to be preserved in the archives of Grace
Church. It was in connection with the marriage of Tom Thumb,
whom Brown (you doubtless recognize his outlines) called a "monstrosity," that Dr. Taylor exploded, "Tut, tut, Mr. Brown, no more
a monstrosity than you are!"

You did not know our predecessor, I think. I wish you had. A
more individual character never lived, and a more delightfully
"spunky" letter than his to—(whoever he may have been—he vanished before my time) one doesn't often read.

Faithfully yours,
H. C. Potter

The Revd. Dr. Taylor.
Sir

The object of my unwilling addressing you this note is to inquire
what right you had to exclude myself and other owners of pews in
Grace Church from entering it yesterday, enforced too by a cordon
of police for that purpose. If my pew is not my property I wish to
know it, and if it is I deny your right to prevent me from occupying
it whenever the Church is open even at a marriage of mountebanks,
which I would not take the trouble to cross the street to witness.

Respectfully
Clarendon Hotel   Your obdt. servt.
Feb. 11, 1863   William Stewart

804 Broadway, New York
February 16, 1863

Mr. William Stewart
Dear Sir,

I am sorry my valued friend that you should have written me the
peppery letter that is now before me. If the matter of which you complain be so utterly insignificant and contemptible as "a marriage of
mountebanks which you would not take the trouble to cross the
street to witness" it surprises me that you should have made such
strenuous, but ill directed efforts to secure a ticket of admission: and

why, permit me to ask in the name of reason and philosophy, do you still suffer it to disturb you so sadly?

It would perhaps be a sufficient answer to your letter, to say that your cause of complaint exists only in your imagination!

You have never been excluded from your pew!—As Rector, I am the custodian of the Church, and you will hardly venture to say that you have ever applied to me, for permission to enter, and been refused!—

Here I might safely rest, and leave you to the comfort of your own reflections in the case. But, as you in common with many other worthy persons, would seem to have very crude notions, as to your rights of *property* in Pews,—you will pardon me for saying that a Pew in a Church is property only in a peculiar and restricted sense. It is not property as your house or your horse is property. It invests you with no fee in the soil, you cannot use it in any way, and in every way, and at all times, as your pleasure or caprice may dictate. You cannot put it to any common or unhallowed uses: you cannot move it, nor injure it, nor destroy it. In short you hold by purchase, and may *sell* the *right* to the undisturbed possession of that little space within the Church Edifice you call your *Pew,* during the hours of Divine Service! But even that right must be exercised decorously, and with a decent regard for time and place, or else you may at any moment be ignominiously ejected from it. I regret to be obliged to add, that by the *law of custom,* you may during those said hours of Divine Service (but at no other time) *sleep in your pew.* You must however do so noiselessly and never to the disturbance of your sleeping neighbors! Your property in your Pew, has this extent and nothing more.

Now if Mr. William Stewart were at any time to come to me and say "Sir, I would that you should grant me the use of Grace Church for a solemn service (a Marriage a Baptism or a Funeral as the case may be) and it is desirable that the feeling of the parties should be protected as far as possible from the impertinent intrusion and disturbance of a crowd from the streets and lanes of the city, I beg that no one may be admitted within the doors of the Church, during the very few moments that we expect to be there, but our invited friends only!"—It would certainly in such a case, be my pleasure to comply with your request and to meet your wishes in every particular; and I think that even "Mr. William Stewart" would agree that all this would be entirely reasonable and proper:—

Then, tell me, how would such a case differ from the instance of which you complain? Two young persons, whose only crime would seem to be, that they are neither so big, nor so stupid, nor so illmannered, nor so inordinately selfish, as some other people, come to me and say,—

"Sir, we are about to be married, and we wish to throw around our marriage all the solemnities of Religion; we are strangers in your city, and as there is no clergyman here, standing in a Pastoral relation to us, we have ventured to ask the favor of the Bishop of New York to marry us, and he has kindly consented to do so, may we then venture a little further and request the use of your Church, in which the Bishop may perform the marriage Service? We assure you, Sir, that we are no shams, no cheats, no mountebanks, we are neither monsters nor abortions.—It is true we are *little,* but we are as God made us,—perfect in our littleness! sir we are simply *man* and *woman* of like passions and infirmities, with you and other mortals: the arrangements for our marriage are controlled by no "Showman," and we are sincerely desirous that everything should be ordered with a most scrupulous regard to decorum.—We hope to invite our relations and intimate friends together with such other persons, as may in other years have extended civilities to either of us, but we pledge ourselves to you most sacredly that no invitation may be bought with money! Permit us to further say, that as we would most gladly escape from the insulting jeers, and the ribald sneers and coarse ridicule of the unthinking multitude without, we pray you allow us at our own proper charges, so to guard the avenues of access from the street as to prevent all unseemly tumult and disorder."

I tell you sir that whenever and from whomever such an appeal is made to my Christian courtesy although it should come from the very humblest of the earth I would go calmly and cheerfully forward to meet their wishes although as many William Stewarts as would reach from here to Kamchatka clothed in fuss and frowns should rise up to oppose me.

In conclusion I will say that if the marriage of Charles S. Stratton and Lavinia Warren is to be regarded only as a pageant, then it was the most beautiful pageant it has ever been my privilege to witness —If on the contrary it is rather to be thought of as a *Solemn Ceremony,* then it was as touchingly solemn as a Wedding can possibly be rendered. It is true that the Bishop was not present but Mr. Stratton's own Pastor, the Revd. Mr. Willey of Bridgeport, Conn., read the service with admirable taste and impressiveness: and the bride was given away by her mother's Pastor and her own "next friend" a venerable Congregational Clergyman from New Hampshire.

Surely there never was a gathering of so many hundreds of our best people when everybody appeared so delighted with everything— Surely it is no light thing to call forth so much innocent joy in so few moments of passing time. Surely it is no light thing then to smooth the roughness and sweeten the acerbities which mar our happiness as we advance upon the uneven journey of life. Sir, it is most emphatically a high triumph of "Christian civilisation."

> Respectfully submitted by
> Your obd. servt.
> Thomas House Taylor
> Rector of Grace Church

Most engaging of all the anecdotes of Rector Taylor comes in a report (transmitted by Lydia M. Child) of his last moments when he lay dying in his Hudson River home at West Park.

"You will soon be with the angels," said his nurse.

"What do I care about angels?" said Thomas House Taylor as impulsively as ever. "I want to be with folks."

❦ The Mad Poet of Broadway

A poet comfortably crazy
   As pliant as a weeping willow
Loves most everybody's girls, ain't lazy
   Can write a hundred lines an hour
With rackety-whackety railroad power

In the twilight of an autumn day in 1819, seventeen-year-old Mary Brundage kissed her stern, rather masculine mother and set out along Broadway for the old Park Theater at the corner of Fulton and Nassau Streets. Big-lettered playbills along her path announced her debut that evening as Ophelia in a revival of *Hamlet*.

When the girl was passing St. Paul's, the tall young poet, Mac-Donald Clarke, stepped out of the shadows and took her in his arms. For a moment of excited whispering they stood there, the pretty girl enveloped in the poet's bright blue cloak, her head resting on the red silk neckerchief carelessly spread under the fold of his Byronic collar. Then, glancing guiltily about, they hurried off in a direction that would not take them to the Park Theater.

At curtain time the manager of the playhouse and the mother of missing Ophelia tried hard to fight off a growing suspicion. When apologies for postponement of the performance had been made to the grumbling audience and ticket money had been refunded, suspicion had given place to certainty. Since August, Mrs. Brundage had angrily protested her daughter's liking for the twenty-one-year-old rhymer. But in Mary's fancy all well-meant advice was outweighed by Mac-Donald Clarke's reflections on the death of his mother at sea while he was a little boy in Connecticut, his intimations that his life had been blighted by the death of an innocent young girl whose trust he had betrayed while he was visiting on the tropic isle of Jamaica, his story of poverty so great that during his summer's stay in Philadelphia he had slept nightly on the cold stone that lay above the remains of Benjamin Franklin.

It was midnight before manager and mother found the elopers and routed them from their marriage bed. The outraged Mrs. Brundage made the girl dress and go home; the businessman, no less concerned over his loss of profits, waited only until the blue cloak and red kerchief were in place to give the frail poet a thorough beating.

Before a week had passed Mary escaped to her penniless poet. They slept in the shelter of a widespread tree when skies were clear, under the roof of a market when storms threatened. Then, on a cold night of torrential rains they could find no dry spot and in despair went to the Brundage house. They knocked long and loud at the door, but the unforgiving lady behind it had guessed who they were and would not answer.

Mary remembered that it was possible to climb from a corner rain barrel to the roof and thence to the window of her former room. She and her husband were hopefully reaching for the eaves when, with an explosive crack, the board they had placed across the top of the barrel gave way, dropping them into the black pool below. At that instant Mother Brundage darted out of the house, seized her daughter by the hair, and ducked her again and again in the icy water. Then, screaming with rage, she hustled the girl inside and locked the door against her son-in-law who was still standing in the rain barrel.

The mother won after that. A divorce was arranged and Mary Brundage resumed her stage career. She was bitterly denounced by the sentimental Bohemians of lower Broadway, but her husband defended her:

"... in the generous hour of maiden imprudence and spirited tenderness," he wrote, "she defied the unjust frown of deluded society and dared to mingle the moonlight of her own destiny with the midnight of mine ... When the name that harmed her is blotted from the ledger of life and the heart that loved her is stiff and silent in its last friendly resting place, prejudice will drop a tear on the dark weeds that cover it and restore her to pardon and peace."

This romantic tragicomedy could not have served better to introduce MacDonald Clarke to the world of Broadway. He became "The Mad Poet," a lion of the pavement by day, of the literary taverns after dark. On the long bench at The Old Shakespeare, Windust's famous rendezvous for the artistic world, he had his accustomed place and there Manhattan's writers and actors roared him welcome. New York's most distinguished poet, Fitz-Greene Halleck, lent him money and introduced him to Washington Irving and James Fenimore Cooper. These gentlemen delighted in his posturing, were surprised by his talent, amused by his facile diatribes when liquor had warmed his eccentric brain.

Each morning he strode along Broadway between Canal and Fulton Streets, stopping always to gaze sadly through the palings that surround St. Paul's churchyard. Each Sunday his noble posturings waked whispers in the pews of aristocratic Grace Church. The whispering spread throughout the town when he let it be known that for three months he had found nightly lodgings in the decorative interior of a hearse and that, evicted, his bed was now a grassy spot between two graves in Trinity Churchyard.

Soon he had put behind him the sufferings caused by his marriage and began to celebrate with his pen the life of the street that had championed him. He had appointed himself poet laureate to Broadway.

His verse paid tribute to "Luke, the Broadway Baker"; "The Clam Cart"; "The Astor House"; "The Rum Hole." Most numerous of the street's inspirations, however, were its pretty girls and he wrote poems to nearly all of them—Margaret, Eliza, Orva, Agnes, Caroline, Ellen, "My Dear Little Pie Girl," and "A Young Female I saw at the Window of Mrs. ——'s Boarding House." Little volumes dripped from his pen and somehow achieved publication. Halleck and the rest of New York's recognized writers, pitying him for the instability of his mind, forgave the printed evidences of it for lines which they admired. The most popular of these,

> Now twilight lets her curtain down
> And pins it with a star.

recently turned up, slightly garbled, as part of a cowboy folk song.

Most of Clarke's readers, however, were attracted to such of his volumes as *The Elixir of Moonshine* and *Afara or the Belles of Broadway,* by their incongruities of expression. They laughed, probably harder than would a contemporary critic, at such lines as:

> I know of nothing better than a dose
> Of naked champagne for a luckless lover
> It makes one's heart lie down so snug and close.

Anecdotes clustered about the Mad Poet.

"It is easy to write like a madman," said a jealous writer.

"Not so easy as to write like a fool," said Clarke.

"Clarke has zigzag brains," said an editor.

"Better zigzag than none," said Clarke.

One morning Fitz-Greene Halleck lent his young friend a two-and-a-half-dollar gold piece that he might eat breakfast and pay a debt. A minute later Halleck saw the money impulsively handed to an organ grinder. Clarke's long legs won the foot race that followed.

Lydia M. Child, whose published letters were an early gossip column, wrote: "Often when he had nothing to give he would snatch up a ragged, shivering child in the street, carry it to the door of some princely mansion and demand to see the lady of the house. When she appeared he would say, 'Madam, God has made you one of the trustees of His wealth. It is His, not yours. Take this poor child, wash it, feed it, clothe it, comfort it in God's name.' "

On December 28, 1823, according to his own telling, MacDonald Clarke was walking down Broadway in the late afternoon when, at the corner of Barclay Street, he saw a girl standing in the window of a pretentious house.

> One of those pale and pretty little girls
> Who looks as if of sifted moonlight made.

He was in love again. Eagerly he asked his friends the name of his new sweetheart. She was Mary, the daughter of the Dutch merchant-millionaire, John G. Coster. In his long rambling poem, *Dutch Dignity,* the Mad Poet eventually told the pathetic story. A dozen nights he waited outside her window until "St. Paul's had spoke the midnight's birth sublime," then wandered over to Daly's for hot whisky punches that made going home a problem. In his visions of her his loved one was haughty and he longed to:

> Plunge amid her weeping dreams
> And drown her reason with love's thinn'd ice creams.

All winter he haunted the corner of Broadway and Barclay Street until the Costers, Astors, Lydigs, and Hosacks must have been sick of the sight of him. Then spring came, and just as he believed the warm sunny days were helping his courting along, he saw a bad omen—a servant fastening a shutter:

> For 'twas a sight that thrilled me through with horror
> The family will rusticate tomorrow.

On the next day his worst fears were realized.

> As I was going down at three o'clock
> I spied her in the carriage by her grandma
> She smiled and looked as if she'd give her frock
> To be with me alone upon a sand-bar.

The Costers were going to their country home on Kip's Bay (34th Street and the East River) for the summer. Despairing, Clarke went to his grandfather's very handsome and respectable home in Canterbury, Connecticut, to moon the summer through.

Broadway reclaimed her Mad Poet in mid-October. The Costers had not yet returned, "But hi-de-hi upon the twenty-three I saw the carriage." In a frenzy of delight he rushed to his new room on Barclay Street which he had taken so that he might be near her.

Young daughters of the very rich were then more carefully guarded than they are today, and the poor poet found no chance to tell Mary Coster of his love. Two years went by and he had not spoken to her. The story of his infatuation became a jest about the town. Little boys told him they bore him sweet messages from Mary and he believed them because he wanted to believe. Older and crueler jokers said she longed for him but was zealously guarded by her father. Her brothers took to speaking to him with exaggerated courtesy when they met him on Broadway.

Then on a mid-June afternoon in 1826, he borrowed gloves and stick from men who pretended to be his friends. They accompanied him to the Coster house and urged him to present himself as a suitor for Mary's hand. A tall footman answered his knock. Clarke asked to see Mr. Coster, and that gentleman came to the door in a towering rage:

> With eyes as red as a first-rate segar
> And face 'twould puzzle God Himself to tame.

The shock of being kicked downstairs was almost more than the Mad Poet could bear. For an hour afterwards he leaned upon a nearby railing, summoning strength of mind and body. Finally he went back to his room to write in verse the story of his humiliation. When he fell asleep he dreamed of old Coster cringing before a jury of love-crazed poets who sentenced him to a never-sleeping hankering for the girls.

Clarke did not recover from this experience as easily as he had from his divorce. Years went by and he still talked of Mary Coster. Some evenings when his fellow writers bought him drinks he made wild speeches in the taverns against the rich Dutchman.

> And did he think I valued his high rank
> Among the gilded drudges of a street
> Where his three millions and a certain bank
> Buy him a bow from all he there may meet.

Each season found his mind more eccentric, his body weaker. Though he was desperately poor he kept his gorgeous trappings. The blue cloak still fluttered in the wind and the red pennon of his courage was still about his throat.

On Christmas Eve 1841, the editor of the *New York Aurora* met him in a public house eating apples and milk.

"You think I am MacDonald Clarke," he said, "but I am not. The Mad Poet dashed out his brains last Thursday night at the foot of Emmet's monument. The storm that night was the tears Heaven wept over him. God animated the body again. I am not now MacDonald Clarke but Afara, an archangel of the Almighty."

About the first of March 1842, a night watchman making his rounds found Clarke on one knee before a poor beggar. He had given the beggar all his money and was writing down in his notebook the poor fellow's story. His tall cloth cap lay beside him in a drift of snow, and his sandy curls hung down over his eyes. The watchman found the poet's talk so incoherent that he took him to the Tombs. In the morning he was ferried to the insane asylum on Blackwell's Island. He died a few days later. An unauthenticated story went the rounds of the city that either on purpose or by accident he had turned on the water faucet beside his cot and thus flooded his cell and drowned himself. Officials said he died of brain fever.

Fitz-Greene Halleck and other friends, many children among them, attended the funeral at Grace Church. A few followed the hearse that took the body of MacDonald Clarke to Green-wood Cemetery in Brooklyn. When alive he had carved three words, "The Poet's Grave," on a wooden plaque and had hung it above the spot where he wished to be buried. Perhaps that is why even now the grassy slope where he lies is called "The Poet's Mound." His monument, standing beside the little lake called Sylvan Water, is of white marble—a square block supporting a truncated column. On one side in high relief is the profile of the Mad Poet. On another are the words he wrote on the death of a poet friend:

> But what are human plaudits now?
> He never deemed them worth his care;
> Yet Death has twined around his brow,
> The wreath he was too proud to wear.

A third surface tells how the monument happens to be there. Perhaps Halleck wrote the lines:

> By friendship's willing hands erected
> By genius taste and art adorned
> For one too long in life neglected
> But now in Death sincerely mourned.

On the remaining side is the epitaph Clarke wrote for himself:

> Sacred to the memory of poor MacDonald Clarke.
> Let silence gaze—but curse not his grave.

The word "silence" is no longer legible.

🐝 Green-Gown

> Under a mushroom's wide umbrella
> Snug
> Glib
> In a world of rain

Squats a knobby green-gowned fellow
Tells
Tales
Again, again.
His roof is pleated and rose madder
Drip
Drop
In a world of rain;
No other shade could make him madder
"No madder!" he shouts
And the echoing ceiling
Answers unfeeling
"No matter."

The new fawn listens, stops his stumbling
Clip
Clop
In a world of rain,
Waits for him to stop his grumbling,
Start a tale again.

The fawn hears tell of a pony talking
Chit
Chat
In a world of rain
While the wild shrimp frisk
In a peppery bisque
And a ladder's walking
To the noonday train.

Tell of a fire engine, nose a-running,
Sniff
Sniff
In a world of rain,
Of a black bat lying on the sand a-sunning
An old-gold river tug foaming at the mouth
And a snowplow wintering in a red-clay south.

Tell of a crow that barks like a beagle
Bow
Wow
In a world of rain,
Of a bull-calf soaring like a blooming eagle
A white white-elephant putting out to sea
A brown trout climbing on a tulip tree.

Now from the madder roof of the mushroom
Swells the
Fellow's
Green-gold voice,
Like a bellowing in a washroom
Like a bell-ring in a classroom
Ding
Dong
For girls and boys.
Green-gown sings of children stepping
Down the hours long gone before
Left
Right
Their feet are tapping
Over the rain-wet forest floor.

Under a mushroom's wide umbrella
Snug
Glib
In a world of rain,
Squats a knobby green-gowned fellow
Tells
Tales
Again—again!

❦   The Family Mountains ·

In the northeast corner of New York State, bounded, roughly speaking, by the St. Lawrence on the west and the line of Lake Champlain and Lake George on the east, lie the "up-histed" counties. There rise the steep and green-clad sides of the Adirondack Mountains, formed ages ago by the upfolding of molten rocks through the sediments that had once lain at the bottom of a great body of water —the Grenville Sea.

Go north from the valley of the Mohawk and you will see the foot-hills rising and come upon the first of the clear-water lakes that dot this region of hemlock, spruce and balsam. You will come upon loneliness, too, for people are scarce in this land of silent forests, high rocks and deep and dark ravines. The solitary log cabin in the woods is still far from a memory here. For many generations now in the summer months Americans have sought relief from the pressures of their busy lives in the clear, cool solitudes of these wooded slopes and gem-set pools.

The Adirondacks were named for the tribe of Indians which once inhabited them. They are not very high mountains but they are sightly with a beauty that many writers have tried to describe, though few have succeeded. Forty-six of the hundreds of summits rise above the four-thousand-foot level. Highest of all is Mount Marcy, its rocky summit, eight hundred feet above the tree line, stands 5,344 feet above sea level. Nestled on its side lies Lake Tear of the Clouds, highest source-water of the great Hudson River. Professor Ebenezer Emmons and his party were first to reach the top of Marcy in 1837.

Everyone who knows and loves the Adirondacks has his favorite way of entering among them. One of the happiest, and certainly the newest, is by airplane. I have flown over the mountains on sunny days and seen the sun bring the little lakes out of shadow far down among the passes. I have seen white cumulus clouds obscure the rocky peaks, then blow away, leaving them pitilessly bare in clean, bright light.

Of the land entries it is hard indeed to choose between the virtues of Keene Valley and the banks of the Black River. Each Adirondack neck-of-the-woods has its own special scenic treasures, its unique traditions.

No one who has driven west from Elizabethtown and the shores of Bouquet River may forget the levels of Keene Valley with the mountains looming above them. Natives and summer residents love this region with a passion approaching fanaticism. Give them less than half a chance and they will tell you the story of pioneer Anson Allen's fight with the bear and recite every stanza of the ballad commemorating the event—with special emphasis on the immortal lines:

> Against the rock with giant strength
> He held her off at his arm's length,
> "Oh God," he cried in deep despair,
> "If you don't help me, don't help the bear."

Summers in this valley are filled with flower-strewn meadows, the sound of rippling water and the sight of friendly mountains—Skylight and Haystack, Table Top, Big Slide and Giant.

An equal number of devotees firmly state that the Adirondacks must be approached from the west. The only way to "go in," they say, is from Forrestport on the Black River or McKeever. Here you may follow old lumber trails in along the banks of West Canada Creek, Moose River or the Black toward peaks that rise above the green into the blue —Tarnesda and Kismet and Snowy and Big Panther. This is lumberjack country—full of songs and tales of timber. If you have friends who live in the tight little houses and cabins, you can hear the fiddles tuning some bright sharp night, hear heels thump the floor, hear raucous voices lifted in the ballads of the "up-histed" lands—*Saranac River, Cold River Line* or *Blue Mountain Lake*:

> Come all you good fellows, wherever you be,
> Come set down beside me and listen to me;
> A story I'll tell you, without a mistake,
> Of the rackets we had around Blue Mountain Lake,
> Derry down down down derry down.

There was the Sullivan Brothers and big Jimmy Lu,
Little Mose Gilbert and Dandy Pat, too,
As fine lot of fellows as ever was seen
And they all worked for Griffen in township nineteen
Derry down down down derry down.

In the winter the "road-monkey" and the "whistle-punk" still go busily about their work of getting the tall trees out to the banks of the river that floats them to the sawmills. Tall tales are still told from the deacon's seat in the bunkhouse after voracious appetites have been satisfied. Lumbering is the Adirondack region's oldest business but it is not the only one.

Americans believe in vacations in the open and they try to see to it that as many of their fellow citizens as possible may have them. Vacationing in the Adirondacks runs all the way from the luxuries of fashionable clubs, such as that on the shores of Lake Placid, where skiing in winter and water sports in summer amuse the well-to-do, to the simplicities of hiking mountain roads and putting up for the night on State lands where lean-tos and grills bid the modest wanderer welcome. All summer long the lakes and woods of the region give the solace which only nature can give to her eager disciples. Every vacationist has his favorite spot and time of year. My own is a log house looking far down on the gleam of Thirteenth Lake. Set me on its porch early on a July morning when the mists that lie close above the surface are breaking—and you will find me a happy man.

Less widely known are the enterprises involving the natural resources of the Adirondacks. A few years ago the iron mines at the foot of Mount Marcy lay in idle disrepair. The demands of war industry brought them again into humming activity. Near Thirteenth Lake is one of the most fascinating of the mountain treasures—a garnet mine.

A friend once said to me that it is impossible to love the Alps, the Rockies, the Andes. They are too massive, he said, to inspire affection. The Adirondacks are lovable mountains. They are remembered for clear, bright waters and shadowed, cool woods. They are not majestic —they are family mountains—green slopes that rise not too far above the curling smoke from the chimneys of home.

❦ Author's Note

Not all of man's wisdom has come from the great. The people in the slow passing of the generations have also learned to express truths—truths proved by their own experience. Using their simple vernacular they create sayings that have been sifted and polished by thousands of retellings until they have reached the ultimate in succinct meaning. From the simplicity and brevity of a proverb, which has been affirmed by a community-as-a-whole on its journey through time, comes beauty that is not often rivaled by individual literary craftsmen.

❦ When a Bronx Cheer Was a Gardaloo

A Review of *Grandfather Stories*
by Samuel Hopkins Adams

Mr. Adams has built for his readers a bridge between the American past and the American present. His grandfather's memories make vivid the early nineteenth century days of the Republic, and his own the decades of the Seventies and Eighties.

The character of Grandfather Myron Adams is so subtly and surely drawn that there are few word-portraits for comparison. It suggests a combination of the virtues of Clarence Day's *Life With Father* with

those of Edward Westcott's *David Harum,* and it adds to these a practical use of period vocabulary which is constantly fascinating.

It is particularly in his affectionate enlistment of old words that
Mr. Adams excels. He must have a prodigious memory and a comprehensive knowledge of archaic uses. He has, moreover, the ability
to bring obsolete words back to us with all their old life and vigor.
His command of nouns of vituperation alone would inspire the envy
of a top sergeant. When Grandfather Adams and his companions utter
such picturesque phrasings as "crawfish-catching, turtle-chasing mud-
chunker," "gyppos, pikies and swing-kettles," "inglers, make-bates,
daw-pluckers, and bunghole sippers," "higglers, federal muckworms,
scrim-shankers, and jimber-jawed politicasters," "blanketeers and
hedgerow campers," the reader can only mourn the impoverishment
of contemporary name calling.

Mr. Adams frequently offers also little-known but very revealing
bits of American social history. He pours them so lavishly into his
paragraphs that a reader following the main thread of the narrative
might easily disregard them or assume that they are fictional. If he
does not do so, he will learn that in the old days an antialcohol organization was called a Sober Society, a cemetery was sometimes designated as "a sorrow of stones," a love letter as a "cupidity," that the
time of day was often documented by reference to the steeple from
which it was read—as "Baptist Time" or "Methodist Time."

Forgotten proverbs lace this text with folk wisdom:

"Let young Loosetongue hire a turnip cart and preach the end of
the world from its tail-piece."

"A pig on credit makes a good winter and a long spring."

"Blow high, blow low, hired money passes with the wind."

Many rich expressions once in common use are also here rehabilitated. A wind is "fit to blow a bespoken boot off a wooden leg"; a ball
player "couldn't hit a rotten punkin with the thill of a four-horse bob";
and an ignoramus "don't know enough to stamp dirt in a rathole."
Grandfather Adams himself contributes to our knowledge of folk expression with forceful comment: "I was not born in the woods to be
scared by an owl" and "I was plugging breach [in the canal] when
you were mumbling pipsissiway suckets in your cradle."

Each of these twenty-three tales is complete in itself, and the book covers a wide spread of significant revelations of America's past. Beginning with the "pribbles and prabbles" of Rochester in a high society described in "A Third Ward New Year's," Mr. Adams proves the catholicity of his and his grandfather's enthusiasms by excursions into transportation, circuses, literary clubs, chicanery, photography and the early cinema, ghosts, the export of ginseng root, precious and semi-precious stones, medicine (patent and otherwise); such competitive sports as pie-eating, single sculling, baseball; and experience with such national figures as iconoclastic Frances Wright, Harriet Tubman, rescuer of slaves, and the great leaper, Sam Patch.

The result of the easy, natural use of such materials is the literary re-creation of the colorful and active world which was America in the days when the nation was getting under way. Mr. Adams' work goes far beyond the quaint and the picturesque. It conveys an atmosphere and a spirit which contemporaries extol while they mourn its loss. In his last days Grandfather Adams had his own say about the subsidence of the general respect for the dignity and worth of the individual "in this thin-blooded age when loyalty is a dull spark and patriotism the echo of Independence Day rhetoric."

Grandfather Stories is an amusing book but it does not arouse laughter. The humor is in the consistently humorous attitude of mind of the author toward his materials. The collection would seem a hodge-podge were it not for Mr. Adams' calm assumption that he has achieved a kind of unity by taking most of the Americana of our yesterdays for his province. Few recent presentations of the American past—fictional or factual—carry so much detailed background, authentic, feelingful atmosphere and engaging charm. The cord with which the bundle is tied together is a strong one—the eager attention of an expert and versatile raconteur.

✐ The Adventures of Cooper's Famous Scout, Natty Bumppo

A Review of Allan Nevins'
The Leatherstocking Saga

When Allan Nevins, Professor of American History at Columbia University, was a boy in Illinois he and his companions played at being the picturesque heroes whose exploits they had read in those five of James Fenimore Cooper's novels which portrayed the most popular of all American fictional figures, Natty Bumppo, known variously to his companions as Leatherstocking, Deerslayer, Hawkeye, Pathfinder and to "the Frenchers and the redskins on the other side of the Big Lakes" as *la longue Carabine*. Inspired by nostalgic memories, Mr. Nevins has now lined in this one volume, *Leatherstocking Saga,* the portions of these books which have pleased him most, omitting or briefly summarizing passages which do not concern Bumppo and such superfluities as reveal Cooper's affected mannerisms, lush sentimentalities and painfully forced humor.

The books are wisely arranged, moreover, in the chronological sequence of Bumppo's life rather than the order in which they appeared in print. This may be somewhat confusing to the student of the development of Cooper as a writer, since *The Deerslayer,* in which Bumppo is at his youngest (in his early twenties) was published eighteen years after the first of the series, *The Pioneers,* which presented the hero in his seventies. The result of the editing and arrangement, however, is a unified and artistically highlighted portrait of the simple and noble master of forest lore whom readers from nearly all nations of the world have long regarded as the supreme characterization in American literature.

Cooper could well take for granted in 1823 the assumption by his readers that his unlettered sage of the forest was based on an existing American type. He acknowledged his debt to the widely known adventures of Daniel Boone, and near his home in Cooperstown lived old men who resembled the woodland sage he was planning to describe. One named David Shipman and one named Nathaniel Shipman were in no way related to each other, but each in many qualities fitted Cooper's descriptions of his famous hunter, and it may be that he made use of both, though to this day separate factions quarrel over which of them was the "original" of Natty Bumppo.

The character emerging from Cooper's pages as edited by Allan Nevins is an original in another sense, "untutored but noble-minded ... a being of great purity of character but of as marked peculiarities." Most readers of Leatherstocking tales find their first admiration, as did Allan Nevins, for the scout's practical and intimate knowledge of life in the woods. Few can resist the appeal of a man who can "journey by the moss on the beeches" or set a back-fire to save his companions from a flaming death, who knows that "grass is a treacherous carpet ... but wood and stone take no print from a moccasin," or that a good hunter never overloads his gun because "a kicking rifle never carries a true bullet."

Add to the scout's knowledge of the forest utter fearlessness, even when Indians have bound him to the stake for burning, an affection for his deep-voiced hound-dog, Hector, and calm assurance that his gun, Killdeer, "the long-barreled, true-grooved, soft-metaled rifle," is the most dangerous of all weapons, and you have a character that will not fade from the memory of the heart. From these attributes alone grew a popularity which resulted in an endless parade of imitative narratives in which the wise old man-of-the-woods played his familiar role.

In *The Prairie* Cooper tells of the death of Bumppo, who had sought his accustomed freedom in the woods of the ever-receding frontier. But the old man had too much blood in him to die. Other writers, less able than Cooper, gave him new names and made him a hero in adventure tales of prairie and desert. And while the would-be Coopers were springing from American soil Gustav Aimard was writing in France novels whose titles—*The Virgin Forest, The Trappers of Arkansas*—betrayed their inspiration.

When in 1860 Erastus Beadle of Cooperstown began to publish in New York his sensational dime novels the number of replicas of Leatherstocking—Seth Jones, Kent the Ranger, Oregon Sol, Pete Shafer—grew apace. Nearly half of Beadle's orange-backed books of western adventure contained such a character.

So greatly loved was this "nature's gentleman" that those who would popularize living flesh-and-blood men gave them the attributes of Leatherstocking. Davy Crockett, half-history and half-legend, became another Hawkeye in coonskin cap and fringed buckskin, listening for the voices of his favorite hounds, Whirlwind and Growler, never missing his target with his long rifle, Betsy. Like Deerslayer, Crockett was an associate of ex-pirates and bee-hunters. Like Pathfinder he was a lover of justice and a champion of the rights of honest Indians.

Kit Carson, to his own occasional embarrassment, became in the public prints as righteous, abstemious and pious as Cooper's fictional scout. And Ned Buntline soon created for a little known plainsman, Buffalo Bill, a set of noble characteristics identical with those of *la longue Carabine*. Van Wyck Brooks wrote only a decade ago of "the young Westerner, Abraham Lincoln, who had something in common with Natty Bumppo."

In *The Virgin Land,* a volume containing studies of the American hero, Henry Nash Smith says that the stalwarts who took the popular fancy after Natty Bumppo supplied remedies for "that neglect of comic possibilities so marked in Cooper." Mr. Nevins also decries the humor of the Leatherstocking tales and has removed by skillful editing many of Cooper's efforts to be funny. By so doing he has brought into sharper relief witty passages that compare more than favorably with the brag-and-boast humor-filled narratives that were to come. Many of early America's funniest anecdotes have to do with the cunning of the trader, and Cooper proves his hero an able precursor of T. C. Halliburton's Sam Slick and E. N. Westcott's David Harum when he reports the sharp exchange between Iroquois warriors who have taken two white prisoners and Leatherstocking, who offers for their release a carved elephant from a recently discovered chess set. The Indians praise their captives and the scout lists their faults and disparages their value so successfully that he convinces the savages that "a beast with two tails is well worth two such scalps."

At another tense bargaining, when asked by a villainous Indian if he will give his life for that of a kidnaped white girl, Leatherstocking refuses, then mildly suggests: "I might go into winter quarters, now— at least six weeks before the leaves will turn—on condition you will release the maiden."

Scholars have apparently accepted Deerslayer's oft-stated assurance that "it don't become white blood to brag" and have not noted that the opinion does not hamper its holder. If they read for evidence of influence on the Davy Crockett, Mike Fink, dead-shot, ringtailed roarer school of comic braggarts already aborning they will not go unrewarded.

More important today than his influence on certain sections of our literary history are Cooper's observations as folklorist and poet. Through the scout's mouth he reports accepted folk-talk of his time —"You burnt your powder to warm your nose" or "A crow would shed tears...to fly across this district"—and in his role as narrator he describes turkey shoots, maple-tappings, militia training days, materials that America has since approved in the writings of Ben Lucien Burman, Jesse Stuart, the late Stephen Vincent Benét, the late Marjorie Kinnan Rawlings and many another.

As for poetry, Cooper said that Bumppo "felt, though it was unconsciously, like a poet." The author gave much of his own poetic expression the common touch by offering it in the unpretentious duds of an unlettered man's dialect, a device that many an American poet from James Russell Lowell to Robert Frost has adopted to advantage. Said Bumppo: "The echoes repeat pretty much all that is said and done on Glimmerglass in this calm summer weather. If a paddle falls, you hear of it sometimes ag'in and ag'in, as if the hills were mocking your clumsiness."

An accomplished American stylist recently described the admirers of Leatherstocking and his ilk contemptuously as "the cult of the sublimated roughneck." Allan Nevins' inspired contrivance has made answer. His peeling of the unessential has left a core of gold. As a result of his taste and skill Cooper's genius has been so illumined that it will need and receive many new and favorable reappraisals.

❦ Foreword to
Legends of the Shawangunk

This is a book of history without history's formal disciplines. This is a book of folklore without the baling wire with which scholars bind their folk-harvests. But to a casual contemporary this book has virtues which compensate. One of these is that it serves as a hill-country tunnel leading to the bright gateway of a forgotten land.

Set off from the present by the ridges of old generations, this region still offers the arc of green earth and blue water in which a people lived a life now too unbelievable to be understood. It was an existence in which burning cabins, the dripping scalps of murdered settlers, captivities lived in slavery under the dark trees of a measureless forest were commonplace.

Nature was as cruel here as the Indians, and whole families died in battles against snows, floods, and windstorms. Merciless outlaws lay in ambush along the trails and added evil notoriety to the names of Claudius Smith (whose skull, after he was hanged, became the center-stone in the arch over the courthouse door at Goshen), Ben Kelley, and Shanks Ben, long before the names of "bad-men" had become infamous in the far west. More widely known than any other Shawangunk villains, however, was Tom Quick, a sadistic slayer of Indians, whether hostile or friendly, whom he shot on sight.

There were ghosts, too, that haunted the old cabins of this wild land. And here men—and boys, too—fought monstrous bear, panthers, and wolves, stabbing them to death with their knives. Mines holding copper and silver gave rich rewards, then disappeared and lay hidden by deceptive boulders for generations.

When Philip Smith wrote [in 1887] of these incidents, he was working, as Washington Irving and James Fenimore Cooper had sometimes worked, with the sort of legendry that adorns the background tapestry of strictly patterned history. His tales were the trivia that never fail to accompany narratives of international rivalry. Inspired, as the more important literary figures of the past were, by the "spirit of place" that even now broods over the Shawangunk area, Smith chose to report not the great movements of world history, not the motives of nations, not matters of intrigue and strategy, but neighborhood gossip about the heroic, the clever, the cowardly persons who had impressed themselves upon his curious mind.

Smith has no formula. He is obviously a talker, not a writer—and he depends upon conversational gambits to entertain his audience. Even when his prose is in print he is unmistakably a teller of fireside yarns and for them he has the true feeling. He does not mold his subject matter, his subject matter molds him. Sometimes he pretends to be a historian, sure and objective, until an undocumented bit of hearsay lures him into recording it. Sometimes he pretends to be a man of letters, genteel, classical, lavish with apt figures of speech, until he remembers a homely colloquialism that he cannot resist.

Though today's inhabitants of the Shawangunk may find this author's prose sententious, overwrought, old-fashioned, it may truly be said that these very attributes inform the reader of an attitude of mind characteristic of the times in which he wrote. While describing a past period of an American region, Philip Smith becomes an informative index to his own period.

Smith struck his attitudes at a time when no demands other than entertainment were made of him. His sources he chose to suit his own moods and whims. And somehow he succeeded in communicating the look and feel of the Shawangunk country. We can be sure of this because today this wide amphitheatre has suffered less than most wooded landscapes of America from the invasions of commerce and industry. While it has more concentrations of residents than it had in early times, it still preserves the image of the America-that-was more successfully than do most rural areas of the nation. Now that Indians and catamounts are few in the Shawangunk, it is for the most part a hunter's delight. Its great hotels occupy only relatively small portions of the wooded acres that lure visitors seeking recreation. Its little communities—Sundown, Grahamsville, Peenpack, Wallkill, and many another—are hardly larger than they were in the days that Philip Smith described.

These anecdotes, gathered like windfall apples, from the unkempt orchards of the past, Smith carried to the cider-mill of a region's memory, and from them he pressed an essence.

❦ Rattlesnake Hunter

When I first saw Bill Clark he was down in one of his back lots mending fence. I had parked my car close to the edge of the narrow winding road that leads over the mountains back of the lake and I had reached his porch, littered with pails, baskets, milk pans, bits of old machinery and ears of seed corn before he saw me. He waved then and came slowly up the rise toward his little house.

"Yesterday was my sabbath," he said, "so that's why you catch me workin' on your Sunday."

"I don't mind," I assured him hastily. "I just wondered if you wouldn't take me out to hunt rattlesnakes with you."

He smiled and his mouth spread to each side of his face—paralleling the lines about his blue eyes. His squat figure was firmly planted on the stony soil.

"Don't get many requests like that," he said. "Folks don't care much about catchin' snakes. But I guess I could oblige you. When c'n ye go?"

"I'm ready any time," I said.

"Ain't no time like the present," said Bill. "We may be a little late startin' since it's near nine o'clock but maybe we can pick one up before very long, certainly before dark."

"One'll be enough," I said. "I just want to see how you do it."

Bill stepped to the wall of the porch and picked up a long stick with some sort of metal contraption on the end.

"You see this," he said impressively; "this is what's known as the

Bill Clark rattlesnake tongs. I do practically all my snake catchin' with
it. Fifty years ago I used to use a forked stick—or my hands—but by
and by I invented this an' it's the best thing for takin' a rattler that
I know."

"How does it work?" I said.

"Well, it's really a broomstick with a wire run through eyelets along
the side. They's a handle at your end and at the business end it's got
a pair of steel jaws like pincers an' they work the same way. When
I see a rattler I get up on him and get his neck between them jaws.
Then I pull on the handle an' the jaws close on his neck, an' I've got
him. I usually carry a basket to put him in because he might be a her
and have five or six little ones down her gullet. I git jest as much
bounty for little rattles as I do for big ones. But if I'm in a hurry I jest
put my foot on his neck and jerk his head off with the tongs. Then
I bury his head under a stone and go ahead. Well I reckon I'm ready.
Here's a pair o' tongs fer you."

We put the tongs in the back of the car and started driving south
along the west shore of the lake.

"How much can you make out of one average-size rattlesnake?" I
said.

"Well, now, that depends," said Bill. "We used to get three dollars
a rattle regardless o' size. Then they reduced it to a dollar 'n a half,
but now it's back up to two-fifty. Then there's all the oil you can try
out of him. May amount to three-four dollars' worth."

"Oil?" I said.

"Sure. Rattlesnake oil. Good for what ails ye', whatever it is. Drugstores buy it an' these doctors that goes out with a tent and an Indian
through the country sells lots of it. Mighty good for rheumatism—
makes ye soople. Feller I know says he knew a man wunst used too
much of it—got so soople he couldn't stand up."

His blue eyes sought mine in kindly seriousness.

"I take it the female rattler carries her young in her gullet," I said
sternly.

"Yep. But they ain't no way o' tellin' unless ye take her home an'
put her in a box an' wait fer 'em to crawl out. Then ye can get bounty
fer all the little rattles. That's a damn sight better than doin' like a

rattlesnake feller on the other side of the lake did a couple of years ago. He broke the big rattles in two an' tried to collect bounties fer both ends. He's still in the penitentiary."

We were crossing the southern end of the lake now. The great cliffs on the east side were looming above us and the water at their feet was very blue. Far to the north green islands seemed to be floating on the still surface.

"I like livin' back from the water," said Bill suddenly. "A lake always looks better when you come up on it. Here's where we stop an' hit a trail."

Through an upward slanting field we strode, tongs dragging behind us, then climbed along a creek bed until we reached a wooded ridge.

"There ought to be some in the rocks at the end of this ridge," said Bill.

"Isn't this business a little dangerous?" I said.

"Ain't been struck in fifty years."

"Yes, but suppose there's more than one at a time."

"More than one!" He struck his thigh with his open palm. "Guess I ain't told ye 'bout the time round ten years ago when Dal Pratt an' I was huntin' on this very ridge. We was separated. Pratt had gone on up the mountain an' I come into a little rocky ravine not much bigger'n a minute and there, by God, was all the rattlesnakes in this whole Adirondack country a-sunnin' 'emselves. They'd jest come out o' their winter dens an' was gettin' ready to move to their summer ones. Five hundred to a thousand rattlers, by God, a-turnin' and twistin' there in the sun an' all of 'em singin' so's you could hear 'em a half-a-mile."

Bill's eyes gleamed, his face seemed contorted with joy. I imagined that he was counting up the grand total of rattles and rattlesnake oil in terms of dollars.

"I called to Pratt an' he heard me and come along the mountain to the edge of the ravine. He jumped down on a boulder just beside my shoulder an' then not payin' any attention landed right beside me an' there we both was with all them rattlers raisin' hell around us. I seen Pratt's eyes sort o' flicker so I says to him, I says:

" 'If you be scared you better git back up thar on that rock.'

" 'Wall,' he says, sort o' slow an' careful, 'I be.' "

Bill waited for this monosyllabic expression of emotion to sink in, his eyes twinkling. Then he said, "I sure was a fool to use my shotgun that day. I got seventeen on the first shot and I got about seventy-five that morning—but I could of got the whole lot if I'd took my time and used these here tongs."

We had come to a pile of dark rocks and Bill began poking around under them with the tongs. Once he turned one over, looking expectantly at the spot beneath while I stepped back and felt frightened. At last he said:

"We'll rest here a bit," and sat down on a rock. Fearfully I sat beside him.

"Why can't you breed rattlesnakes?" I said. "Then you wouldn't have to go to all this trouble and you'd get your bounty and oil just the same."

"I thought o' that," said Bill reflectively. "Fact is I tried it once. I got a lot o' rattlers an' put 'em all in box all winter and all spring an' nothin' happened. Didn't get no little rattlers at all. Then Henry Hall, friend o' mine lives down in the town o' Lake George, come by and he says, 'Ye won't git no little ones unless you put a blacksnake in there.' So I put a blacksnake in there and by God it wan't no time 'fore there was six little fellers crawlin' around. So I'd say it would be my conclusion after fifty years o' huntin' rattlers that the blacksnake is the papa rattler."

"I didn't know they ever mated," I said.

"Oh, sure. One mornin' I seen a big blacksnake come out from under a rock and a rattler followed him out and they mated right there— you know how they do—twistin' and turnin' sort of like they was dancin'. Well then, I'm damned if he didn't get back under that rock and bring out another rattler and mate with her, and then he went back again and when a third rattler come out I jest went on about my business."

"You haven't told me why you aren't breeding blacksnakes with rattlers to get more rattlers," I said.

"Well, that was Henry's fault, too, really. He seen I had some luck, so he tried it. He put some blacksnakes and rattlers in a big wire cage and kept 'em there a long time. But nothin' happened. So he kept 'em a couple o' months more and still he didn't get none and somehow he got to blamin' it on the female rattlers. Henry's house is right plumb on the street in Lake George an' one mornin' his wife woke up and there sits Henry in the doorway with his shotgun on his knees.

"'You goin' huntin'?' she says.

"'Nope,' says Henry.

"'What you plannin' on?' she says.

"'I'm figgerin' on shootin' the first female that comes down the street.'

"'You can't do that,' she says.

"'I'm goin' to,' says Henry.

"Well, then she screamed an' some men come in an' satcheled onto Henry an' by God they had to take him to the crazy house. He's sane enough 'bout everything else except females but he's bound to take a shot at the first one o' them he sees. So they have to keep him locked up. He's up there now."

Bill pulled some sandwiches and two bottles of milk from his basket and we ate and talked awhile. Then we dozed off and midafternoon had come before we felt like continuing our quest. Neither of us expected it to have so sudden an ending.

For as Bill rose, the rock on which his foot rested tilted slightly. From under it came a prolonged buzz not unlike the note of a cicada but lower and harder. The shambling ease of the old man vanished. With one quick movement he kicked the rock over and there beneath it in a writhing coil lay a snake. His head was already moving back making ready to strike. His mouth was open very wide and his eyes were darkly gleaming beads above it.

"See if you can catch him by the neck," said Bill and I pushed my tongs awkwardly forward. As I pulled the wire handle the rattler struck and his head lunged up the pole, the jaws at the bottom catching him toward the middle of his body. Again he struck, coiling about the steel teeth that held him, his dripping fangs reaching halfway up to my rigid hands while I stood paralyzed, gazing at him.

"Hold tight," said Bill sharply, and I heard the sharp click of his tongs as they bit into the snake just behind the head.

I must have had sense enough to loosen my hold then, for I remem-

ber Bill's raising the twisting burden and turning away from me. Then
he had the snake firmly held, his right hand close up to the head, and
he was stuffing it into a wicker fish-basket lined with felt and hung
by a strap over his shoulder.

"Well, that's one," he said.

"I was too scared to do a good job," I said miserably.

"It takes practice," said Bill, "but you weren't in much danger. I was
ready to hit him if he got too close to ye. A rattler ain't much of a
fighter. One lick and he gives up and runs. Looks like we might find
some today. Blamed if I didn't think that C.C.C. camp had driven most
of 'em back into the mountains."

"No," I said, "I've had enough."

Bill followed me down the trail in reproachful silence. Finally he
said:

"I reckon you'll want this one killed so's you can show it to your
friends. We better stop and kill it now, for it takes a rattler a long
time to die."

"How long?" I said.

"Depends—but my son and me cut the heart out of a big one once
and laid it on a rock in the hot sun. It was beatin' forty-seven times
a minute then and when we come back three hours later it was still
beatin'—twenty-three times a minute."

"You'd better keep it," I said as we reached the car and climbed in.
"Perhaps," said Bill pessimistically, and then we both lapsed into a long
silence as we rolled along the side of the lake. The sun was out of sight
somewhere beyond Bill's house and its rays were almost level as they
struck against the rock cliffs on the eastern shore. The water below
them seemed covered with a golden sheet.

We were approaching Bolton's Landing when Bill spoke again.

"Sometimes," he said, "the rattlers cross the lake."

"Ever see 'em?" I said.

"Sure," he said. "Lots o' times. They take the little ones down their
gullets and set out. You can see the mother snake's head above the
water and she keeps her tail out, too. You can hear it rattlin' away—
sort o' like an outboard motor. In the spring o' the year, in the moonlight, it makes a mighty pretty sight."

🐝 The Lavender Evening Dress

A few years ago the postmaster in a village that lies beside the lonely waters of the Ramapo River, dappled by light and leaf shadow in the morning and darkened by hill shadows in the afternoon, talked often about a lithe, tawny girl with hyacinth eyes and wheat-yellow hair. He was a sophisticated gentleman, traveled and urbane, a member of a distinguished family in those parts. To atone for his sins, he said, he taught a boys' class in a Sunday school that was in session on the first day of each week after the preaching in a tiny weathered church back in the Ramapo hills.

From the summits of those hills, on a clear day washed by recent rain, the slim gray towers on Manhattan Island seem to advance into sight and hang, like figures long ago worked into the tapestry on the old blue sky wall. None of the boys in the Sunday school had ever entered the city on the horizon, and only a few of them had been to Hillburn or Sloatsburg in York State or any of the New Jersey towns to the west. They were a shy lot, but wild as wood animals are wild, and they found the simple lessons in Christian ethics the postmaster was trying to teach difficult at best and impossible at those times when that girl was around.

She went through his class, the postmaster said, like a slow pestilence. A boy would be gone for a month, sometimes two months, and then he would come back on a Sunday, glowering and sheepish, and one of his schoolmates would be absent for a while. The Sunday school teacher would sometimes see him and the girl picking wild blackberries on a hillside or, on a Saturday night, walking the road, shoes in hand, to a country dance.

There was much talk about the girl among the hill-folk gossips, and the postmaster, whose job gave him speaking acquaintance with most of these, gathered from what they said that she was gay and hot-tempered and amoral—feeling that the general admiration gave her the privilege of disobeying the somewhat eccentric conventions of her own community. The only time he had a good look at her was during a Wednesday-night prayer meeting at which, according to an announcement the previous Sunday, the contents of three barrels of old clothes from the members of a New York City church would be distributed. The girl came in after the service just as the preacher beat in the head of the first barrel. She was barefoot and it was obvious that she wore only a stained and patched calico-check dress much too small for her. She sat in the back pew and paid no attention as the usual pathetic garments that are contained in such shipments were displayed and granted to those who could argue the greatest need.

There was a gasp when the preacher pulled from the middle of the second barrel a lavender evening dress covered with sequins that glinted like tiny amethysts. It was cut low off the shoulders, and as soon as the preacher saw that, he rolled it up into a shapeless bundle and held it helplessly, waiting for someone to speak for it. No one did, but the girl stood up and padded swiftly down the aisle. Without saying a word, she grabbed the dress from the good man's hands and raced out of the church.

From that time on, the postmaster said, no one ever saw the girl in other costume. Rain or shine, day or night, she was a brush stroke of lavender against the brown of dirt roads, the green of hill slopes, the khaki-colored shirts and pants of whatever boy strode beside her.

Frost came early that year and leaves dropped. The air was clear and the New York towers came nearer and stayed longer. The hill people were all talking about a letter that had come to the girl from cousins in Jersey City. The postmaster had told one of his Sunday school boys that the letter had come, and the next day she had stood before his window and quietly asked for it, the sequins glinting purple in the shadowy room. People who dropped in the next day said her cousins had invited her to visit them and they had sent the money for her bus fare. A week later a witness regaled the postmaster with a description of the expressions on the faces of the bus passengers down on the asphalt highway twelve miles away when the girl climbed aboard, holding her long skirt about her waist.

In mid-December came a cold snap, and the thermometer outside showed eighteen degrees below zero when the postmaster opened his window for business. The people in the line of waiters-for-mail were more eager to give him the news than to receive their letters. The body of the girl in the lavender dress had been found frozen and stiff on the road a few miles above the bus stop. Returning from Jersey City, she had left the bus and begun the long walk home, but the evening dress had proved too flimsy wear for such a night.

The postmaster said that after this tragedy all the students in his class came regularly to Sunday school, and that was the end of the story of the girl.

The girl froze to death about 1939, and for a decade nothing reflected doubt on the postmaster's conclusion. But now a growing number of people feel that his narrative, the truth of which is easily provable by many witnesses, has had an inexplicable consequence, overtones that have transcended his matter-of-fact realism. For a strange report recently began its rounds of upstate towns and, particularly, colleges. It had many variants, as such tales do, but in none of them was it in any way connected with the account of the girl, her dress, and her death, a factual record known only in the vicinity of her Ramapo home, and the suggestion of such a connection is made here possibly for the first time.

As I heard it, two Hamilton College juniors motoring to a dance at Tuxedo Park after sunset of a warm Indian-summer Saturday on the road that runs through the valley of the little Ramapo River saw a girl waiting. She was wearing a party dress the color of the mist rising above the dark water of the stream, and her hair was the color of ripe wheat. The boys stopped their car and asked the girl if they could take her in the direction she was going. She eagerly seated herself between them and asked if they were going to the square dance at Sterling Furnace. The thin, tanned face with high cheekbones, the yellow hair, the flashing smile, the quicksilver quality of her gestures enchanted the boys, and it was soon a matter of amused debate whether they would go along with her to Sterling Furnace or she would accompany them to the dance at Tuxedo. The majority won and the boys were soon presenting their new friend to the young couple who were their hosts at the Park. "Call me 'Lavender,'" she said to them. "It's my nickname because I always wear that color."

After an evening in which the girl, quiet and smiling, made a most favorable impression by her dancing, drifting dreamily through the waltzes in a sparkling cloud of lavender sequins, stepping more adeptly than any of the other dancers through the complications of revived square dances—Money Musk, Hull's Victory, Nellie Gray—the boys took her out to their car for the ride home. She said that she was cold, and one of them doffed his tweed topcoat and helped her into it. They were both shocked into clichés of courtesy when, after gaily directing the driver through dusty woodland roads, she finally bade him stop before a shack so dilapidated that it would have seemed deserted had it not been for a ragged lace curtain over the small window in the door. After promising to see them again soon, she waved good night, standing beside the road until they had turned around and rolled away. They were almost in Tuxedo before the chill air made the coatless one realize that he had forgotten to reclaim his property, and they decided to return for it on their way back to college the next day.

The afternoon was clear and sunny when, after considerable difficulty in finding the shack, the boys knocked on the door with the ragged lace curtain over the window. A decrepit white-haired woman answered the door and peered at them out of piercing blue eyes when they asked for Lavender.

"Old friends of hers?" she asked, and the boys, fearing to get the girl into the bad graces of her family by telling the truth about their adventure of the day before, said yes they were old friends.

"Then ye couldn't a-heerd she's dead," said the woman. "Been in the graveyard down the road for near ten years."

Horrified, the boys protested that this was not the girl they meant—that they were trying to find someone they had seen the previous evening.

"Nobody else o' that name ever lived round here," said the woman.

" 'Twasn't her real name anyway. Her paw named her Lily when she was born. Some folks used to call her Lavender on account o' the pretty dress she wore all the time. She was buried in it."

The boys once more turned about and started for the paved highway. A hundred yards down the road the driver jammed on the brakes.

"There's the graveyard," he said, pointing to a few weathered stones standing in the bright sunlight in an open field overgrown with weeds, "and, just for the hell of it, I'm going over there."

They found the stone—a little one marked "Lily"—and on the curving mound in front of it, neatly folded, the tweed topcoat.

🐝 The Lesson

He took her to town
Through miles May green
Showed her far doings
Flashed on a screen,

Said driving home,
"Pictures and words
Fly the blind air
Like so many birds,"

Said when sun-up
Snuffed stars with light,
"Stars shine always
Come day, come night."

Late June he died
"Don't mourn," said she,
"Things keep on
That folks don't see."

☙ "You Can't Win Looking Back"

As the wild melee of trotters, sulkies and men thundered around the last curve of the track, all racing split-the-creek for the wire, I saw a driver's maroon-and-gold sleeves rise high, saw his lifted reins slapping the trotter's flanks and heard above the cracking of whips his shrill "Hi-yah!" The big stallion, Rodney, lunged forward with an unbelievable burst of speed.

In all my years of watching trotting races I had never seen such a homestretch drive as on that August afternoon of 1947 at the Good Time Track in Goshen, New York. It was the first of three heats of the annual Hambletonian Stake, in which the swiftest three-year-old trotters in the nation were trying for one of the largest purses then offered in harness racing. Rodney had beaten the favorite, a bonny colt named Hoot Mon.

I hurriedly turned to my program. Rodney's owner was R. Horace Johnston, of Charlotte, North Carolina. His driver was Bion Shively, aged sixty-nine.

In the next two heats Hoot Mon went out ahead early and stayed there. As his owner and admirers gathered at the paddock where the Hambletonian trophy would be presented, I drifted toward the stables. Bion Shively, bright-eyed and contented-looking, sat before Rodney's stall. I said, "It looked as if the boys ganged up on you in the last two heats. They had you in a box so tight you couldn't have got through them without going around the grandstand."

Driver Shively's eyes twinkled. "Track's a little rough out there."

"When did you begin driving?" I asked.

"You'd have to trot the wrong way round a parcel of laps to start even with me," said the driver. "Draw up a chair."

In the next two hours I learned the facts of Bion Shively's career. The first time he saw trotters race was at a Nebraska country meet. He was nine years old. They pulled old-style sulkies then, with wooden wheels higher than his head. But from what he saw through the spokes he knew what he wanted to do for the rest of his life.

One day his uncle let him drive his old pacer, Stratton, and gave Bi some advice: "The first thing you have to know about harness racing is you can't win looking back."

There were mornings when Bi drove from one Nebraska fairgrounds to another, with Stratton between the shafts. Then came the day, in 1893, when, sitting between the high wheels and yelling like a Comanche, the boy rattled down the stretch to a first place. So began a career that lasted for more than sixty-seven years. And, dusty or muddy, win, place or show, it was all the same to Bi.

While drivers like Pop Geers, Ben White and Tom Berry were making themselves famous on the Grand Circuit, Bi was driving his unpredictable plugs, his in-and-out-of-the-money nags, in the half-mile "twice arounds" of Kansas, Oklahoma and Missouri, on a calendar dubbed the Punkin or Leaky Roof Circuit. At matinees when the thermometer registered 100 and the iron shoes drummed loud on the stretches, his silks turned dark with sweat and his trotters turned white with lather.

Bi was forty-eight when, in 1926, the first Hambletonian Stake—the promised land all drivers hope one day to enter—was trotted by three-year-olds at Syracuse, New York. He was fifty-two when the race was shifted to the Good Time Track at Goshen. Eighteen more years of driving for assorted owners followed before R. Horace Johnston of Charlotte saw this old-timer get more speed out of his racers than his younger drivers could, and made him his chief trainer.

Long since, Bi had married sweet-faced Miss Gertrude, and they had a son who learned to tell time by the minutes and seconds of mile trots, geography by sunrises over Midwestern fairgrounds, physiology from veterinarians, arithmetic from reckoning prize money. As the seasons passed, young Jerry became his father's right-hand man.

Now, with sixty years of driving behind him, Bi and the big stallion, Rodney, had won the first heat of the 1947 Hambletonian. "I reckon that's close enough," he said as I rose to leave him. "I'll be working for Mr. Johnston a while longer and then I'll make my last go-round and turn myself out to pasture."

Later I read that Mr. Johnston had died and I was sure that Bi Shively—or "Old Folks" as some of the sports columnists called him— was in the restful meadow of retirement.

Rain poured down on Hambletonian Day morning in 1952. The great race was postponed to the following afternoon, and I was disconsolately picking my way across the Good Time Track when I saw Old Folks, now in his seventy-fifth year, measuring the depth of the mud with a ruler. He recognized me and said, "Ought to put the colt in the sulky and have me pull him. But it's too late to get him a driver's license and I don't know as I could pass as a three-year-old."

I spent the afternoon chatting with the old driver, and I learned why Bi was for the third time to race a colt for the big stake. At the Lexington, Kentucky, sales he had seen an ungainly and uncertain colt ambling about inside a circle of quiet men. The beginning bid was low. Bi wasn't thinking of bidding. But his sharp brown eyes noted the oversized haunches of the dark and homely colt.

"I was at the Lexington sales mostly out of habit," Bi said. "Then C. W. Clark of Dearborn, Michigan, showed up. He said he'd like me to pick out a colt and train him. At first I said no. It meant starting where I did sixty years before with a cheap horse and an off-chance of making him into something. Then I thought of what my uncle told me: 'Boy, remember you can't win looking back.' So I gave Mr. Clark the go-ahead. 'One thousand dollars,' he said, and we had us a colt. His name was Sharp Note."

The endless circling of the practice track, the calm talking to the nervous young trotter, the patient timing of each quarter began all over again. Sharp Note was soon responding. His uncertain gait became swift and precise. He was filling out in body and he began to know what was expected of him. He became a three-year-old in January of 1952, and Old Folks entered him in a spring meet at which early Western candidates for the Hambletonian are appraised. Sharp Note won. The crafty old man immediately canceled all entries in the other meets that usually determine the odds at the Hambletonian, and shipped the colt to Goshen. Day after day that spring and summer Sharp Note sped by the judge's tower, the big grandstand. When the

Hambletonian came around in August, Sharp Note would know every inch of the mile he would trot.

On the afternoon of the race the sunlit tote board showed Hit Song and Duke of Lullwater as the favorites. I bought a tip sheet and asked about Sharp Note. The tout said quickly, "Don't bet on him—cheap colt, greenhorn owner and driver so old he's loco."

"Why loco?"

"Didn't give his entry no race experience. Colt's had too little and the driver's had too much," said the tipster.

During the parade to the post, Bi Shively was slumped easy on the sulky seat, his thin legs spread wide along the thills. As all drivers turned the colts into place behind the wide wings of the mobile starting gate, Sharp Note, unused to the obstacle, hit its bar. He started the race trotting unsteadily and before he reached the half-mile mark he broke gait and galloped. Shively leaned back, pulling desperately on the reins to bring the colt again to a trot. Hit Song was well ahead at the wire. Sharp Note finished tenth.

Hit Song was an even greater favorite in the second heat. Bi put all his strength into holding Sharp Note from the bar, and the colt started the race trotting fast. Bi kept him behind the leading horses all the way to the three-quarter mark.

Then came one of the shattering events that fill harness racing with almost intolerable excitement. Suddenly the spectators saw a dark spot begin to move forward with the relentlessness of a perfect machine. As the horses reached the curve into the straight homestretch, the old driver, not daring to risk being boxed behind the madly trotting colts ahead, took Sharp Note out around them! Straight in front was the wire, and the colt was passing his rivals. The voice of the announcer in the judge's box shrilled into a scream: "It's Sharp Note, no it's Duke of Lullington, no it's Sharp Note, it's *Sharp Note!*"

Once Old Folks had established his pattern, he stuck to it and won the last heat. The Hambletonian was his. To Sharp Note's owner came the winner's share of the purse—$47,236.64. To the impassive leather-faced driver of seventy-five came a storm of congratulations. Said a reporter, "How does it feel to win the Hambletonian when you're the oldest driver in the business?"

"There's Howard McKinley out in Missouri," Bi replied. "He's got to be older'n me."

Nineteen fifty-two turned out to be the beginning of Old Folks' golden period. He won the Futurity at Indianapolis that year and threw in the Kentucky Futurity at Lexington for good measure—all winnings counted, Sharp Note was the first trotter to win $100,000 in one season. In San Francisco that year there was a dinner for America's world-champion athletes. The guests of honor were youngsters in their teens and twenties and—Old Folks.

When he was eighty-one, some officials tried to bar Old Folks from certain tracks as too old; he answered this insult by winning six one-heat stake and overnight races in six days. No one has criticized his driving since.

In 1960 he gave out he was retiring. At about the same time son Jerry married Bertha McKinley, whose father is the same Howard McKinley Bi called "older'n me." Howard, at the age of eighty-nine, trains trotters for meets on Midwestern tracks. He has never won a world championship, but now that the Hambletonian Stake has been moved to Duquoin, Illinois, nearer to his business, Howard feels that he still has time to win it. There is a rumor that Bertha and Jerry, knowing that both their fathers believe the old adage, "You can't win looking back," are urging them to buy qualifying two-year-olds and drive them in the next Hambletonian. *That* would be a race.

🐝 The Wraith on Cedar Street

Though I have given ghosts and other spirits from beyond the grave every opportunity to manifest themselves to me, none of them has ever, so far as I know, made the effort. I have tried tipping tables by placing my finger tips upon them, have sought out well-known mediums recommended by my friends as being positively unfailing in ability to put anyone in touch with relatives who have

passed on, have spent dark hours in houses guaranteed to be haunted.
I have never had an experience which could in any way be connected
with the supernatural—that is, with the possible one exception when
I may have seen a ghost.

My wife had sent me to a delicatessen which is on the south side of
Cedar Street in Dobbs Ferry and I was to bring back a pint of French
ice cream for our dinner's dessert course. It was in a summer when
Daylight Saving was adding to the length of days—the summer of
1952. I parked my car about half a block from the store to which I was
bound, and walked slowly along the sidewalk. Sunset was still red in
the sky above the west bank of the Hudson, and little of the day's
bright light had faded from the street. Then I saw the woman who
may have been a ghost.

She was tall and dressed entirely in white. Her hat was of the large,
round "garden party" sort, lacy about the edges, and its whiteness was
so stark I remember being surprised that her long, oval face nearly
matched it. Obviously, it seemed then, she had so covered her features
with talcum powder that any semblance of flesh color had disappeared.
Only her eyes—black, with no tinge of brown in them—stared beadily
out of the whiteness that surrounded them. Even her lips were so white
that the line which divided the upper from the lower was almost indis-
tinguishable. A high collar circled the whiteness of her neck and seemed
to be stretched upon narrow white bone supports. Above her shiny
white belt white embroidery made an indistinct pattern against the flat
whiteness of her dress, and below it a plain but voluminous white skirt
fell in folds to the top of her white high-button shoes made of a leather
that once long ago I had come to recognize as "vici-kid."

The woman neither hastened nor dawdled as she walked toward me.
Her pace was rhythmic, but its rhythm seemed exact and precise—like
that of a machine. She moved quickly, but there seemed to be no sense
of determination about her pace. It was impersonal and somehow inevitable. And when we passed each other I had the feeling that she
was unaware of me, though my eyes sought to meet hers. When she
reached the corner of Broadway I stopped and turned my head to see
which way she would go. I do not know whether she would have
continued straight ahead if the automobiles on the road had been mov-

ing against her progress. I felt that she would have—but the traffic
light was with her, and as she passed by it there was a moment when
its beam turned all the whiteness of her to a pale green—a green like
that which shows when a stone has been lifted from an April lawn.
In another moment she was across Broadway and had begun climbing the slope on the other side. Dusk was now settling swiftly and I
saw lights flash from an ornate Victorian mansion that has long stood
on the campus of Miss Masters' School, which crowns the rise toward
which she moved. When I lost sight of her she was moving toward
those lights, and I remember that she did not bend forward as most
people do when they climb a hill. Indeed, her straight figure seemed
to be moving up the slant at an unnatural angle.

I went on then to do my errand, and I suppose I would never have
thought of the incident again had I not recently found in an old book
which contained some Hudson River tales a strange narrative. I read
in its faded pages that once there had been a rambling and elaborate
mansion on the hill where the school now stands. Gardens surrounded
it, and replicas of classic statues dotted its smooth lawns. To it had
come a long time ago a family named Dobbs—but these people were
very unlike the descendants of the sturdy and honest boatman from
whom the town took its name. They left their home only occasionally,
and then only in impressive silver-decorated carriages drawn by spirited
teams of black horses which trotted swiftly and steadily along the river
roads. On summer nights the people living in the town below could
hear laughter and sometimes music drifting in the air above them and
faltering into silence above the moonlit Hudson. This obviously rich
and cultured family employed gardeners and house servants from the
town below, and those thus privileged to work in and about the big
house were often eagerly questioned by their fellow townsmen as to
what went on up there. They inevitably made vague replies, and when
they were reproached for this, they would answer that, while their employers were pleasant and paid them well, they seemed to dwell behind
a curtain of reserve which was never drawn aside.

One summer day, the tale said, a tall woman clad entirely in white
appeared on the streets of Dobbs Ferry. The inhabitants were im-

pressed by her strange presence, and when she began to walk toward the estate at the summit of the hill many eyes were upon her.

That night no laughter, no music, no light came from the high windows of the house above the town. The servants said that soon after the arrival of the lady in white they had been called together and told that they might go to their homes below for the rest of the day. When they returned in the morning they found an empty house. Sheets of music lay upon the piano beside violins that had not been returned to their cases. Apparently no meal had been eaten the night before. All of the family—and the white lady—were gone, never to be seen again. Years went by, the grass grew tall and wild, the formal gardens were overgrown with weeds, rain seeped through the rotting roof and dripped onto the rotting floors. I do not know how or when the property was sold. The book I read did not say. But its pages have left me wondering whether once, on my way to buy ice cream in Dobbs Ferry, I saw a ghost walking on Cedar Street.

❦ The Womanish Man

A carnival come to Honeoye once. It had a merry-go-round an' a Ferris wheel. An' a lot o' small-size tents with gamblin' games under 'em. You could toss hoops at prizes an' you could have what you ringed. Or you could throw baseballs at a nigger's head an' get cigars for it. An' Miz Simmons tried what they called a Wheel of Chance an' got a funny-lookin' long doll, kind o' slimpsy in the middle an' with a look on his face like he had the bellyache. She's got four gals but she wouldn't give it to none of 'em—keeps it on her bureau in her bedroom an' won't let nobody touch it. Bet it could tell plenty by now if it could talk.

Well, the first time I seen the womanish man, he was sellin' tickets outside the tent where the feller begins by shoutin': "Now women an' children'll find a lot o' instructive an' worth-while exhibits further on down the street. This here show's for men only an' believe me it oughta be." I pushes up my quarter an' this feller looks down at me, an' fer a minute I thought it was a woman. Damn if I don't believe he was wearin' a little paint on his cheeks. Anyway, they was sort o' pink an' white an' his hair was yellow an' curly an' he wore it sort o' long.

"Thank you very much," he says, an' his voice is sort o' prissy an' womanishlike. I was goin' to say, "You oughta be in there dancin', too," but I got shoved on by the crowd. By the time I got inside I plumb fergot about the feller. Boy! That was some show. An' after it was over the talkin' feller says: "Now just a few of us is goin' to stay on in here fer a little somethin' extry special. It's goin' to cost a dollar but it's goin' to be worth it—there ain't goin' to be no limit this time." So I stayed on fer that an' I tell you I never hope to see more for my money.

Well, when I come out it was just beginnin' to get dark an' most the crowd was home to supper. I was just about t' set out myself when I seen a fat man with a cigar in his mouth talkin' to the curlyhead. He'd got down from the ticket stand an' he was fidgetin' roun', swingin' his hips like a woman, an' complainin' in his woman's voice.

"But I can't be leavin'," he was sayin'. "You told my friend I could have the job."

"I hadn't seen you then," says the fat man. "Serves me right fer bein' a sucker. I'm tellin' yuh, you're through," he says, shakin' his fist at the feller. "I don't want nobody like you in my shows. Gives 'em a bad name. You want to make trouble about it?"

"No, no," says the fella, shakin' his head so's his long hair fell in his eyes. "I don't want no trouble. Jest give me my fare back to New York."

"You'll play hell gettin' it," says the fat man an' walks off chewin' on his cigar.

I went on home t' supper an' didn't think no more about it—that is, till about three days later when the carnival was gone and I goes into Woods and Bogue's flour an' feed store t' get some alfalfa seed. I was sort o' lookin' round when by God up switches curlyhead.

"May I be of service?" he says in that high prissy voice.

"I ain't no cow," I says, "an' you couldn't service me if I was—'cause

you're a mighty long way from a bull," I says an' busts out laughin'
fit to kill. I could see that got his goat, for he turned sort o' pale an'
got twitchy round the mouth an' walked off. When Vic Woods come
out to wait on me I says: "You must be goin' t' put in a line o' flowers,
too. I see you got the young lady to sell 'em all hired," an' I breaks
down laughin' again.

When I got m' seed I stepped over to the Elite Poolroom for a few
minutes an' it wasn't no time 'fore I had the boys in there plumb near
bustin' their sides over what I said about the cow an' the bull, an' about
Vic sellin' flowers. I had so much fun at it I begun thinkin' up somethin' else to tickle the boys with.

"Listen," I says, "I've heard tell about these womanish guys. Ain't
nothin' they like so much as a good-lookin' young boy. I got an idea.
We'll each put in a quarter an' we'll hire George Woods, Vic's boy,
to get him to go fer a walk in the moonlight tonight. We'll get George
to lead him around to the vacant lot behind his pa's store an' we can
be hidin' behind the barrels back there an' listen an' if he starts anythin'
we can jump out an' beat the livin' Jesus outa him. We don't want
no such bastards in this town anyway," I says.

All the fellers said sure, that was a great idea—so we waited till
George come by the store after school an' called him over to the poolroom an' told him what we wanted. He said he wouldn't do it at first
but after I went over to the barbershop an' got two more quarters from
fellers over there, that wanted to be in on it—makin' two dollars in
all—why, he says he guessed he would. He went over to the store an'
stayed a little while an' then he come back an' says it's all fixed. He says
the feller jumped at the chance o' goin' fer a walk after supper. So
I says: "Jest as soon as it gits dark, 'round eight, you tell him how nice
the moon looks from that lot behind your pa's store an' get him over
there. You lead him on," I says, "an' don't be afraid 'cause we'll be
just waitin' to get a chance to knock hell outa him."

So after supper an' gettin' my chores done, I walks down to town an'
picks up the other fellers an' all eight of us sneaks out behind Vic's
store an' waits. The moon come up early that night an' it was big an'
yellow. We didn't dast talk much 'cause somebody on the street might
hear us and want to be in on it an' spoil it all. So everythin' was damn
quiet except the peepers over by the marsh was raisin' hell.

Well, sir, it got to be eight an' nothin' happened. An' it got to be quarter past an' the boys began gettin' restless. Jim Butler was jest sayin', "Aw, t'hell with it," when we heard 'em comin'. "Duck," I says an' we all got down behind the barrels jest in time.

They come into the lot walkin' arm in arm an' curlyhead was talkin'. "I never knew anythin' more beautiful," he says. "The air is full of moonlight an' that crying," he says, pointin' toward the marsh. He kep' still fer a while. Then he says, "You know I'm glad I stayed on here after I got fired. I've got along good here, an' I've found a friend." At that he unhitches his arm from the boy's and puts it around his shoulder.

I riz up from behind the barrels an' walked right over to him.

"Take your dirty hand off that boy," I says, "you stinkin' womanish bastard," an' I let him have it on the nose. He went down like an empty feed bag, didn't seem to be nothin' to him. Then he sort of screamed an' got up an' started to run. But the boys by that time had got in a circle round him an' no matter which way he run somebody fetched him a clip that stretched him out again. Finally he jest laid there on the ground an' begun to cry, makin' a high noise jest like a woman. I reached down an' grabbed him by the collar an' yanked him onto his feet. His watch fell out of his pocket an' he reached down to pick it up but I stomped on his hand.

"My father give it to me," he says between sobbin' and carryin' on.

"I don't give a goddam *who* give it to yuh," I says. "You get the hell out of this town or *we'll* give you somethin'. This ain't no place fer any womanish son-of-a-bitch," I says, an' all the fellers says, "You bet it ain't" an' "You're right, there."

"Get goin'," I says, an' starts to hit him again. Well, he made one jump that landed him outside the circle an' he run like a jack rabbit. We chased him at first but he run too fast for us an' we stopped. When he got out on the concrete headin' toward Canandaigua he was still hollerin' an' carryin' on. I thought we'd die laughin' to hear him cryin' way down the road. When we couldn't hear him no longer I went back an' picked up the watch. It was real gold an' I been carryin' it ever since.

✿ Three Decades and a River

More than thirty years ago I was commissioned by a publisher to write a book about the Hudson. It was a welcome assignment, and I spent the next three years in river towns and on river roads. Librarians revealed to me the secrets of the wide waterway's past; friends, old and new, told me of its present. Recently, because that present is a part of history, I have had another look.

Perhaps the most surprising impression I have gained from my reunion with The Great River of the Mountains, as the Elizabethan sea captain, Henry Hudson, called it, is that in many respects it looks younger than it did in 1935. I believe I can safely venture the statement that no American river is more cognizant of its past. The people of its valley are so proud of its place in the nation's history that they have chosen not only to preserve its landmarks but to create replicas of some of those that no longer exist in their original state. Restoration of past glories has been a major project of the last three decades. Thanks to the Rockefeller family, Sunnyside, the many-angled home of Washington Irving, at the boundary between Irvington and Tarrytown, may be seen as it was when America's most popular author lived in it. The architectural traditions of Holland, Scotland, China, and Spain went into Irving's alterations of an old Dutch house and somehow produced a harmonious whole.

Only a short distance north of Sunnyside stands the most recent of the area's restorations, Lyndhurst, a "Hudson River Gothic" castle. In the first half of the nineteenth century, foreign visitors almost invariably compared the Hudson to the Rhine—but mourned the absence, in the American river's valley, of castles such as made its German counterpart highly romantic. These criticisms were answered immediately by the rich families of Manhattan. Literally dozens of castles were erected above Hudson waters. Lyndhurst was built for the prosperous merchant Phillip Paulding by architect Alexander Jackson Davis, about 1840. Soon thereafter it was purchased by Jay Gould, and it was later occupied by his daughter Anna. Her heirs presented Lyndhurst to the National Trust for Historic Preservation, thus preserving happy evidence of America's most romantic architectural period (the early nineteenth century) when sentimental estate owners constructed tumbledown ruins to give their acres a "sense of antiquity."

Phillipse Manor, Upper Mills—another Rockefeller project—has been added to the Tarrytown area but will not be open to the public for some time.

One further Rockefeller restoration that renders this section of the old Albany Post Road a joy to all visitors is the Van Cortlandt Manor House on the banks of the little Croton River near Harmon. That this was a distant outpost of the manor holdings is proved by the narrow windows (mere slits in the thick walls) designed to protect occupants from the arrows of Indians.

Both Phillipse Manor and Van Cortlandt Manor are Dutch residences of the seventeenth century, and they furnish delightful contrasts with the later British-influenced buildings of the region. Most impressive and important of all these is the lovely riverside mansion of Boscobel, built at the beginning of the nineteenth century by States Dyckman, descendant of a Dutch family.

The history of the Hudson valley began as Henry Hudson's *Half Moon* lay at anchor beside the wooded island of Manhattan in the dusk of the second day of October in 1609. The keeper of the ship's log recorded that he saw a cliff "of the colour of a white greene as though it were either Copper or Silver Myne." Wishful thinking, perhaps, yet though the mining of minerals along the Hudson has been abandoned occasionally, productive mines are now being operated throughout the whole length of the river. Near Lake Tear-of-the-Clouds, the Hudson's source, I found, in 1933, that the iron mines at the village of Tahawus were closed down. In recent years the whole town—houses, stores, churches—has been moved several miles downriver to Newcomb because that little town was discovered to be situated above the largest titanium deposit in America—perhaps in the world.

Most romantic of mined products along the Hudson are the garnets that are taken from the side of Gore Mountain in the Adirondacks. There the Barton Mines produce not only the semiprecious gleaming red stones used in costume jewelry but, in greater profusion, the hard garnet used in the making of sandpaper, the grinding of optical lenses, the production of TV sets, even in the cleaning of red hulls from peanuts. The road from the river to the summit of its high mountain bank still offers a motorist a garnet-covered passage.

The Hudson is a river of bridges now. Steel haunches rest on solid, rocky banks and the new bridges they support carry on their backs more traffic in an hour than all the chuffing ferries used to transport in a day. Though the valley dwellers protested the constructing of the great spans, they have discovered that it is difficult for those who build them to erect an ugly bridge. Bitter objections met the announcement that the lovely Tappan Zee would be crossed by three miles of elevated steel roadway. Now inhabitants of Irvington and Tarrytown invite their friends to lawn parties on the east bank at dusk, when the lights of the long bridge suddenly become a jade necklace that repeats itself in a mirror of Hudson water. The Newburgh-Beacon bridge, the Kingston-Rhinebeck, the Castleton (which sends riders of the New York State Thruway rolling into New England), all have admirers who boast of their beauty.

The Hudson is a petroleum river and a grain river. Even the inhabitants of its banks are not aware that the most recent deepening of its channel has made Albany an international seaport. That old and unpretentious city of Dutch origins has been welcoming to its docks freighters of twenty-eight-foot draft. The upriver channel has now been deepened to thirty-two feet, enabling the city to receive the majority of oceangoing commercial craft. The Army Engineers have designated Albany a twelve-month port, and the winter ice that used to ban all water traffic on the river is now broken, whenever necessary, by Coast Guard cutters.

Albany ships millions of bushels of grain to distant ports when the foreign market is good. The demand has been sufficient to justify the presence of an elevator with a capacity of thirteen and a half million bushels. When a grain-laden ship bears from Albany downriver toward the open sea, she passes the "mothball fleet" that once carried supplies to our overseas armies. Now grain is stored in these holds, and once in a long while all of it is run through an Albany elevator to keep it in condition.

The Hudson is a molasses river. Albany is a port of such sweetness as few of New York State's citizens realize. Ships from the hot countries of the world move up the mountain-lined stream in a never-ending chain. The faraway Indian Ocean's British island of Mauritius dispatches two or three cargoes of molasses to Albany every year. From Salaverry, Peru, from the African ports of Angola and Mozambique, from Penang, from Townsville, Australia, come the juices of many widely separated canebrakes, and the cattle of many northern states chomp ensilage from these faraway lands.

On Albany docks laze Hindu sailors from India, Portuguese sailors, Turkish sailors, Greek sailors, British sailors (in shorts). Freighters arrive bearing wood pulp, tapioca, flour, and asphalt to Albany and set out with return cargoes of scrap iron. Even our New England ports in the days of their glory were no more picturesque than this inland seaport 150 miles from the Atlantic. The increase of commercial traffic on the Hudson has created a new breed of river pilots—a dozen or more—who find every voyage up or down the constantly changing channel a test of their skills.

Happiest of all the more recent facts research has uncovered is that the Hudson is a Christmas-tree river. Each November the Adirondacks and the Catskills resound to cries of "Timber!" and the crackle and thump of falling evergreens. Two areas near the Hudson produce about one third of the two and a half million Christmas trees used in the Yuletide season. Those grown near the great river are Scotch pine, balsam, and white spruce. Some of the largest come from a little town called Landon Hill in the Adirondack mountain area, where the Hudson is hardly more than a trout stream.

If most of these changes make the Hudson visually more glamorous than ever, the honest chronicler must admit that the river is very far from attaining the goals set for it a generation ago. I pleaded then for curbs on pollution. The answer has been that pollution between Albany and Manhattan has increased immeasurably, and almost every tributary adds its filth.

The railroad trains that bore thousands of travelers along the river's shore are no longer profitable, and there has been talk of destroying many of the stations. The days of the glittering steamboat packets—our "floating palaces"—are gone. The Hudson River Day Line that was once the joy of passengers and shoreline observers runs only occasional excursions upriver as far as Bear Mountain Park.

One stimulus to economic progress is the moving of the administration offices and experimental laboratories of big corporations from Manhattan to campus-like acres along the river's banks. These installations demonstrate an enlightened effort to preserve and enhance the Hudson's beauty. However, controversy over the construction of large industrial plants on the banks has led to a nation-wide realization that the first explored and most beautiful of our Eastern rivers faces a crisis. The Hudson may benefit from President Johnson's conservation program recently laid before Congress. Thus conservationists have reason to hope that the Hudson may still remain, as its first explorer once called it, "The Great River of the Mountains."

ℰ How Boscobel Was Saved

When sensitive humans become enamoured of houses, they lose their common sense quite as happily as in love affairs with each other. No matter how strongly well-meaning friends advise logic, objectivity, and cooling off periods, they gladly surrender themselves to prejudice and see no imperfections in the objects of their admiration.

Recent studies in the motives of these dreamers have shown that the majority are emotionally moved because of historic incidents that happened within the dwellings, because of the importance of former occupants, or because of the sheer aesthetic beauty of the architecture of a previous age. Sometimes, unknowingly, they even confound these motives. I have heard ladies coming out of Jefferson's Monticello talk enthusiastically of that shrine's architectural excellence when actually they were walking in a daydream with a spare, florid gentleman who played the violin, invented practical gadgets for the kitchen, wrote immortal prose, and taught his tame mockingbird to whistle *Yankee Doodle.*

Many another imaginative soul has wandered among the trees outside Washington Irving's Sunnyside and praised the graceful lines of the many angled Dutch "snuggery" with its added (and somewhat inconsistent) "Chinese Tower," while her mind was re-creating a past in which the lonely bachelor found in her a worthy successor to lovely Matilda Hoffman—fiancée who died in youth and left him her everfaithful lover (with only an occasional exception) to the end of his days.

Indeed it is something of a problem to judge a house exclusively by its aesthetic qualities and this conclusion leads to my effort to document it.

I first heard of a Hudson River house named Boscobel about thirty years ago. I was then an assistant editor of the magazine, *Theatre Arts,* and the author of a small book of poems. In a morning's mail came a letter from the late Charles Messer Stowe, conductor of a column on Americana in the New York *Sun.* Mr. Stowe wrote that a poet whose major interest was obviously in our native culture should be interested in the preservation of an old house of incomparable beauty and he asked me to join a committee which would make the effort to save it from threatened demolition. Its name, he said, was Boscobel.

More impressed by Mr. Stowe's being aware of my poems than by his request, I wrote him I would be glad to help on his project. So far as I can remember I heard no more of the house for about ten years. Then I believe I read in a New York paper a report that the Westchester Park Commission had sold Boscobel and the lands around it to the U.S. Veterans Administration which planned to build a hospital nearby. The new owners, the report said, planned to make use of Boscobel in a capacity they had not yet determined.

By this time my memory of childhood reading in stories from English history recalled to me the flight of King Charles II after the disastrous battle of Worcester and his hiding from Cromwell's troops all of

the next day in the thick foliage of an oak tree on an estate named
Boscobel. Much later, royalists had dubbed the tree the "Royal Oak"
and set aside a holiday on which to celebrate both the Restoration and
the wide-spreading leafy refuge that made it possible.

It was with a somewhat guilty conscience then that on a motor trip
northward in the late winter of 1955 I turned from the Post Road toward the gleam of the Hudson. A number of massive buildings and
a big sign reading: "The Franklin Delano Roosevelt Hospital, Erected
by the United States Army Veterans Administration" were before me.

I stopped my car in the presence of countless dark windows and
trudged away from them over soiled snow toward the Hudson. Then
as if materializing from the failing light of the afternoon a frame house
that had once been white and had, perhaps on this day, assumed the
color of twilight, was before me.

While I stood at the foot of its steps the wooden swags that hung,
like fluted gray velvet, from the roof of the pillared second story balcony, slowly faded into dusk. All shadows had disappeared from the
landscape and I remember thinking that perhaps, through some supernatural agency, the dwelling had vanished. Then lights danced into
a few windows of the enormous building behind me and the image of
the house called Boscobel settled into my consciousness to stay.

When I returned to the lower Hudson valley somewhat later, I discovered that Boscobel had admirers other than myself and that they
had been embattled. The Veterans Administration, despite previous
assurances that the house would be preserved, had judged it an encum-
brance and, to be rid of it, had sold it to a wrecking company for thirty-
five dollars.

The wreckers were about to tear down the walls when they were
faced by a few outraged valley residents. The distinguished American
architect, Harvey Stevenson, who lived nearby, rushed downriver to
say to all who would listen that Boscobel was a gem too priceless to be
cut into salable pieces. Charles and Constance Stearns set out from
their Bird and Bottle, a tavern since the days of the American Revolution, and took their stand beside Harvey. And from his hundred-and-
fifty-year-old house high above the Hudson stalked sturdy, balding,
Benjamin Frazier, who had saved and restored river houses before.

Confronting the wrecker-boss Benjamin announced that Boscobel must not be destroyed.

"I'll sell it to you," said the wrecker whose pockets had been lightened by the thirty-five dollars.

"At what price?" said Benjamin.

"One thousand dollars," said the wrecker suddenly aware that he had bought something of value.

The would-be rescuers agreed to pay the price and took possession. During a month's grace granted by the Veterans Administration they made frantic efforts to raise the money and paid what they obtained on their purchase. At the same time they undertook to remove from the house its most beautiful parts—the Adam-style fireplaces, the graceful doors, even the magnificent façade. On a Saturday morning before the month had ended, however, a letter from the wrecker announced that their rate of payment was too slow and that he would begin demolishing the house on Monday morning at eight.

Benjamin Frazier spent the rest of the day and all of Sunday trying to solve an unsolvable problem. He could get no relief from the courts on a weekend and he became with the passing of time increasingly desperate. Seeking solace he went to a cocktail party where to his horror he learned that his colleagues had sold Boscobel's façade to a lady who was building a new house on Long Island. Nevertheless, on Sunday, he wrote and delivered a message to the wrecker suggesting to him many dire events that might happen if he let his heavy metal ball swing against the old walls of Boscobel on the morrow. He said that the givers of the money already paid would immediately enter suit against him. He said that he and his friends were the legal owners and they would summon the State Police to protect their property. He said that if a single board of the house was demolished, the demolisher would rue the day. Then he and a friend or two, through telephone calls and visits to nonresidential areas of the cities of Ossining and Peekskill, made arrangements that have never been fully explained.

Whatever Mr. Frazier's activity may then have been, it was noted by the defenders of the lovely house who had gathered beside it early Monday morning that a number of rather large young men whose interests would not seem at first glance to be aesthetic had drifted into the area and were waiting for something or other. They waited several hours and then, looking disappointed, scattered. The message had accomplished its purpose. The wreckers would not come.

Given extra time now, the champions of the house set out to accomplish its preservation. They sought the support of foundations, the generosity of philanthropists. But, though they had enlisted in their campaign because of the sheer beauty of Boscobel, they found few people who shared their point of view.

At this time, as I remember it, about three decades after I had first said I would like to help save Boscobel, I said it again and tried to find answers to questions which possible supporters were asking. "Who built it and when? Was he important in our history? What did he do?" were the usual inquiries and we found that if we were to obtain contributions we must know what to say in reply.

Our early researches gave us little aid. When we said Boscobel had been built by one States Morris Dyckman who had been an accountant for the British general officers during their occupation of New York City, some possible contributors said they would not encourage the restoration of a house "built by a Tory" and no amount of assurance that the War of Independence had ended late in the eighteenth century could change their negative decisions. Others refused to trust their own judgments on our project until they were told that the beauty of Boscobel was attributable, in part at least, to the influence of the great Scottish architect Robert Adam. Slowly, painfully, we obtained funds until we could claim that we owned the house.

Since the Veterans Administration had delayed destruction of Boscobel until we could take it away, Benjamin Frazier's first act after the purchase was to do exactly what we all had been trying to prevent. He demolished the house. Under his careful supervision, however, every important board had been numbered and its place in the structure had been noted. In a short time many a barn in Putnam County (of which Benjamin was then official historian) was storing the materials of which Boscobel had been made in 1804.

Now all that we needed was the money to purchase a site on which to rebuild, the money for digging a foundation, the money for restoring the exterior to its former state, the money for furnishing the rooms, the money to pay back a debt of five thousand dollars or so which we had recklessly incurred. We began to despair of finding anyone who agreed with us that beauty alone was an argument worthy of support. Again and again we were told by solicitous and knowing friends "Beauty is not enough." And we had no way of knowing that all the old buildings in the Hudson valley, now safely rescued for a proud posterity, were providing us with the conventional deep darkness before a happy dawn.

The end of our hopelessness did not come dramatically or at least it does not seem so now. It came so casually that at first we forgot to dance in the streets, send fireworks into the sky, or leap fully clothed into the Hudson. Perhaps, in the depths of the pessimism that had been forced upon us, we could not fully realize our own happiness.

At this moment, however, came the turning point in the fortunes of Boscobel. We had written an appeal to Mrs. Lila Wallace, who, with her husband, DeWitt, was co-editor of *The Reader's Digest,* the magazine they had founded together in 1922. Mrs. Wallace's reply assured us that *of course* she agreed with our point of view. Shortly thereafter she began to provide a steady flow of financial aid, which became and continues to be the mainstay of Boscobel.

A site even more beautiful than that on which Boscobel had first stood was purchased. The materials of the house were brought to it and housed under a work-shed. Walls rose. Under the supervision of the late Colonel Campbell Lorini, who dedicated the final months of his life to the project, blueprints were converted into realities. Suddenly the perfect façade, generously returned by the Long Island lady who had purchased it, was looking straight downriver—past the grey towers of West Point toward the southern gateway of the Hudson Highlands at Bear Mountain. A rose garden was growing on the north side of the house. Behind it an apple orchard partly concealed a carriage house, designed in the Adam tradition by Harvey Stevenson.

As the building neared completion, trucks bearing precious freight were arriving. Old books from States Dyckman's library were once more at home on his library shelves. A Waterford glass chandelier glittered above a flowered blue Moorefield carpet designed by Robert Adam. Two young decorators, William Kennedy and Ben Garber, were already searching diligently through Europe and the United States for the most beautiful furniture of the late eighteenth and early nineteenth centuries (Dyckman was known to have spent much time in England). Their discoveries were amazingly rewarding and led to painstaking research on the part of members of the Board of Directors of Boscobel Restoration, Incorporated. The organization's Committee on Historic Research uncovered old records, family papers, books of history and folklore materials that students of both architectural and social history may find interesting. They have discovered:

1. A charming story of the love of States Dyckman for his young wife. They were married when he was thirty-nine and she eighteen. Their letters when they were apart were poignant and beautifully phrased.

2. The annals of Dyckman's friendship with William Cobbett, a crotchety English politician of considerable importance who made life difficult for those who disagreed with him both in the United States and England.

3. The account of a wedding at Boscobel. The bride was fifteen and her descent of the central staircase in her wedding gown was unquestionably dramatic.

4. The traditional story that during night thunderstorms lightning flashes disclose on the same staircase the ghost of Betsy Corné Dyckman clad in a gown her husband sent her from London.

While all these items might well have attracted aid to those who preserved the old house, the rescuers are proud that its beauty alone gave them the inspiration and impetus to save it. They are never happier than when they sit in the audience on pleasant evenings and behold the presentation of "Sound and Light," recently adopted to add effectiveness to the exhibiting of Boscobel's exterior. They listen to the voices of the narrators, Helen Hayes and Gary Merrill, and eventually they hear music from the house itself. Then light pours from all the windows and Boscobel stands in a glow of timelessness.

Boscobel now attracts thousands of visitors each year and suggests to the world an image of early nineteenth century Anglo-American country-house living. It furnishes the American of today a happy link with the highest beauty his predecessors were able to produce, and it is therefore an important contribution to the nation's history.

Too often, however, members of the little group who decided that Boscobel provided a beauty that must be saved are asked "How did you do it?" So far as I can ascertain from them the answers are: "We don't know how we did it. The techniques were completely impractical and were invented out of utter commitment to a cause." The point that is all too often lost in the notable story is that we should not have had to go it alone for so long. Even today, financial contributions to Boscobel would be most welcome. The nominal fee charged for admission does not begin to meet the financial burden involved in maintenance of the building and grounds. Nor, indeed, should it. Boscobel was saved by some of us for all of us. It should be supported by all of us. The alarming frequency with which beautiful and historical landmarks are being exchanged for parking lots, supermarkets, and the like makes all the more urgent a change in our thinking. There are few Boscobels, perhaps. But there are many other houses that carry behind their portals the charm, the beauty, and the historical values that we shall never be able to replace once we lose them. Are we to rely for their salvation on the same last-minute reprieves that saved Boscobel?

Those of us who would preserve the noble houses of the past are continuously made uncomfortable by our knowing that other dwellings along America's most historic river should—some of us say "must"—be saved. We become a bit edgy when we are reminded that in Westchester stands a simple salt-box house once known as Odell's Tavern. There, after Washington's army had been driven north from Manhattan, a few grim strategists—the Committee of Safety—ate a hasty lunch while they considered what should be done next to keep the redcoats from capturing the long line of the river. The little tavern of patriot Jonathan Odell still preserves the clean short and long slopes of its roof, and the rooms that it offered on the day the horses of the anxious officers were tethered outside. Here is no serious problem of a financial or aesthetic nature to hinder restoration.

Gay with gables, its vergeboards carved into wild vagaries by valley carpenters, the gatehouse of the old Wilson estate (once near the home of brewer Matthew Vassar who made Vassar College possible) is known up Poughkeepsie way as "The Pink House." That great designer of river estates, Andrew Jackson Downing, planned it, and it happily represents the "Hudson River Bracketed" era when male quartets sang above moonlit waters, and morning breakfasts were garnished by readings from the new American poets, Lowell and Longfellow. The Pink House, now lying in well-marked fragments in Benjamin Frazier's barn, should stand again on the east bank of the wide stream which it graced for more than a century and a half.

More ambitious and infinitely larger stands Olana, former home of Frederic Edwin Church, one of the most famous painters of the Hudson River School. As might be expected from the creator of canvasses depicting the glories of the Andes, this great house seems limitless in its colorful detail. Church built it with the aid of architect Calvert Vaux (a protégé of the distinguished Downing). Church called it the "Center of the World," and to prove his claim he crowded it with treasures from Persia, China, India, France, and dozens of other countries whose creative achievements had won favor in his fertile and catholic mind. Olana is a universal kaleidoscope exhibiting countless gems and since these are timeless—having been chosen from many periods—their dwelling is not so much an index to the period of its building as a monument to the unique vitality of its builder. Surely Church knew well that this strange oriental masterpiece which he had raised above the waters of a mighty river was peculiarly his own—his gift to posterity. Whether this castle be a sample of late Victoriana, an echo of the amazing personality of Church, or both, it deserves to be preserved.

The admirers of other river houses of dignity and beauty, having looked upon Boscobel, importune those of us who, by happy circumstance, chose that early American masterpiece to save and, by even greater good fortune, won the most generous and essential support of Mrs. Wallace. They would have us protect and preserve such stately and spacious Federal period residences as Christie House in which William Few, a signer of the Declaration of Independence, once lived. There is no historian who would deny its importance as an historic shrine, no architect who would question its aesthetic values.

Miracles do not often repeat themselves and despite the general realization of this truth I sometimes see a gleam in the eyes of my associates and some of their friends. They have recently been told of a big, elegant Dutch house, built at the tiny river town of Coeymans in 1716 and still standing in a pitiful state of disrepair.

It was constructed at the order of Ariaantje Coeymans, and an existing portrait of her shows a tall, angular, homely, aging woman clad in an obviously expensive dress and holding a rose. Her early life with her stern, rich father was miserable, and the events of her love story (which included the building of the elaborate dwelling) were also unhappy. Still this is a mansion which (if restored) could be a permanent memorial to the beauty which the earliest of the Hudson River settlers most admired in the days of the beaver trade. Descendants of the Dutch pioneers are legion. Do I hear among them the cries of volunteers?

❦ Twilight of the Storm King

The sometime warrior
Sun-stained, caped, and vizored
Guides his aluminum craft
On waters greened and darkened by the hills.
Between him and his prow his lady lies
White samite shifting toward her knees—
Snow that spreads on earth's rounded furrows
To lose itself in valley shade

And now the riverbank
Unveils its wound,
Opens its violated mouth
And the vessel—
Silver arrow—
Streaks into the witch-hill's belly

Behind it waters swell,
Spray batters a tube of walls,
The current smacks a dead ungiving end,
Roars upward!

Unhorsed, the warrior and the maid
Climb ladders of foam
Until—drowned and beautiful—they float
Among uphoisted rocks
The grey-lichened,
The slime-coated.
This high Avernus
Mirroring no sky
Waits for dusk,
And the newly deads,
Drifting to each other,
Wait with it.
Their movement quickens.
Together
They slither
Over lusterless cascades
And plunge
Down the tall terraces
Inside the mountain.
Their arms flail white
From ebony,
Their legs twist in the races
Of mills glittering below,
And then
The circling stones crush a new grist
Into the fluid of tamed lightnings,
Custom-made and salable
(At reasonable profit)
Pro bono publico.

❧   The Heart's Memory

"The heart hath its own memory, like the mind."
                    —HENRY WADSWORTH LONGFELLOW

When I was a boy in an upstate New York village my father gave me a big-league-size baseball and a fielder's mitt. Trying them out was instantaneous, and for nearly an hour the giver and the ecstatic receiver played catch. When my mother called us to dinner I saw that the palms of my father's bare hands were bruised to an over-all purple and realized his painful sacrifice.

Now I cannot see a ball game without remembering that incident. It takes precedence over many another because, as Longfellow wisely said, "The heart hath its own memory."

It is not difficult to separate the memories of the heart from those of the mind. At first thought the latter category seems more important. It includes getting the first job, the successful strategy that won an election over a hard-fighting opponent, the time the head of a company asked for advice, "breaking ninety" at golf, being included in a *Who's Who* listing of men in a business or profession, meeting the President of the United States—these things and others like them live in the mind's memory.

But from deeper wells, closer to the essence of the man himself, may come less impressive but more influential facts which inhabit the heart.

When I was in the fifth grade my life was immeasurably and permanently enriched by my teacher, Miss Mattinson (I never knew her first name), who said, "No color is as beautiful as that on the feather jacket of a scarlet tanager."

Once I heard a mother trying to sound modest and objective over her son's having won a Phi Beta Kappa key.

And on a day of a major operation I heard over the hospital telephone "I know you have worries but I can end one of them. I've added a couple thousand to your bank account. Pay it back when you're well."

Makers of the memory of the heart are rarely young because only experience provides the understanding necessary to their exercising their unique gift. "Memory," says an old adage, "is the power to gather roses in winter." Makers of the heart's memory are living sources of that power. And when they go, their mantles fall upon those who remember them and are left behind.

❦ Index